"Stylistic Arrangements"

"Stylistic Arrangements"

A Study of William Butler Yeats's *A Vision*

Barbara L. Croft

Lewisburg
Bucknell University Press
London and Toronto: Associated University Presses

© 1987 by Associated University Presses, Inc.

Associated University Presses
440 Forsgate Drive
Cranbury, NJ 08512

Associated University Presses
25 Sicilian Avenue
London WC1A 2QH, England

Associated University Presses
2133 Royal Windsor Drive
Unit 1
Mississauga, Ontario
Canada L5J 1K5

The paper used in this publication meets the
requirements of the American National Standard for
Permanence of Paper for Printed Library Materials Z39.48-1984.

Library of Congress Cataloging-in-Publication Data

Croft, Barbara L., 1944–
  "Stylistic arrangements".

  Bibliography: p.
  Includes index.
  1. Yeats, W. B. (William Butler), 1865–1939.
A vision. 2. Yeats, W. B. (William Butler), 1865–1939—
Knowledge—Occult science. 3. Occult sciences in
literature. 4. Mysticism in literature. I. Title.
PR5904.V53C76   1986   821'.8   84-45453
ISBN 0-8387-5087-7 (alk. paper)

Printed in the United States of America

Contents

List of Illustrations 7

Preface 9

Acknowledgments 11

1. An Irish Heresy
   Critical Response and the Question of Belief 15
   Man and Mathematics: Tensions within the System 30
   An Eye for Symbolic Systems: Yeats's Early Occult Essays 40

2. Circuits of Sun and Moon: A Comparison of the Systems
   1925 Book 1. "What the Caliph Partly Learned," and
     1937 Book 1. "The Great Wheel" 57
   1925 Book 2. "What the Caliph Refused to Learn," and
     1937 Book 2. "The Completed Symbol" 66
   1925 Book 2, Section 10. "The Great Year in Classical
     Antiquity," and 1937 Book 4. "The Great Year of the
     Ancients" 72
   1925 Book 4. "The Gates of Pluto," and 1937 Book 3.
     "The Soul in Judgment" 78

3. Unnatural Stories: A Comparison of the Fiction in the Two
   Versions of *A Vision*
   Aherne and Robartes 93
   Michael Robartes's Discovery 110
   Robartes's Friends: Biography Changed into Myth 117
   Hudden, Dudden, and Donald O'Nery 128

4. Style: The Playing of Strength
   Sources of the Change in Style 135
   Farce and Absurdism 146
   Self-Dramatization 156

Notes	173
Select Bibliography	184
Index of Book Titles and Section Headings in *A Vision*	189
General Index	190

Illustrations

Theosophical Seal and Yeats's Cones	35
The Great Wheel	36
Basic Diagrams of Yeats and Blake	44
Blake's Chart of the Twenty-seven Heavens	46
Blake's Chart of the Descending and Ascending Reason	47

Preface

A VISION is a book perhaps more written about than read, and this is particularly true of the 1925 edition. Yeats's elaborate philosophical system is, admittedly, tough going, even for occultists; for those who do not share Yeats's eccentric and eclectic scholarship, it is at best, highly difficult, at worst, a bore. Northrop Frye voiced our frustration once and for all when he called Yeats's sacred book "an infernal nuisance" that we "can't pretend doesn't exist." We feel, somehow, that we must master the book, bring it under the sway of the intellect. Frustrated when we cannot do so, we may then try to dismiss the work by minimizing its importance or translating it into more familiar terms.

Yet perhaps mastery is not our proper aim in reading *A Vision*; perhaps we should take, as Yeats advised, a less logical and a more intuitive approach. There is ample evidence that Yeats himself did not fully master the raw material of *A Vision*, and much of the book is flatly arbitrary or deliberately veiled. The work is not definitive; it gives no answers and reaches no conclusions. If one is stringent about truth, it is not true. Instead, it is generative; it sets the mind dreaming, wandering in a vast, endless speculation that is, in itself, satisfying. We would have been surprised, even disappointed, to have had anything else from Yeats.

Thus, the proper approach to *A Vision* should suggest, to borrow Yeats's own metaphor, a spiral staircase, a constant return to the same puzzles, but each time with more understanding. With this, there must be at least a temporary suspension of the scientific bias toward logic and proof and a partial agreement with Yeats that what the imagination seizes with intensity is a kind of truth.

Yeats was preoccupied throughout his career with the tension between antinomies, and *A Vision* is his major attempt to unite these antinomies in a work of art, a "stylistic arrangement." Thus, the book is of obvious importance to the understanding of Yeats's mind and to his work as a whole. Current critical readings of *A Vision*, however, are often inadequate in two respects: first, they fail to distinguish between the 1925 version and that of 1937, toward which Yeats took a decidedly different attitude; and, second, they fail to consider the surrounding fictional and introductory material both as important literary documents in themselves and as integral parts of the larger work.

When the two versions are compared, it becomes clear that they are, in fact, quite different books. Between 1925 and 1937, the philosophical system itself undergoes significant modifications, losing for example, its personal reference and becoming more largely concerned with history. Attempts to tie the system to Yeats's early occult studies or to Christianity fall away, as does any specific attempt to interpret contemporary art and history according to the system. The more significant changes, however, occur in the tone of the work. The addition of "Stories of Michael Robartes and His Friends" and other introductory material adds a tonal tension to the work and is evidence of the different attitude Yeats took toward his vast project in the 1930s. By 1937, he saw that an "explanation of life," as he had subtitled the first edition, conflicted with the modern scientific perspective; and he dramatizes this conflict in the later version, using himself as the central persona.

Obviously, the system was not modern subject matter, as Yeats realized. Modernity brought pressure to bear upon the system, distorted it perhaps—if not in itself, at least in the way in which Yeats wrote about it. In this struggle with the material, a personal artistic drama emerged; and it is, in part, the purpose here to trace the evolution of that drama through *A Vision*, that elaborate and controversial book which stands, in some ways, as Yeats's most central work.

This study grew out of work begun in 1971 at the University of Toronto under the direction of Robert O'Driscoll, whose comments and suggestions greatly improved it. The work was also helped along by the comments of Michael J. Sidnell. Conceptually, it divides into two parts: the system itself, and Yeats's manner of presenting the system—in other words, content and form. The aim is to discover what the material is, where it came from, and what form Yeats gives it; then, how this material and form change over the years and why.

In attempting to keep my focus tightly upon *A Vision*, I have had to ignore the temptation to cross-reference that work with Yeats's poems and plays except in very general ways. A more detailed—and much longer—study would pin down associations I have merely suggested. In other places, notably in chapter 4, I have tried to suggest new ways of thinking about Yeats's work, but have left much open for future study. Necessarily, too, I have slighted the work of other critics or, perhaps unfairly, taken issue with their viewpoints; but in writing thus, my purpose has been to reopen consideration of a work that many students of literature have shelved away as eccentric or irrelevant or both. Of course, no single discussion of the book, my own included, represents the final truth about *A Vision*; and I would guess, that is exactly how Yeats would have wished to let matters stand.

Acknowledgments

I AM grateful to Michael B. Yeats and Macmillan London, Ltd. for permission to quote from William Butler Yeats's *The Works of William Blake* (London: Bernard Quaritch, 1893); *Fairy and Folk Tales of the Irish Peasantry*, edited by W. B. Yeats (London: Walter Scott, 1888); *Oxford Book of Modern Verse: 1892-1935*, edited by W. B. Yeats (Oxford: Clarendon Press, 1936); *W. B. Yeats and T. Sturge Moore: Their Correspondence*, edited by Ursula Bridge (London: Routledge & Kegan Paul, Ltd., 1953); *Autobiographies* (London: Macmillan and Company Limited, 1966); *The Collected Plays of W. B. Yeats* (London: Macmillan and Company Limited, 1966); *The Collected Poems of W. B. Yeats* (London: Macmillan and Co. Ltd., 1969); *Essays and Introductions* (London: Macmillan and Company Limited, 1961); *Explorations* (London: Macmillan and Company Limited, 1962); *John Sherman* and *Dhoya* (London: T. Fisher Unwin, 1891); *Letters on Poetry from W. B. Yeats to Dorothy Wellesley* (London: Oxford University Press, 1940); *Memoirs: Autobiography—First Draft Journal*, edited by Denis Donoghue (London: Macmillan London Limited, 1972), reprinted by permission of A. D. Peters & Co. Ltd.; *Mythologies* (London: Macmillan and Company Limited, 1959); *The Speckled Bird* (Toronto: McClelland and Stewart, 1976); *Stories of Michael Robartes and His Friends: An Extract from a Record Made by His Pupils: And a Play in Prose* (Dublin: The Cuala Press, 1931); *Uncollected Prose by W. B. Yeats*, edited by John P. Frayne and Colton Johnson (London: Macmillan and Co. Ltd., 1970, 1975); *The Variorum Edition of the Plays of W. B. Yeats*, edited by Russell K. Alspach (London: Macmillan and Company Limited, 1966); *A Critical Edition of Yeats's "A Vision" (1925)*, edited by George Mills Harper and Walter Kelly Hood (London: The Macmillan Press, Ltd., 1978); *A Packet for Ezra Pound* (Dublin: The Cuala Press, 1929); *A Vision: An Explanation of Life Founded upon the Writings of Giraldus and upon Certain Doctrines Attributed to Kusta Ben Luka* (London: T. Werner Laurie, Ltd., 1925).

Quotations from the later edition of *A Vision* are reprinted with permission of Macmillan Publishing Company from *A Vision* by W. B. Yeats. Copyright 1937 by W. B. Yeats, renewed 1965 by Bertha Georgie Yeats and Anne Butler Yeats. Selections from *Mythologies* are reprinted with permission of Macmillan Publishing Company from *Mythologies* by W. B. Yeats. © Mrs. W.B.

Yeats 1959. Portions of Yeats's letters are reprinted with permission of Macmillan Publishing Company from *The Letters of W. B. Yeats* by W. B. Yeats, edited by Allan Wade. Copyright 1953, 1954 by Anne Butler Yeats, renewed 1982 by Anne Butler Yeats. I am also indebted to Macmillan Publishing Company for permission to quote from *Explorations* by W. B. Yeats (© Mrs. W. B. Yeats 1962), *Essays and Introductions* (© Mrs. W. B. Yeats 1961), *Autobiography* (Copyright 1916, 1936 by Macmillan Publishing Company, renewed 1944, 1964 by Bertha Georgie Yeats), and *The Collected Poems of W. B. Yeats* (Copyright 1919, 1924 by Macmillan Publishing Company, renewed 1947, 1952 by Bertha Georgie Yeats. Copyright 1940 by Georgie Yeats, renewed 1968 by Bertha Georgie Yeats, Michael Butler Yeats and Anne Yeats), and from *The Variorum Edition of the Poems of W. B. Yeats*, edited by Peter Allt and Russell K. Alspach (New York: Macmillan Publishing Co., Inc., 1973).

"Stylistic Arrangements"

1
An Irish Heresy

Critical Response and the Question of Belief

IN May 1917, Yeats published *Per Amica Silentia Lunae*, which, he implies in *A Vision*, is his spiritual history, the necessary precedent to obtaining "the secret";[1] but the ideas of this essay are old, familiar ones to Yeats, dating back, as Harold Bloom has suggested, to the Yeats-Ellis edition of Blake in 1893. They were present, too, in the early essays, particularly in *Ideas of Good and Evil*, as a later remark regarding the themes of that early work shows:

> I have written of all these things in *A Vision*, but that book is intended, to use a phrase of Jacob Boehme's, for my "schoolmates only."[2]

In the fall of 1917, Yeats married and, with the help of his wife, continued the spiritualistic explorations that had led him to write *Per Amica*. The result was *A Vision: An Explanation of Life Founded upon the Writings of Giraldus and upon Certain Doctrines Attributed to Kusta ben Luka*, privately printed in 1925.[3] In 1937, a second edition was published with significant alterations. The 1925 edition contains a dedication by Yeats, an introduction and a mythological story called "The Dance of the Four Royal Persons" by Owen Aherne, and four books: 1, "What the Caliph Partly Learned," an account of the wheel and the twenty-eight personalities; 2, "What the Caliph Refused to Learn," an explanation of the cones; 3, "Dove or Swan," the historical cycles; and 4, "The Gates of Pluto," which considers the condition from death to birth. There are five poems: "The Phases of the Moon," Desert Geometry or The Gift of Harun Al-Raschid," "Leda," and "The Fool by the Roadside," each of which introduces one of the four books, and "All Souls' Night," which concludes the volume. In 1937, only "The Phases of the Moon," "Leda," and "All Souls' Night" are retained, and the untitled poem about Huddon, Duddon, and Daniel O'Leary is added. In both editions, the poems, except Huddon, Duddon, and Daniel O'Leary, which will be discussed later, are essentially as they appear in *Collected Poems*.

"Dove or Swan" and "What the Caliph Partly Learned," which is Book 1 of the 1937 edition, "The Great Wheel," are revised least; but in general, the 1937 version represents a radical reorganization of the material and a significant change in approach. The major differences in the system itself are that, in the 1925 version, there is more attention given to the period between death and birth, book 4, and more specific consideration of the coming antithetical era as it is reflected in literature, notably the conclusion of "Dove or Swan," omitted in 1937. The 1925 version, like *Per Amica*, is much more personal in its perspective, much more concerned with the individual and with the creation of art through the interaction of the man and his Daimon; the 1937 version is more oriented toward the larger historical perspective as illustrated by the fact that a fifth chapter, "The Great Year of the Ancients," is added to develop the idea of historical cycles. Walter Kelly Hood notes, too, that Yeats's frame of reference changes from that of Christianity in 1925 to Neoplatonism in 1937.[4]

A final distinction is that the 1925 version uniformly maintains the deception that Michael Robartes discovered the book of Giraldus and the Judwali tribe and that he and Yeats and Aherne quarreled, first about "Rosa Alchemica" and later about the 1925 *Vision*, a deception that Yeats also mentions in his notes and letters. As the quotation cited earlier illustrates, Yeats was uneasy about the first edition; the deception, he hoped, would make it seem less obscure and "mystical," more acceptable to his general readers. When he writes to Edmund Dulac in 1923, thanking him for the portrait of Giraldus that appears in both editions and that looks so much like Yeats himself, he remarks:

> I doubt if Laurie [the publisher] would have taken the book but for the amusing deceit that your designs make possible. It saves it from seeming a book for specialists only and gives it a new imaginative existence.[5]

This deception continues in the 1937 version, somewhat, in John Aherne's letter; but there, of course, the Michael Robartes material is specifically classified as fiction, and Yeats includes the account of the origin of the material in his wife's automatic writing and the supposed reason for his suppression of that account, or at least, of its disguise in "Desert Geometry," in the 1925 edition.

The issue of automatic writing is something of a critical red herring, taking scholars off on false trails to what Yeats *really* meant and asking readers, often, to accept a ridiculous pseudo-Yeats half-witted enough to believe in such nonsense. Critics, reluctant to take the matter at face value, have been, perhaps, too willing to accept comfortable explanations. In the traditional scenario, for example, a sly, womanly-wise George Yeats, aware of her new husband's lingering passion for Maud Gonne and her daughter, dupes the credulous old man with the most transparent of carnival flimflam. In another common interpretation, automatic writing is no more than a metaphor for the creative process.

In fact, the idea of poetic inspiration coming in a state of trance or through supernatural agents has a long and honorable tradition in literature, notably in Coleridge and Blake, both of whom Yeats studied extensively; yet even if the account of the automatic writing were pure fiction, it would certainly be justified, like the story of Robartes, by the "imaginative existence" it adds to the work. The drama of the instructors, which will be examined later, is fascinating material in its own right, and it intensifies the drama of myth-making by including Yeats in the historical cycle as an antithetical prophet, like Kusta ben Luka, opposed to the primary figure of Giraldus and his abstract book.

There is a direct explanation of the strange events Yeats records in *A Vision*: They simply happened. Perhaps Mrs. Yeats did undertake the experiment out of jealousy; but once underway, the automatic writing seemed to take on a purpose of its own, and events, one must assume, occurred in much the same manner Yeats says they did. Whatever the case, the writing was not faked. As George Mills Harper and Walter Kelly Hood point out in their critical edition of *A Vision*, the symbols and ideas of the book evolved from Yeats's own thinking and from the psychic experiments he and his friends conducted as members of the Hermetic Order of the Golden Dawn and the Society for Psychical Research,[6] specifically from an automatic script produced by Lady Edith Lyttelton and a hastily written warning from his skeptical friend, William Thomas Horton.

About 1913, Lady Lyttelton, inspired and encouraged by her friendship with the occultist, W. B. Yeats, began to experiment with automatic writing and produced in April 1914 a curious reference to Yeats and the "double harness" of Phaeton. A few months later, in July 1914, Horton, concerned about Yeats's preoccupation with spiritism, scribbled the poet a note in which he, too, referred to the dark and the white horse of the myth, warning that the dark horse, if not conquered and subordinated to the white, would drag Yeats's chariot into "the enemies camp."[7]

Undoubtedly, Horton meant by the dark horse Yeats's avid interest in spiritism which he probably associated with the irrationality or the unworthy aims and desires that that creature symbolizes in the myth. The white horse, to Horton, was probably a symbol of poetry. When the double-harness motif reappeared in George Yeats's automatic script on 5 November 1917, Yeats, already deeply involved in the ideas that he had just published as *Per Amica Silentia Lunae*, recognized the two horses immediately as emblems of the sun and moon. As Harper and Hood interpret the symbolism from the automatic script:

The dark unruly horse of the moon is equated symbolically to the inner subjective, and "antithetical self"; the white horse of the sun to the outer, objective, and daily or "primary self."[8]

Yeats notes in the card file that he kept to record the results of his experiments with George in automatic writing that the system of *A Vision* developed from Lady Lyttelton's script and Horton's warning; the image of a dual influence established the "psychological polarities," as Harper and Hood put it, from which the work evolved.[9]

From all this it seems obvious that the issue of automatic writing cannot simply be dismissed as a metaphor or humored as a psychological quirk in an otherwise sound mentality. Automatic writing was no hoax, no game, and taken in the context of modern parapsychological research, it perhaps no longer seems as incredible as early critics found it to be. Yet, though Yeats himself believed, he was well aware that others, like Horton, did not; and he is careful in the 1937 edition, where the issue first surfaces, not to insist that the reader share his faith. Instead, he invites the reader to participate in an imaginative experience. In "To Ezra Pound," Yeats explains his book in terms of the opposition of Oedipus and Christ and concludes:

> What if Christ and Oedipus ... are the two scales of a balance, the two butt-ends of a seesaw? What if every two thousand and odd years something happens in the world to make one sacred, the other secular ... What if there is an arithmetic or geometry that can exactly measure the slope of a balance, the dip of a scale, and so date the coming of that something?[10]

The repetition of "what if" in this passage is obviously meant to intensify the significance of the system, but surely it also solicits the "willing suspension of disbelief" necessary for aesthetic appreciation. Likewise, the analogies between his book and Pound's poem, "The Return," or the art of Wyndham Lewis and Constantin Brancuşi indicate that Yeats classified the book as art, not philosophy.

The proper classification of *A Vision* has been a problem for critics since the first edition appeared. Although Yeats at times did refer to his book as philosophy, it is clearly a mistake to read *A Vision* as philosophy if the term calls to mind the rigid intellectual discipline of Spinoza or Hegel; for Yeats's book is not a logical argument but a systematic complex of images forming one symbol—and that a symbol, roughly, of the universe or more precisely (Yeats being a Berkeleian), of the Divine Essence. In fact, Yeats may have included the account of the automatic writing in part deliberately to cut off the possibility of intellectual debate. When he says, for example, that he has been *told* to make the numbers of the personality classifications correspond to the phases of the moon,[11] there can be no logical argument against such a personal revelation.

To say that *A Vision* is immune to logical refutation does not imply, however, that the book is chaotic or unintelligible; such a qualification merely points out that *A Vision* begins in imagination or in vision itself—that is, in Yeats's privileged glimpse of Anima Mundi—and not, as philosophy does, in the objective, natural world of fact that is available to everyone. Once the reader agrees to suspend disbelief in regard to Yeats's initial assumptions, the rest of the book follows logically. The work has, in other words, an inner logic that, although it may be built of natural facts randomly selected, is not, like philosophy, dependent upon the objective world for verification of its truth as symbol. More will be said of *A Vision*'s logic as a work of art later; for the time being, it may be helpful to compare it to a science fiction fantasy or a utopia in which the reader must make an initial leap into the subjective landscape of the author.

A more acceptable approach than the philosophical is to hold, as Northrop Frye does, that *A Vision* is a cosmology like those of Dante, Blake, and Milton.[12] By a cosmology, Frye means a poet's structure of imagery, his "world of images," patterns of association so habitual that they have become an "associative construct":

> These associative constructs, considered apart from whatever assertions they may make about the structure of the external world, become a framework of associations of imagery, in other words, "metaphors for poetry," which is what Yeats's instructors said they were bringing him. In this context we can understand Valéry's remark that cosmology is one of the oldest of the *literary* arts.[13]

In other words, the systems of Dante, Blake, and Yeats are, in a way, total metaphors or great, singular symbols for the entire cosmos; and as such, they control the less-encompassing images contained within them.

These cosmologies, however, are not unique to the individual poet, according to Frye. In a sense, there is only one cosmology, the language of poetry itself, and it is the business of the literary critic to be the grammarian of that language, "interpreting the symbolic systems of religion and philosophy in terms of poetic language."[14] Poets of the nineteenth century, Yeats foremost among them, suffered from the lack of a "coherent tradition of criticism which would have organized the language of poetic symbolism for them."[15] They were driven to other and, Frye implies, inferior traditions: occultism, paganism, nationalism, and forms of decadent romanticism, for example.[16]

According to Hazard Adams, who has also written extensively on *A Vision*, it is precisely this failure of the critical tradition that accounts for the strange and difficult symbolism of the work. Yeats's book is a "grammar of poetic symbolism, conforming to the categories of the literary universe or symbolic form."[17] That is, the work is to be taken as but one "poem" in the larger homogeneous literary tradition, but because the tradition of such "grammars" has declined, it is a badly mangled example, distorted by the occult filter through which Yeats viewed the tradition. Thus, according to Adams, *A Vision* is not unique in any sense except its strange occult terminology. Yeats does not want us to believe in his symbols, but to see them as the "language" of poetry, of a piece with the many works that form the larger context of literature in general.[18]

If Yeats's wheels and cones, his Daimon and instructors are merely parts of a language and that the same language used by every other poet, it is difficult to imagine what a unique idea might be or how one might separate Yeats's thought from another poet's; but that seems to be Adams's position, and it is definitely Frye's when he writes, "Poetic symbolism is language and not truth, a means of expression and not a body of doctrine, not something to look at but something to look and speak through, a dramatic mask."[19] It follows, then, that all poets (or perhaps, all good poets) use the same language of symbols, and that they inherit this language from the tradition.[20]

Frye's standard, traditional framework for poetic symbolism has four levels: the Logos vision of God and the heavens; the Eros vision, an ascent of the fallen soul back to the Logos vision via human love (divided into allegro and penseroso visions—that is, explicit and sublimated sexuality); and the Thanatos vision of death and hell.[21] The best example of this fourfold pattern is, of course, Dante, but distinct problems arise when Yeats's occult perspective is grafted onto Dante's Christian intention. Frye assumes that because Yeats's gyre resembles Dante's mountain, both poets are engaged in the same sort of quest; but in fact, Yeats's stance in relation to the content and intention of his work is totally different. Yeats stands outside the process; Dante is immersed in it. The fact that Yeats was *given* his material (a fact that Frye rightly thinks excludes Yeats's work from the tradition of poetic frameworks like Dante's)[22] makes the point emphatically. Yeats is, in a sense, perhaps symbolically, passive; Dante is active. *A Vision* is not really a romantic quest, and it does not fit traditional Christian patterns.

The problem is that no "grammar" exists for speaking of *A Vision*, precisely because it lies outside the largely Christian literary tradition. By definition, *A Vision* comes out of the submerged tradition of occultism; even more to the point, it comes out of Yeats's own private psychic experiments.[23] It is, to use Yeats's vocabulary, an antithetical vision thrust into a primary critical tradition; and it creates a new grammar for which there is no model, one in which separating language from ideas becomes a little like telling the dancer from the dance. In this new form, the structure is the poem; the language, to use Frye's terms, is the truth.

Yet a second problem exists with the cosmological approach: Looking at Yeats's ideas as mere structure gives *A Vision* little more status as a work of art than the notes to the poems:

It seems obvious that *A Vision* should be approached as a key to the structure of symbolism and imagery in Yeats's own poetry ... If we did not have *A Vision*, a critic could still do with Yeats what Yeats did with Shelley: extract a poetic cosmology or created world of images from his work. Such a cosmology would have, or at least begin with, the same general outline as *A Vision*.[24]

In the cosmological interpretation, the stature of *A Vision* as art is obviously reduced; as Frye says elsewhere, "It is to the student of Yeats what *De Doctrina Christiana* is to the student of Milton: an infernal nuisance that he can't pretend doesn't exist."[25] *A Vision*, seen in this way, is little more than an outline, a filing system for the poet's images, yet even as such, Frye finds the work an "often misleading guide to the structure of imagery in Yeats."[26] If this is the case, it would seem more reasonable to conclude that *A Vision* was not intended as a catalog of Yeats's imagery and that readers are, perhaps, doing the work, and Yeats's other work, a disservice by insisting on seeing it in that light.

Helen Vendler's view of *A Vision* is similar to Frye's in that she sees the book primarily as a key to other works, but whereas Frye calls the book a cosmology—a symbol of the cosmos—Vendler calls it a poetics—a symbol of the poetic process:

> Yeats is obsessed by the nature of poetic inspiration—not its definition, but rather its workings in the poetic mind. In *A Vision*, as we have seen, Yeats traces the waxing and waning of inspiration in the individual life and in the life of history, while describing the types of mind receptive to that inspiration. He continues by describing inspiration in its unconscious sources as well as in its conscious labors, gives an exposition of the state of the mind being purified in order to create, and finally invokes historical symbols to convey his sense of the power and order of the creative act.[27]

Vendler's argument seems a prominent example of the kind of distortion Yeats's works often undergo in order to make them fit some preconceived notion about the nature of Yeats's mind. Certainly, he was a great poet, but he was other things as well. Many critics, for example, refuse to see Yeats as a skillful, serious dramatist, despite the fact that he wrote drama most of his life (exclusively for a decade) and that his plays were not only very popular but extremely stageworthy.[28] Others are uneasy with Yeats's occultism and either ignore it completely or force it to serve more orthodox concerns. Hazard Adams, for example, speaking of Yeats's Blake book, writes, "The truth is that when Yeats speaks of mysticism and the mystical vision of experience, he is in spite of his terminology speaking of the language of poetic symbolism."[29] Like many critics, Adams believes that one can read "poet" for "mystic" in much of Yeats's work, ignoring the careful distinction Yeats himself made between the two.[30] Vendler disassociates *A Vision* from mysticism altogether[31] in order to make it a work of Yeats the Poet, despite Yeats's famous remark in an 1892 letter to O'Leary that "the mystical life is the centre of all that I do and all that I think and all that I write."[32]

This is not to say that *A Vision* has no connection with poetry; clearly, it does. Both Yeats's essay, "Magic," and *The Speckled Bird* were written in part to expound the relationship of magician and poet.[33] But, poetry follows from the mystical life; the mystical life is not poetry, nor is it explored for the sake of poetry. There is considerable danger in confusing one's own preferences for Yeats's in an argument that runs: Yeats was primarily a poet (by which is usually meant that one prefers his poetry to his other writing); therefore, everything he wrote, *A Vision*, for example, was either about poetry or, like the plays, an excuse for poetry. In the matter of mysticism especially, one must take Yeats at his word.

Furthermore, while it is true, as Owen Aherne points out in the introduction to the 1925 *Vision*, that Yeats had a preference for the antithetical phases,[34] he did not neglect the primary to the extent that Vendler's study would indicate; for the tension between the two gyres made the wheel turn. To tie all Yeats's concepts to creativity, a distinctly antithetical characteristic, is to see only half of the symbol, but this seems to be Vendler's approach when she writes:

> If we treat the statements in *A Vision*, then, as assertions in mythical form of what we are to believe about poetry rather than as "philosophy," we will be reading them as Yeats intended them to be read, and using them somewhat as he used them himself, when he wrote of *A Vision*, "I am longing to put it out of reach that I may write the poetry it seems to have made possible."[35]

Such a reading of *A Vision* must, like Northrop Frye's, reduce the book to a mere tool for interpreting Yeats's other work. As Vendler writes elsewhere, "*A Vision*, then, exists to provide a 'systematic' background against which Yeats's poetry and plays must be read to acquire their proper resonance";[36] or "It is as a stylistic arrangement of experience—a poet's experience—that *A Vision* must be seen if it is to shed light on Yeats's poetry and plays."[37] Ironically, this seems to be a most damning criticism of the book, coming, as it does, from a critic who insists that *A Vision* deserves "sympathetic reading and consideration, not dismissal out of hand."[38] For, on the basis of her own criticism, even Vendler has difficulty in finding reasons why the book is worth reading and concludes, somewhat weakly:

> The post-1917 poetry is made clearer, Yeats's characteristic thought processes emerge, his symbols are further defined. Both *A Vision* and the plays have intrinsic worth too. They contain splendid pages, and they incarnate Yeats's poetics.[39]

To say that a book has "splendid pages," a concession that even hostile critics make to *A Vision*, does not seem to imply that it has intrinsic worth. Surely, no artist would be satisfied with praise that ignores the artistic unity and integrity of his or her work, for as Yeats says, "We love nothing but the perfect";[40] a work that depended upon other works for its resonance would be, by design, an imperfect work. Artists simply do not write for the reasons Vendler cites. They write because, as Yeats puts it, they have "a marvellous thing to say." Cross-referencing between *A Vision* and Yeats's other work is, of course, illuminating, but no more so, really, than between any other Yeats works. *A Vision* does not prove or settle anything.

In all fairness to Vendler's position, Yeats does give his reader some reason for seeing *A Vision* as an explanation of the other works, as for example, in the 1925 dedication, where he writes:

> I can now, if I have the energy, find the simplicity I have sought in vain. I need no longer write poems like "The Phases of the Moon" nor "Ego Dominus Tuus," nor spend barren years, as I have done some three or four times, striving with abstractions that substituted themselves for the play that I had planned.[41]

Yeats's lifelong battle against abstraction and his search for a sacred book are well documented; and the implication here is that his artistic and personal needs merged and were answered in *A Vision*. Certainly, Yeats felt the need for a mythology, and he describes *A Vision* elsewhere as "one of those statements our nature is compelled to make and employ as a truth though there cannot be sufficient evidence."[42] Richard Ellmann writes in *Yeats: The Man and The Masks* that *A Vision* was for Yeats both a personal religion and a poetic device for controlling the intrusion of abstractions into his work, a sacred book for both his life and his art.[43] This position, however, seems biographical only; there is a difference between an author's personal motives for writing a book and the substance that that book embodies once it is finished. One must remember that Yeats offered to abandon poetry altogether and spend his life piecing together the system.[44] His letters speak often of the work as a fascinating experience. Writing to Olivia Shakespear in 1928, Yeats says that he is "pottering" over a new edition "which should be ready some time next year";[45] yet the second edition did not appear until nine years later. Apparently Yeats was not eager then to put *A Vision* aside. In a discarded dedication to his wife, Yeats remarks that George will accept the tribute only if he agrees to write verse exclusively for a year.[46] The implication again is that the work was a fascination he could not easily put by. Surely, so experienced a poet as Yeats was by 1917 would not have needed or taken twenty years away from writing verse simply to put his thoughts in order and clear the way for poetry. *A Vision* was more than a poet's notes or a personal exorcism. Yeats was fascinated by the material. If critics are not, there is, perhaps, little hope that they can meet the book on its own terms.

One wonders, too, how much an understanding of *A Vision* really serves to illuminate Yeats's other work. If, to take an example, one applies *A Vision* to *A Full Moon in March*, one can say that the play opens with the Queen in Phase 15, the Swineherd in Phase 1. The action of the play is that the wheel turns. The Queen moves out of the quarter of beauty and into the quarter of violence; the Swineherd is called out of the quarter of wisdom, which is unity with God, and into the quarter of temptation. Or in other terms, he moves toward self-realization or the discovery of strength, and she away from it to the breaking of strength. Since at Phase 15 "all thought becomes an image,"[47] one can say that the two characters have changed places; where she was the image for which he strove, now he is her image, and this reversal occurs in a sudden and violent interchange of the tinctures.

Yet one sees on stage in dramatic terms that the Queen represents ideal beauty and the Swineherd, natural man, that they are opposite, that one seeks the other, and that violent sexuality is both the actual means and the image of this reversal. One does not need to know the pattern beforehand because one sees it acted out on stage, and anything that is not acted out on stage is not in the play. The terminology of *A Vision*, which is all that is really added when one interprets according to the system, cannot add to the dramatic impact. Terms like "Phase 15" or "interchange of the tinctures" are neither plot nor characterization; they are only names for concepts that already have adequate names. To put it simply, art is the treatment of a theme, not the theme alone.

If Vendler's study tends to deny a serious purpose to *A Vision*, Harold Bloom's work, *Yeats*, takes the book almost too seriously. Like Northrop Frye, Bloom considers *A Vision* to be a cosmology; and like Frye, he sees it as one with not only a poetic, but a moral purpose. To Bloom, Yeats is a romantic: "Yeats's temperament and tradition alike were High Romantic."[48] He sees *A Vision* as an apocalypse, "and the purpose of an apocalypse is to reveal the truth, and so help stimulate a restoration of men to an unfallen state."[49] Yet, although he grants Yeats's work a high moral theme and purpose, ultimately Bloom finds *A Vision* disappointing because it seems to deny to man his free will, and thus it seems to be reductive. His judgment is similar to Northrop Frye's. Because Yeats's vision is a cyclical repetition rather than a linear ascent, and because Yeats received it in a passive state, Frye sees the work as "infernal" and ironic, a Thanatos vision,[50] but one, surprisingly, that lacks any sense of evil.[51] Too much can be explained away, excused; there is no realm of evil, only the endless whirling of the gyres. Both critics feel that Yeats has somehow betrayed his subject by failing to represent it completely, and both seem to be asking nearly the same question: Does *A Vision* have sufficient scope and vital tension to sustain it as a work of art or are the ideas expressed within it too naive and shortsighted, too eccentric to make the work anything more than a sketchy catalog of Yeats's imagery?

Such criticism meets the work on legitimate grounds, but the questions raised are too complex for any quick and easy answer. Clarification may well lie in an examination not only of *A Vision*, but of the often uncomfortable, subjective experience of modernity that, since we are in the midst of it, we cannot always see clearly. Yeats did speak of himself as a romantic, but the term is misleading if one fails to take into account his efforts to remain contemporary. His career spanned more than fifty years, and during that time, his style changed often.

"Apocalypse" sounds as right for *A Vision* as "romantic" does for Yeats himself; but this term, too, can be misleading, especially if it calls up visions of the end of the world, which Yeats certainly was not predicting despite the grim images with which he sometimes surrounds the coming of the antithetical age. If the term refers to prophetic revelation, it is legitimate to ask what is being revealed. "The truth" is no satisfactory answer. If truth means God's will, readers are clearly carried beyond their depth; if the poet's truth is meant, there seems to be no way of separating an apocalypse from any other sort of poetic inspiration, or, indeed, from creativity itself. Truth becomes a matter of preference and no standard of judgment, not to mention the fact that truth becomes confused with the poet's skill in expression.

One might say that *truth*, which is taken here to be synonymous with *reality* and which implies belief, is a term that has narrowed in meaning since the advent of the scientific perspective and now seems to imply simply the correspondence of a statement to the world that science has verified. Thus, in modern terms, a newspaper or a physics textbook is true; *Paradise Lost* is not true. Obviously, this idea of truth is difficult to apply to mythology or art, yet art and myth may still be said to be true if by this one means that all of the statements within a given work cohere—that is, if the work has an organic unity in itself, regardless of what may actually exist, in scientific terms, outside the work of art, and if that unity seems to symbolize some common thought or emotion.

This artistic truth cannot be eccentric, however; it must conform to a sense of spiritual reality as a given age or community perceives it. Here the problem gets especially difficult because within Western civilization there is no longer any widely agreed upon body of spiritual truth as there was, say, in Dante's or Milton's time. Further, spiritual truths depend upon revelation and faith; when reason has eroded these ways of apprehending truth, it is difficult to argue that spiritual truth is anything more than individual preference.

The point may seem belabored, but it is a crucial one,[52] for almost all of Yeats's work until 1925 had been an attempt to unite symbolically the material and the spiritual world in which, despite the modern materialistic trend, he still had a total and passionate faith. In *A Vision*, his most elaborate attempt at this unity, he begins to doubt whether such a synthesis is possible in the modern world. As he writes in the final pages of "Dove or Swan" in 1925:

> It is as though myth and fact, united until the exhaustion of the Renaissance, have now fallen so far apart that man understands for the first time the rigidity of fact, and calls up, by that very recognition, myth—the *Mask*—which now but gropes its way out of the mind's dark but will shortly pursue and terrify.[53]

The 1925 edition of *A Vision* is a conscious attempt to bridge the schism between the imaginative or spiritual and the scientific perspectives—between myth and fact—and as Bloom demands, "restore men to an unfallen state." In fact, the book concludes, "That we may believe that all men possess the supernatural faculties I would restore to the philosopher his mythology."[54] Yeats was attempting in 1925 to create mythological truth in defiance of fact; in 1937, he attempted to create artistic truth that included both myth and fact.

The question of truth and belief is particularly relevant to Harold Bloom's discussion of *A Vision*. Because of Yeats's lifelong study of Blake and Shelley, Bloom compares the book to *The Marriage of Heaven and Hell*, *Prometheus Unbound*, and in the interest of fairness, to what he supposes to be the modern mythology of "Psychological Man," Freudianism:

> Even analytical maps of the mind become mythologies; perhaps the Freudian mythology of ego, superego, id, libido, imago, is the only one now held in common by Psychological Man.[55]

Bloom has accurately identified Yeats's problem: the lack of a commonly held mythology. He is wrong, however, to believe that Freudianism can fill the void. Freudianism is analytical; mythology is synthetic and creative. Psychoanalysis heals the sick; mythology celebrates health. Psychoanalysis would bring men and women down to the democratic level of the normal; mythology would inspire them to soar with Icarus in aristocratic eccentricity. Faced with the lack of a modern mythology, Bloom shrinks the vast realm of mythology to the dimensions of a single human mind, substitutes medicine for cultural unity, and praises as its core the one characteristic true mythology could never incorporate—"restraint of imagination":

> The most admirable restraint of imagination, in our time, is to be found in the writings of Freud, who does not quest after a cure that cannot be found. He offers neither Unity of Being, nor the simplicity of the Condition of fire. Yet he understood that poetry might be a discipline roughly parallel to psychoanalysis, one in which the poet and his reader, like the analyst and his patient, would find not cure but a balance of opposites, not ulti-

mates beyond knowledge but self-knowledge, not a control over fate but self-control. There are a few modern poets, of the highest achievement, who have the Freudian wisdom that accepts limitation without prematurely setting limits; Stevens, I think, is the major example of this diminished but authentic Romanticism, which might be called still a possible humanism.[56]

Bloom overestimates the extent to which Yeats sought a cure that could not be found; but the discussion of that point will be saved for chapter 2 where, in conjunction with the concept of the interaction of man and Daimon, the basic human core of Yeats's thinking on self-knowledge can be more easily explained.

Because Bloom, like Northrop Frye, insists upon seeing Yeats as the heir of the visionary tradition, a tradition that "sought to make a more human man, to resolve all the sunderings of consciousness through the agency of the imagination,"[57] and neglects the modern context in which Yeats was writing and of which he was keenly aware, he finds Yeats's work disappointing in comparison with Blake's or Shelley's. It lacks, in his view, a clear sense of human free will:

> *A Vision* is most heavily indebted to Blake, but it is not at all a Blakean book, *A Marriage of Heaven and Hell* for our century. Its vitalism, like all modern vitalisms since Rousseau's, is a protest against reductiveness, against the homogenizing of experience, but its dialectics are themselves reductive, and tend to diminish man.[58]

Bloom refutes Yeats's "inhumanism" with Martin Buber's criticism of the Gnostic and his "'composite God' of 'possession by process, that is by unlimited causality.'"[59] Free will, the power to reverse the processes of history and causality, is, according to Bloom and Buber, the most real of all revelations about the human condition; this is, apparently, the "truth" that Yeats's apocalypse should have revealed. Bloom concludes:

> One longs for Yeats's comment on the following critique [Buber's], while feeling for him nevertheless the reverence due to the last of the High Romantics, the last of those poets who asserted imaginative values without the armor of continuous irony. That so great and unique a poet abdicated the idea of man to a conception of destiny, however Homeric, is not less than tragic.[60]

Bloom's position regarding the power of free will to reverse the process of history reveals the core of his disappointment with Yeats's system. He conceives of history as linear, and although he faults Yeats for reductiveness, the tone of his comments indicates that he himself sees history as a linear reductive movement that man must combat with his free will. Linear movements, almost by definition, necessitate the concept of a goal; history moves *toward* something, either total good or total evil. Deprived of the Christian perspective, in which history moved toward union with God, the destruction of this world and the establishment of the New Jerusalem, modern man tends, because he still thinks in linear terms, to foresee a movement toward total destruction. Thus, he tends to regress; he clings to the patterns of the past and attempts to return to the old Eden.

Further, Bloom's argument begs the question in still another way, for where did this reductive tendency originate, what drives it on, if not man himself? In a sense, the argument blames Yeats for failing to save man from what man himself has chosen. It sets up an ideal human nature consisting of imagination and free will, which in fact may not be eternal truths about man, but simply illusions, values of the past or even transitory, random characteristics. Then it asks the poet to defend this nature against what Frye might call the vision of evil, the thirst for mechanism and destruction, which is also, modern history has demonstrated, a part of human nature.

Yeats's perspective is larger, cyclical; each side of human nature in turn has its era. Yeats hated the idea of progress and makes clear that he is considering a cyclical, not a linear, pattern of history. The historian considers each age as an advancement on or a falling away from the previous one, but Yeats sees all civilizations as equal.[61] He rejects the Cabalistic linear pattern[62] and Plotinus's pattern[63] because a descent of divine power is linear, whereas his system is an irrational whirling. Likewise, he rejects logic in favor of instinct because instinct is vivid experience; logic, being bound in time, is linear and abstract. Far from reducing the stature of man, Yeats's cyclical system gives full play to the complete spectrum of human nature. It is difficult for the modern reader, perhaps, trapped in a one-sided primary perspective, to appreciate the chaos of the coming antithetical, just as the classical era could not value Christianity, but no other pattern—certainly not the linear Christian one—seems large enough to contain all that is human.

In its insistence upon giving full scope to the potential of man, both for good and evil, Yeats's system seems highly romantic. Evil is a perspective, not an absolute. It changes as the cycles move, and what was sacred becomes secular; what was divine, devilish.[64] In the Cabalistic tradition, evil is an imbalance between opposing forces.[65] In Yeats's system, one exorcises evil after death, but one also exorcises good. The purpose of exorcism is not to be made good as in the Christian purgatory, but to have the question of good and evil dissolved, to have the imbalance corrected, to be freed of the definitions of good and evil that arise from living in particular circumstances of time and place. More will be said of Yeats's concept of evil in chapter 2; it is enough to suggest here that the lack of the vision of evil or the lack of free will may not be flaws in Yeats's system, but considerations that he saw were resolved in the larger perspective of the cycle.

Yeats's view of evil, incidentally, accords well with modern Jungian psychology. Erich Neumann, author of *Depth Psychology and a New Ethic*, sees many modern neuroses as a result of the impossible attempt to annihilate the evil within rather than accept it as a part of human nature. The evil that is now breaking through the rigid, Christian facade is humanity's dark side seeking expression. Neumann does not, of course, refer to the modern upsurge of evil as the coming antithetical era, but his phrasing is strikingly like Yeats's and suggests the same pendular or cyclical movement between the antinomies of good and evil:

> Life is a continual balancing of opposites, like every other energic process. The abolition of opposites would be equivalent to death ... There is no good without evil, and no evil without good. The one conditions the other, but it does not become the other or abolish the other.[66]

It should, perhaps, also be noted that the necessary connection between free will and human worth or dignity is traditionally a specifically Western bias and should not be made a standard of universal judgment, much less a standard for Yeats, who was greatly influenced by Eastern thought, and whether he believed in free will, a consistant defender of human dignity. It is Bloom's insistence upon the idea that free will is a necessary condition of humanity that drives him to select Freud as the modern mythologist, despite the fact that psychology's god is Norm, a composite god of averages and hardly Promethean. The choice of Freud's diminished romanticism is defensive and does not solve the problem the modern world poses for the dignity of man; for if man's scope is narrowed, the ability of free will to maintain his human dignity—and consequently that dignity itself—is weakened proportionally.

Further, what triggers man's free will if not his imagination, the faculty which both perceives that things could be different and creates change? Imagination is the motive of free will. Thus, if Bloom thinks it "admirable" to restrain imagination, he must accept the consequent restraint of free will. In fact, Yeats's system is not so harshly deterministic as many critics suppose; but even if it were, Yeats would remain a strong defender of human dignity because he continues, like the romantics, to place mankind at the center of a vast historical drama.

One might answer the charge of determinism by saying that, while man is free to choose any action, all possible choices have been anticipated by the system and imply a determined consequence. In other words, the system is deterministic, but man is not determined. In this sense, Yeats's system is no different from Christianity, where free will versus determinism also poses a philosophical problem. The object of man's passing through the phases and the cycles of reincarnation seems to be to learn the eternal rightness or goodness of the system—that is, to bring the individual will into accord with the eternal will and thus to enter the Thirteenth Cone, a kind of "unfallen state." The faster one learns, the faster one passes through the cycles, but theoretically, the individual will seems free to choose error, the false Mask, almost indefinitely. This individual freedom to err seems highly romantic, in fact, Byronic; what has altered is the concept of the universe in which it operates. Nature is no longer supportive, no longer even actively hostile, but indifferent; and man has now, according to modern materialistic thought, no intuitive means of knowing, no innate empathy with the world, but only, like Congal in *The Herne's Egg*, his reason to subdue it.

Thus, it may be suggested that Bloom's quarrel is not with Yeats so much as it is with modernity, its scientific perspective and its loss of faith not only in the Christian God, but in the concept of a melioristic universe with a final goal of human perfection. Like Christianity, *A Vision* is not accessible through reason alone; no mythology can withstand scrutiny solely in terms of the scientific perspective. Yeats was aware of the problem of belief and took pains to instruct the reader in how to approach *A Vision* through intuition. To some extent, Bloom's disappointment is well founded; but Yeats also sometimes found the bare mathematical system yielded less than he had hoped from it, and the final version dramatizes his struggle to unify all thought within the one vast symbol.

It is somewhat unfair to fault the work because it is not what one wanted by calling what one wanted, or what one remembers from the past, the truth. This is, after all, the twenty-third phase. The works of many modern writers, Camus's *Myth of Sisyphus*, for example, or Kafka's *Trial*, express the theme that man is permanently fallen, always guilty and at odds with his universe; they illustrate the fact that, given what has been discovered about humanity and the universe, Blake's model will no longer serve and Freudianism does not fill the gap. As Susanne Langer points out, there is no modern mythology; as Yeats points out, none is possible until civilization has passed the absurd perspective, with its tense and ironic disjunction between man and his universe, and enters the antithetical age again.

Man and Mathematics: Tensions within the System

The critical viewpoints explored in the previous section each have a distinct validity and testify to the fascination and richness of a work that can be approached from a number of directions. No one, for example, could deny Richard Ellmann's contention that *A Vision* served Yeats both as a personal religious satisfaction and as a tool for perfecting his artistic craftsmanship. Yeats admits as much when, in the introduction to the 1937 version, he cites

The Tower and *The Winding Stair* as evidence of his increased poetic power,[67] or when, in the 1925 version, he writes to Vestigia that the documents are the answer to his early "need" for a system.[68] There is a sense, fully explored from a Jungian point of view in Erich Neumann's *Art and the Creative Unconscious*, in which every artist is caught up in a personal mythology that mirrors the psychic history of the race.

To summarize Neumann briefly, the male child in the early developmental stage of unconscious perception, like the race at a primitive level, perceives unity flowing through the archetypal mother figure, often symbolized by a great bird.[69] This is the condition of creativity. As he develops a differentiating consciousness, the child's world divides into mother and father figures (unconscious and conscious perception). Gradually he identifies with the father figure, whose conscious ability to act unites him with the community and, through a symbolic matricide, rejects the creative unconscious side of his nature represented by the mother. In other words, the normal man sacrifices his creativity for consciousness, but the creative man suffers loneliness—isolation from the consciousness-oriented community—because he cannot renounce allegiance to his mother figure and the unified creative world she represents.[70] He continues to see himself in service to her as the hero-son, often as her lover as well, and may symbolically slay the father figure by destroying or ignoring the community's collective values and spend his life in search of a spiritual father, which may be accomplished in finding an "unknown God."[71] In short, the creative man has a strong instinctual loyalty to his childhood world: Ideas and images acquired there persist throughout his life:

> Precisely because the child, with its undeveloped consciousness, still lives in the mythical world of primordial images and like early man has a "mythological apperception" of the world, the impressions of this period, in which the profoundest strata can be expressed or rather "imagined" without falsification, seem to anticipate the whole life.[72]

So exactly do these comments seem to fit Yeats that one can only wish Neumann could have discussed the poet rather than Leonardo da Vinci as his representative type of the artist. Yeats's autobiography reveals the same persistence of childhood memories and the same strong allegiance toward an early mystical landscape. What is particularly striking in Yeats's case, however, is how visible and systematic, how conscious was his awareness of the artist's psychic conflict, a conflict that, Neumann implies, usually goes largely unrecognized by the artist himself. Yeats's study of magic, for example, certainly reflects a deliberate attempt to unite these two worlds. Although in the 1930s, as will be shown later, his tendency was to swing his full weight upon the side of instinctual, joyous allegiance to the unconscious, most of Yeats's work strives for a balance between the conscious and the unconscious. The bias (natural in an artist) in favor of the unconscious is deliberately disciplined; and the struggle is characterized by Yeats's evenhanded and systematic approach as opposed to the blind, emotional rejection of collective values Neumann would lead one to expect. *A Vision,* with its balance of the primary and antithetical tinctures is, of course, a prime example of this same evenhandedness.

This tension between the conscious and the unconscious or between reason and instinctual belief as it worked itself out in the writing of *A Vision* is a central concern of this study; but in order to understand it, one must look briefly not only at Yeats as a personality, but at the world of ideas he inhabited. The need for a modern mythology was a constant preoccupation of Yeats's throughout his life, and his work shows several deliberate attempts both to revitalize old Irish mythology and to mythologize contemporary events and persons. When he received the system in 1917 and later—and it is important to note that he received only the system in outline, not the entire book—he must have seen that it could serve as the doctrinal structure for the mythology he had been seeking. He clearly states in the 1925 edition that his aim is to restore to the world of modern philosophy the concepts of immortality and human supernatural faculties—in short, to restore mythology. He seems to have seen, too, that a mythology must be a continuum, rooted in antiquity yet flexible enough to refute the modern depreciation of man, for he writes in the 1925 dedication:

> I wished for a system of thought that would leave my imagination free to create as it chose and yet make all that it created, or could create, part of the one history, and that the soul's. The Greeks certainly had such a system, and Dante—though Boccaccio thought him a bitter partisan and therefore a modern abstract man—and I think no man since. Then when I had ceased all active search, yet had not ceased from desire, the documents upon which this book is founded were put into my hands, and I had what I needed, though it may be too late. What I have found indeed is nothing new, for I will show presently that Swedenborg and Blake and many before them knew that all things had their gyres; but Swedenborg and Blake preferred to explain them figuratively, and so I am the first to substitute for Biblical or mythological figures, historical movements and actual men and women.[73]

The substitution of historical figures for mythological ones is ingenious, for it both makes Yeats's system modern (in a way that Blake's and Dante's no longer seem to be) and revives the sense of reality mythology once had. One cannot think of *A Vision* as a pure poetic construct because actual historical persons are involved in it. History is a way into the deadened modern imagination, and it gives the raw rationality of the book its emotional force. Yeats writes elsewhere:

A book of modern philosophy may prove to our logical capacity that there is a transcendental portion of our being that is timeless and spaceless, and therefore immortal, and yet our imagination remain subjected to nature as before. The great books—Berkeley's "Principles of Human Knowledge" let us say—beget new books, whole generations of books, but life goes on unchanged. It was not so with ancient philosophy because the ancient philosopher had something to reinforce his thought, —the Gods, the Sacred Dead, Egyptian Theurgy, the Priestess Diotime.[74]

The problem of restoring to the philosopher his mythology arose, of course, from the very cause of the decay of mythology in modern times: Modern man had no gods; there was, it seemed to Yeats, no spiritual authority to refute the scientific view of man as a natural object, confined by natural law. As this passage suggests, however, Yeats's studies had taught him to look to the dead for answers and inspiration; his vast occult knowledge, his contact with Japanese Noh drama, and his early research into Irish folklore, with its firm links between the living and the dead, provided obvious models for a contemporary mythology. If modern man had no gods, he did have an interest in history, and since historical events and persons could not, like the gods, be refuted, they served as a type of spiritual authority.

In one sense, Yeats's approach was not radically new; for mythology is always based upon a selection of culturally significant events and persons that are supposed to be historically true. These figures and events represent idealized, as opposed to scientifically documented, histories that support the religious, creative, and progressive ideals of the society. In this sense, Yeats is writing the only sort of modern mythology that is possible, one that is explained historically, not poetically or, as Yeats writes, figuratively. In doing so, he avoids the sterility of reason alone on the one hand and the dismissal that a purely poetic or figurative construct would invite on the other. In short, the historical aspects of *A Vision* provide the characteristic Yeatsian balance.

This interest in history was also a manifestation of the symbolist movement that influenced Yeats's early thinking. History furnished a kind of proof of the disembodied moods, the unseen realities these poets were attempting to express. John F. Lynen, in his study of Robert Frost, has provided one of the clearest explanations of how history could verify poetic values through symbolism. Lynen writes:

> Their use of a deep historical vista and their characteristic interest in archaeology, anthropology, and philology indicate their intent to find for intuitions of value a firm basis in scientific fact.[75]

Lynen sees the patterns symbolism imposed in relation to time and from a dualistic perspective: On the one hand, symbolists were compelled to accept the linear time perspective of science, but they could do so only when the linear was combined with its opposite, the cyclical.[76] Yeats and Eliot are his examples.

Northrop Frye discovers the same duality of perspective in *A Vision*. He suggests that what is called the pattern of the system is properly two patterns based upon two principles of association: the cyclical pattern based upon identity or metaphor, and the "dialectical rhythm" based upon analogy.[77] In Yeats's total vision the two patterns, while retaining their separate characteristics, are united in a recurrent process, but the fact that there are two patterns, rather than just one, accounts for the sense of a progressive structure and a dramatic tension both in the work and in the plays and poems based upon it.

Yeats's total vision is based upon the interaction of two whirling cones, one called primary and one antithetical, which move toward one another, merge, separate, and move toward one another again in an endless process. The antithetical cone is opposed to the primary in its qualities and aspects as individuality is opposed to unity, discord to concord, tragedy to comedy, aristocracy to democracy, evil to good, art to science, war to peace, freedom to necessity, Robartes to Aherne, subjective to objective, and lunar to solar.[78]

At first glance, the characteristics of the antithetical and primary gyres seem to be merely a collection of opposites; but as Frye points out, basically these gyres represent the "two great rhythmical movements in all living beings: a movement towards unity and a movement towards individuality."[79] In diagram, they form a figure something like Solomon's seal: two triangles intersect, apex to base; one is black, representing the primary gyre, and one white, signifying the antithetical gyre. (Yeats explains, incidentally, the troublesome business of having the primary—the solar—represented by darkness. In the wheel of the faculties, these are phases of the moon, looked at always from the lunar perspective. Thus, Yeats writes, "when one uses the phases, in popular exposition or for certain symbolic purposes, one considers full Sun as merely the night when there is no moon, and in representing any phase visibly one makes the part which is not lunar dark.")[80]

The point at which either gyre's characteristics are at their fullest expansion is, of course, at that gyre's base. Thus, if the gyres are diagramed as triangles with the black, primary gyre's baseline forming a perpendicular boundary at the extreme left of the diagram, and the white, antithetical gyre's baseline forming a similar boundary on the right, and if the apex of each gyre is drawn so that it touches but does not intersect the baseline of the opposing gyre, then the point where these lines meet on the left will represent Phase 1 or total objectivity, since that is the point at which the primary gyre has almost total dominance over the influence of the antithetical. The opposite point on the right of the diagram represents Phase 15, where the antithetical has full dominance; the lower and upper intersections are phases 8 and 22 respectively and represent mixed states in a movement toward full antithetical subjectivity (Phase 8) or full primary objectivity (Phase 22).[81]

Harbans Rai Bachchan, who traces Yeats's occult sources thoroughly in *W. B. Yeats and Occultism*, finds that the intersecting triangles, which Madame Blavatsky used in her own personal seal, represent in theosophy the two opposing principles of fire and water, the human and the divine, the one ascending, the other descending. When they are superimposed in full integration, as in Solomon's seal, they represent harmony. In Yeats's dia-

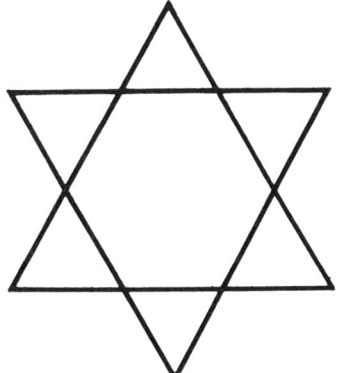 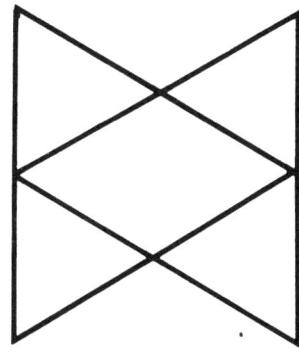

THEOSOPHICAL SEAL (*left*) AND YEATS'S CONES (adapted from Bachchan, *Yeats and Occultism*, appendix 6).

grams, however, the two triangles never merge in complete equilibrium; one or the other is always dominant because these diagrams represent life, which is continual conflict, not an ideal state. For the same reason, they are drawn with reference to right and left, not as ascending and descending.[82]

Since Yeats was instructed to identify the different subjective-objective ratios of his diagram by numbers corresponding to the twenty-eight phases of the moon, it is more convenient for purposes of visualization to round this angular pattern into a circle.[83] It is the same pattern, now called the Great Wheel: the extreme left intersection (which is totally dark) is Phase 1, its totally white opposite is Phase 15, and the remaining twenty-six mixed states are spaced counterclockwise around the circle.

Each human soul, although it is by birth of a particular phase in a series of reincarnations, moves during the course of its incarnate life through all of the phases of the wheel with the exception of phases 1 and 15. These are pure states of being and thus, since life is a tension of opposites, inaccessible to the living man. He passes first through the primary phases, sharing their characteristics, then moves toward individualization and subjectivity in the antithetical phases, and finally moves back toward objectivity and the primary char-

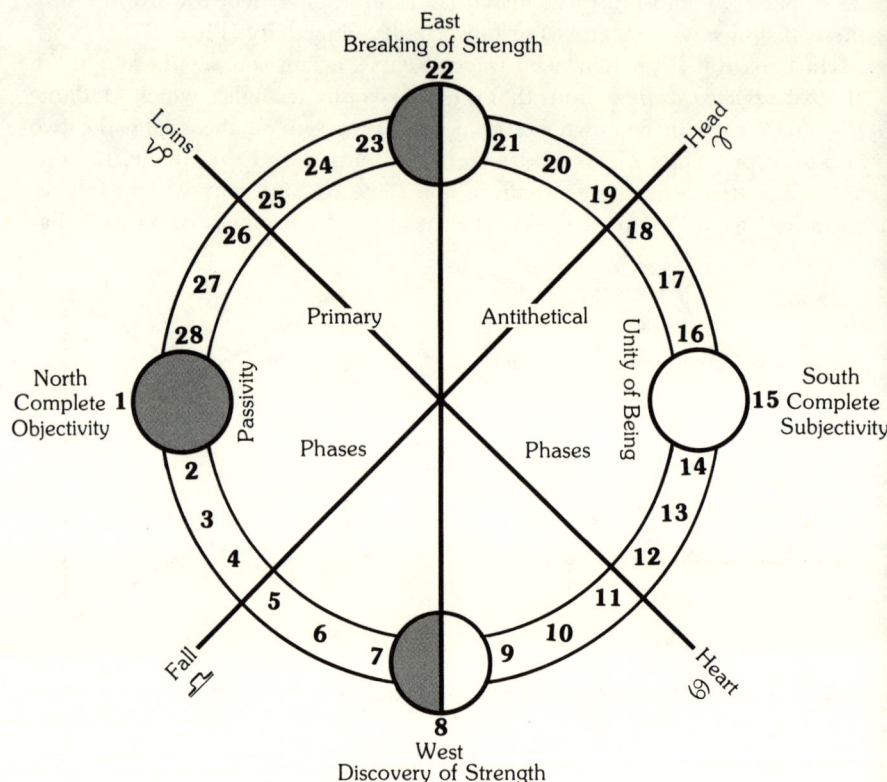

THE GREAT WHEEL (W. B. Yeats, *Vision*, 1962, p. 81).

acteristics in phases 22 to 28. As Aherne remarks in "The Phases of the Moon":

> Before the full
> It sought itself and afterwards the world.[84]

In completing this movement, the soul employs the Four Faculties: Will and Mask, or will and its object, "the Is and the Ought," which are antithetical; and Creative Mind and Body of Fate, or thought and its object, "the Knower and the Known," which are primary.[85]

This cyclical pattern as a metaphor for poetry, that is, as an all-encompassing total metaphor, naturally imposes unity and order upon a work or life. In itself, it signifies completeness:

> This wheel is every completed movement of thought or life, twenty-eight incarnations, a single incarnation, a single judgment or act of thought. Man seeks his opposite or the opposite of his condition, attains his object so far as it is attainable, at Phase 15 and returns to Phase 1 again.[86]

Its danger, artistically, is that it might, in its apparent determinism, produce a static, didactic work of art and thus miss the dynamic quality of life as experience, the exercise of freedom and the pursuit of goals. It might be, in short, too perfect and thus inhuman. Yeats's poetry avoids this pitfall, however, as Frye suggests, by preserving the dialectical rhythm or the principle of analogy within the larger context of the cycle that is governed by the principle of identity. Louis MacNeice, who insists that Yeats was first a poet and second a philosopher, might argue that the desire to preserve the emotional effect of these dialectical rhythms (as against the rational appeal of the cyclical system) is instinctual in the poet; in fact, as MacNeice points out, even the poems like "The Phases of the Moon," which Yeats intended to be didactic, affect the reader emotionally.[87] Yeats's famous remark that man can "embody" truth but cannot "know" it seems appropriate here, and MacNeice is thinking along the same lines when he writes:

> *A Vision* with its seemingly arbitrary complexities is to be regarded as a diagram for something which Yeats knew to be unknowable; that he knew how any such diagram must be unjust to its concrete subject is proved by those poems which are professedly on the same theme; here what was static becomes dynamic, what was abstract concrete.[88]

Regardless of what may be argued of the poetic instinct, *A Vision* itself provides two clear-cut loopholes through which this dynamic rhythm may enter the system: the doctrine of the Mask and the Thirteenth Cycle. The doctrine of the Mask preceded *A Vision* in Yeats's thinking, originating, according to John Unterecker, as a technique to objectify the personal expression of his early poems and thus avoid sentimentality.[89] The full theory as it appears later in *A Vision* is complex, but in outline it complements both the idea of a struggle of antinomies or the dialectical rhythm and the idea of the consciously created life.

For Yeats, the antithetical personality was a matter of "constantly renewed choice,"[90] and it is in this connection that Yeats's contrasting tendencies toward both abstract systematizing and lyric expression become reconciled. His search for order and his love of magic might have produced poetry of the type of T. S. Eliot's; but whereas Eliot sought escape from personality—intellectualism—Yeats pursued personality to the point of unity between the actual and idealized self. This resulted in a kind of negative capability. From a person analyzing his personality, a trait that is constant in his writings and one mark of the last romantic, he became a universal personality through which poetry and vision would naturally flow:

> We should write out our own thoughts in as nearly as possible the language we thought them in, as though in a letter to an intimate friend. We should not disguise them in any way; for our lives give them force as the lives of people in plays give force to their words.... "If I can be sincere and make my language natural, and without becoming discursive, like a novelist, and so indiscreet and prosaic," I said to myself, "I shall, if good luck or bad luck make my life interesting, be a great poet; for it will be no longer a matter of literature at all."[91]

This artistic stance of personality also informs *A Vision*; without it, the work would be simply a strange and perhaps negligible diary.

Achieving such a stance, however, was a struggle, and it is the struggle with the Mask that provides the dialectical rhythm. Even Robartes must suffer the pain of antinomies in love, the agony of ideals and goals.[92] Like the young girl in the Japanese play, the flames of his torment would cease if he ceased to believe in them, but he cannot do so.[93] When Denise, perhaps the most worldly of the characters of *A Vision*, comforts him by saying, "It is necessary to keep in existence the symbol of eternal love,"[94] she is voicing an affirmation of the dialectical rhythm. As Unterecker has noted, this struggle is the basis for art:

> "Reality," for Yeats, is neither to be found in that buried self which directs and orders a man's life or in its Mask, the anti-self, but in the product born of their struggle. Extroverts, Yeats felt, must flee their Masks. Introverts—painters, writers, musicians; all creative men—must recognize their own proper Masks, ideal opposites, and in trying to become those nearly impossible other selves create the dramatic tensions from which art arises.[95]

The tension comes from the fact that a man may choose between true and false Masks, and it is this feature of the system that helps to break its determinism and provide the dialectical rhythm. There is both an internal tension between man and Mask, and a tension between man (with his linear sense of goals and his freedom) and the larger mystical rhythm of identity, the cycle where choice and chance are at one.

The second opening for freedom within the system is provided by the Thirteenth Cycle, which Aherne refers to in "The Phases of the Moon" as the "escape."[96] As Yeats describes it in the concluding pages of *A Vision* in 1937, this cycle, also called the Thirteenth Cone, both defeats and extends the system, and in its lack of resolution, injects the artistic and human tension into the work. Yeats specifically identifies this cycle as man's "freedom," but he also insists that it is "secret,"[97] so the Thirteenth Cycle, which will be more fully discussed in the final chapter of this study, remains essentially a mystery.

Yeats describes life as "an endeavour, made vain by the Four Sails of its Mill, to come to a double contemplation, that of the chosen *Image*, that of the Fated *Image*."[98] The very duality of life and death in the system implies that ultimates cannot be known:

> Much of this book is abstract, because it has not yet been lived, for no man can dip into life more than a moiety of any system.[99]

Perhaps for this reason, Yeats does not explore the Thirteenth Cone, the origins of life, or its final goal, if any, except in the vaguest of terms or by metaphor:

> I see the Lunar and Solar cones first, before they start their whirling movement, as two worlds lying one within another—nothing exterior, nothing interior, Sun in Moon and Moon in Sun—a single being like man and woman in Plato's Myth, and then a separation and a whirling for countless ages, and I see man and woman as reflecting the greater movement, each with zodiac, precession, and separate measure of time, and all whirling perpetually.[100]

The egg symbol of Plato thus becomes the representation of the source of life in the beginning and the constantly self-renewing movement of the cones, the egg "that turns inside-out perpetually without breaking its shell."[101]

Critics have shown some irritation with Yeats's reluctance to explain and with the sudden, inexplicable interjection of freedom into what has seemed otherwise a deterministic system. This "escape" does humanize the cycles and add the sense of an ultimate goal, rest in the Thirteenth Cycle; but, coming as it does, as a brief coda to the intricate pattern of cones and wheels and not fully integrated into Yeats's thought throughout, it seems too little and too late to offset the rigidity of the system. It is, in short, unbelievable, untenable as philosophy.

If one reads the final few paragraphs of *A Vision* as an artistic gesture, however, they make more sense. Critics have been, perhaps, too serious about *A Vision*. Yeats adopted his characteristic personal artistic stance in regard to the system, and especially in the second version, this stance was often ironic and playful. What right has Yeats, Edmund Wilson asked in 1931, to "bore" us with such "stuff"?[102] Yeats might reply that he is simply relating an "incredible experience,"[103] and the fault is the reader's if he tries to *think* a vision rather than *see* it. A vision cannot be reasoned over; it must, like poetry, be expressed and grasped as an experience. As "The Second Coming" tells us, vision comes suddenly and is as suddenly gone; we are "overwhelmed by miracle"[104] or we are not. The sudden appearance of the instructors and the sudden departure of the vision, leaving only the fixed, almost ineffable conviction of intuitive certainty, present the experience itself in 1937, not a rational examination of it. In this sense, the 1937 version is more satisfying than that of 1925; it is more nearly art, and like all art that Yeats admired, it has the grand, casual gesture of the hand. The system is elaborately built up, then simply tossed aside, dismissed;

> All things fall and are built again,
> And those that build them again are gay.[105]

This is the message of the system, and the characteristic arc from the world to vision and back again, of Yeats's most moving works. It is a posture of supreme personal strength, caring and not caring, and in its understatement, a magnificent final gesture.

An Eye for Symbolic Systems: Yeats's Early Occult Essays

In *Per Amica Silentia Lunae*, the immediate forerunner of *A Vision*, Yeats writes of "certain thoughts so long habitual that I may be permitted to call them my convictions."[106] The wording is deliberately cautious, for while Yeats believed emphatically in the existence of the spiritual world and had specific theories regarding its interaction with material life, he was never able to prove these ideas. Unable, on the other hand, to renounce them, he was set "among those lean and fierce minds who are at war with their time."[107] The conflict carried over into his writing; without the sort of scientific proof the modern age demanded, his convictions might seem foolish or even, like Blake's, mad. At best, the themes of occultism required a special form of presentation. Further, his research took him into the realm of hidden things, gave him information that, for one reason or another, he felt bound to keep secret. "Yet I must write," he decided, "or be of no account to any cause, good or evil" (*E. & I.*, p. 51).

This concern with how to select and present occult material is evident in the Yeats-Ellis edition of Blake, published in 1893. Both editors are eager to defend Blake against the charge of madness; but in doing so, they will not compromise Blake's visionary power by attributing it to any modern theory of brain physiology[108] or the unconscious, for the "first postulate of all mystics" is the absolute distinction between the spiritual and the material (*Works of Blake*, p. 236). Yeats ridicules the German scientist who describes the soul as a "volatile liquid capable of solution in glycerine" (*Works of Blake*, p. 236), for the soul is spiritual, different in nature entirely from the body. Yeats and Ellis base this first postulate on the Swedenborgian distinction between discrete and continuous degrees. Continuous degrees differ on a continuum or scale, like light or heat intensity that diminishes in relation to the distance from the source. Discrete degrees, like cause and effect or prior and posterior, imply one another but are distinct things. Spiritual and material are associated by discrete degrees; there is "correspondence" between them, but no identity (*Works of Blake*, pp. 236-37).

The German scientist, however, has an advantage; he speaks a language comprehensible to the modern mind:

> The scientific German has, however, a great advantage over the mystic, in the perfect intelligibility of his statement. He has not been forced by the essential obscurity of truth to wrap his utterance about with symbol and mystery, and to expound the nature of mind and body by "correspondence," or "signature," as Boehmen [*sic*] called it. (*Works of Blake*, p. 237)

Material science, though it is not true, or perhaps *because* it is not true, is easy to understand and therefore widely accepted; but the occult science, now still in its infancy in terms of what can be proven, will one day firmly establish itself in the popular mind again:

> Occultists who have made vision their especial study are inclined to believe that we are still in the infancy of those experiences which will show the majority of us some day how firm a land is the land of dreams. (*Works at Blake*, pp. 95-96)

Yet, even if Yeats and Ellis could have been as explicit as the German, it is unlikely that they would have chosen to be; they were clearly laboring in the service of art, not science, and felt themselves, like Blake, to be a part of a new vatic movement in poetry:

> As the language of spiritual utterance ceases to be theological and becomes literary and poetical, the great truths have to be spoken afresh; and Blake came into the world to speak them, and to announce the new epoch in which poets and poetic thinkers should be once more, as they were in the days of the Hebrew Prophets, the Spiritual leaders of the race. (*Works of Blake*, p. xi)

For the artist, not only truth but also beauty is a criterion for any symbolic system. Later, in the 1925 *Vision*, Yeats would express his dissatisfaction with systems that prove transcendence to one's logial capacity, yet leave the imagination "subjected to nature as before."[109] Any system that would become a living reality must seize the imagination as well as the intellect, and it was this sense of total engagement with the system that Yeats attempted to present in 1937. Even as early as the 1890s when, as the story goes, he sought out Ellis in order to have Blake explained to him, he was after more than raw facts:

> Very little could be given him to satisfy so large a demand, but with his eye

for symbolic systems, he needed no more to enable him to perceive that here was a myth as well worth study as any that has been offered to the world, since first men learned that myths were briefer and more beautiful than exposition as well as deeper and more companionable. (*Works of Blake*, pp. ix–x)

When he met Ellis, Yeats was already a "student of mysticism" (*Works of Blake*, p. ix), but the Yeats-Ellis edition of Blake's works is the first published record of Yeats exercising his critical mind on a fully elaborated symbolic system. His interest, as has been shown, is not only in explicating the system, but in defending vision as a means of perceiving truth, a defense he would continue throughout his life until, at last, in "A General Introduction for My Work," the convictions he defended had become a faith:

I was born into this faith, have lived in it, and shall die in it; my Christ, a legitimate deduction from the Creed of St. Patrick as I think, is that Unity of Being Dante compared to a perfectly proportioned human body, Blake's "Imagination," what the Upanishads have named "Self." Subconscious preoccupation with this theme brought me *A Vision*, its harsh geometry an incomplete interpretation. (*E. & I.*, p. 518)

Clearly, the Blake edition is the starting point for Yeats's system building, an early forerunner of *Per Amica* and *A Vision*. There one finds the fourfold universe (*Works of Blake*, pp. 246, 250), the embryonic idea of the Daimon in Blake's "poetic genius or central mood" (p. 241), what Yeats called the "supernatural artist" (*E. & I.*, p. 43), and perhaps, a precursor of the Mask in the "Covering Cherub," a "mask of created form in which the uncreated spirit makes itself visible" (*Works of Blake*, p. 288). It is not the purpose here to explicate Blake's system or to compare it extensively to Yeats's; Virginia Moore, Hazard Adams, Kathleen Raine, and many others have already done so. The Yeats-Ellis *Works of Blake* is of interest here only because it is the first of several attempts by Yeats to write out his occult convictions. Furthermore, a comparison of Yeats's and Blake's ideas may be misleading. Literary critics tend to think in terms of influences: material means of transmitting ideas, provable by logical methods. For a mystic, such pedestrian means are not absolutely necessary. Yeats writes that "those beings" who gave Swedenborg his knowledge could have given the same knowledge to Blake; Blake need not have read Swedenborg.[110] Yeats need not have read Blake, since visionary truth is essentially the same for all who can break through to it.

From a critical standpoint, then, one can say that Yeats and Blake were working from within the same tradition and may have arrived at similar systems from studying the same documents and phenomena independently. Mary Catherine Flannery (whose book, *Yeats and Magic: The Earlier Works*, explores Yeats's study of the occult, including the supposed influence of Blake, in considerable depth) writes:

> What we will see is that Blake did not so much influence Yeats as serve to give him confidence that a major poet could work from an occult system. Yeats did not find a system in Blake but rather confirmed ideas he was adopting from Theosophy and Cabbalism. And when Yeats moves away from Blake in his interpretation of Blake's work, it will always be toward what he had learned from Blavatsky and Mathers.[111]

The fact that this tradition has been largely ignored by critics accounts for what may be an overemphasis on Blake's influence. Yeats may have taken from Blake only confirmation of what he already believed and more poetic ways of saying what his various mystical sources had already taught him.

Yet there are facets of Yeats's study of Blake's system that bear directly on his own. For example, in the crosslike diagram given for Blake's scheme of mind, matter, instinct, and feeling—a fourfold time-and-space continuum (*Works of Blake*, p. 257)—one senses the cross of subjectivity and objectivity, time and space, which, diagramed and set spinning, provides Yeats's gyre:

> A line is a movement without extension, and so symbolical of time—subjectivity—Berkeley's stream of ideas—in Plotinus it is apparently "sensation"—and a plane cutting it at right angles is symbolical of space or objectivity. Line and plane are combined in a gyre which must expand or contract according to whether mind grows in objectivity or subjectivity.[112]

Both diagrams are really three dimensional and both are in motion.

Yeats, however, seems to be reading Blake's scheme as much more dynamic than it actually is. Blake, as Yeats and Ellis interpret him, seems more interested in the Fall and Redemption of man and the moral implications of the division of matter and spirit. In Yeats's later system, there is little attention given to the creation of the material world, eschatology, or morality, more emphasis on why the world is as it is, how the various symbols in the Great Memory arrange themselves into an elaborate epic.[113] In this sense, Blake seems more the prophet, Yeats more the poet. William H. O'Donnell, writing in *Yeats and the Occult*, sees Yeats as forced to the choice between the life of an adept, concerned with the spiritual world exclusively, or the life of an artist, which must be rooted in the material world.[114] Even at this early stage, and in what should be an objective critical discussion, one can see Yeats's allegiance to the process itself, the life, rather than the abstract, spiritual schema.

For example, Yeats notes that Blake, unlike most mystics, largely ignores the zodiac in his system. Blake charts the twenty-seven heavens, or churches,

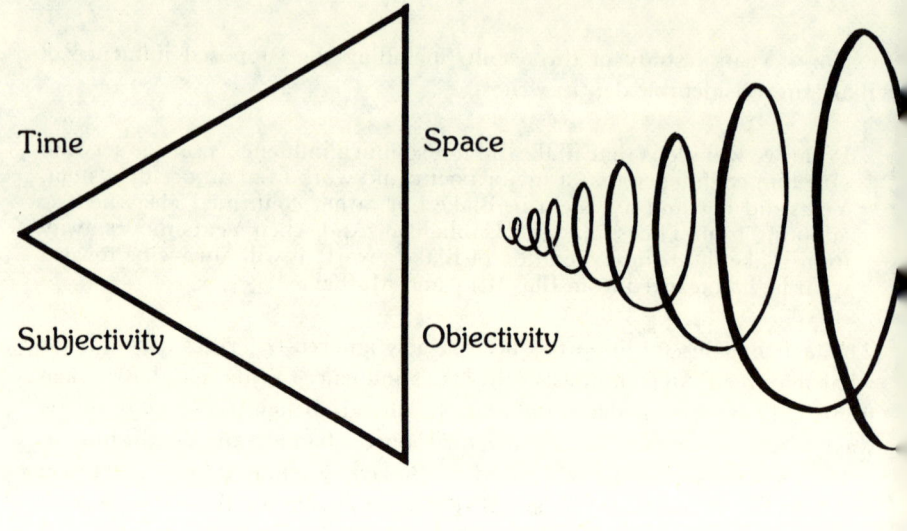

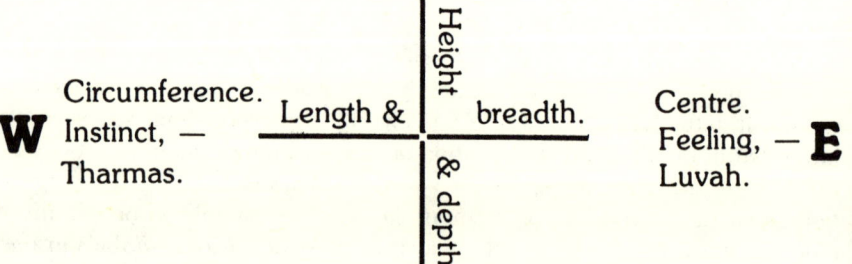

BASIC DIAGRAMS OF YEATS (*top*, *Vision*, 1962, p. 71) AND BLAKE. In the Blake diagram, Urthoma should read Urthona. The designations "Center" and "Circumference" suggest that this figure should also be interpreted as a gyre (*Works of Blake*, 1:257).

on the sun's daily path, moving "Westward and down under the earth through the darkness and up into the east" (*Works of Blake*, p. 300). This, in Yeats's terms, is a diagram similar to the Great Wheel. Using his mystic knowledge to go beyond Blake's system, Yeats superimposes the zodiac, making the wheel correspond to the year, rather than the day (*Works of Blake*, p. 304). He justifies this addition, it seems, not from Blake, but from mysticism in general:

> It must be remembered that all these complex symbols contain the others in miniature within them. All is within all, and every one of the twenty-seven churches contains the whole twenty-sevenfold symbols in minature. Thus, too, this great circle of day and night contains also many days and nights, many winters and many summers. The succession of the churches, and of the symbolic days and nights and seasons, is going on always; we are all passing through it. (*Works of Blake*, p. 308)

This seemingly simple bit of tinkering changes the import of Blake's scheme considerably. Blake seems to have been using east and west, sunrise and sunset, light and darkness simply for their value as images. In other words, the pattern was abstract, a metaphor. Yeats's modification relates the diagram to an actual process, the movement of the planets; and because the planets shift location in the sky over the course of the year, the diagram not only ceases to be abstract, it becomes dynamic in that the forces of the zodiac on one plane interact with and influence actions of the lower plane. The system also becomes mathematical in nature rather than theological. When Yeats modifies Blake's simple diagram, adding the zodiac signs, the result, due to the turning zodiac, is a spiral.

The spiral may be implicit in Blake, but it is Yeats who brings it into focus. Northrop Frye has said that the *Works of Blake* is full of false symmetries,[115] but what may actually be happening is a merging of Blake's mature system and Yeats's embryonic one. In *A Vision*, 1925, Yeats promises in the dedication to "show presently that Swedenborg and Blake and many before them knew that all things had their gyres."[116] Yet he does not actually do so. His instructors sometimes stressed the relationship between Blake's system and their own, using "The Mental Traveller" as their example,[117] and Yeats often interprets the poem according to his own system in order to prove that his and Blake's systems are the same:

> When Edwin J. Ellis and I had finished our big book on the philosophy of William Blake, I felt that we had no understanding of this poem: we had explained its details, for they occur elsewhere in his verse or his pictures, but not the poem as a whole, not the myth, the perpetual return to the same thing; not that which certainly moved Blake to write it; but when I had understood the double cones, I understood it also.[118]

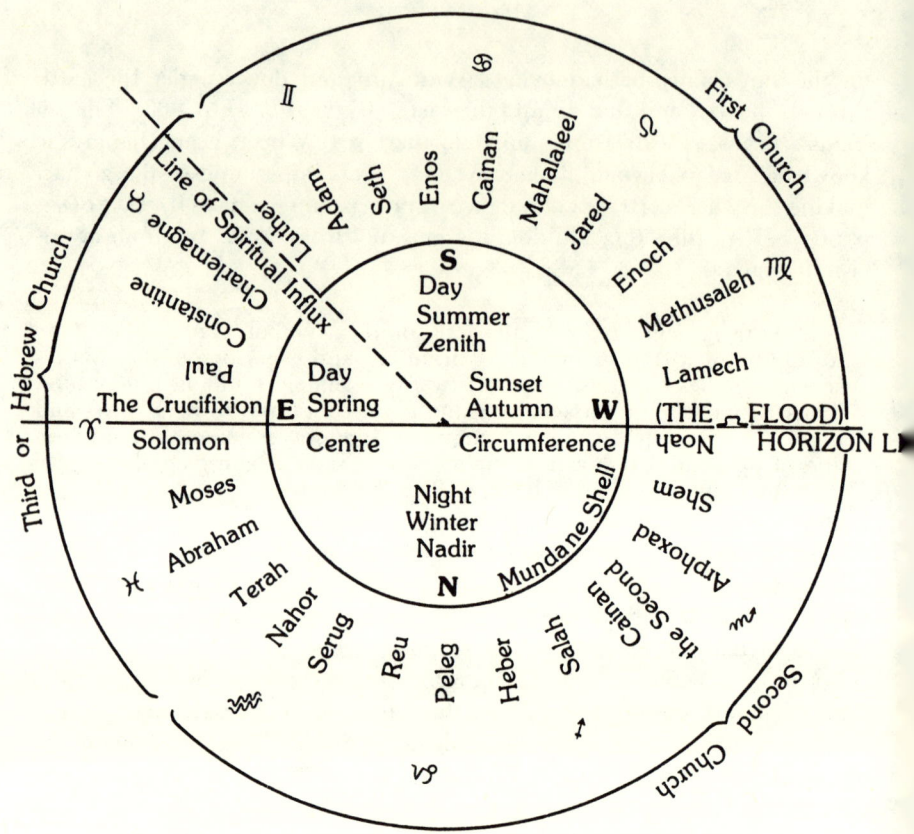

CHART OF THE TWENTY-SEVEN HEAVENS (*Works of Blake*, 1:301).

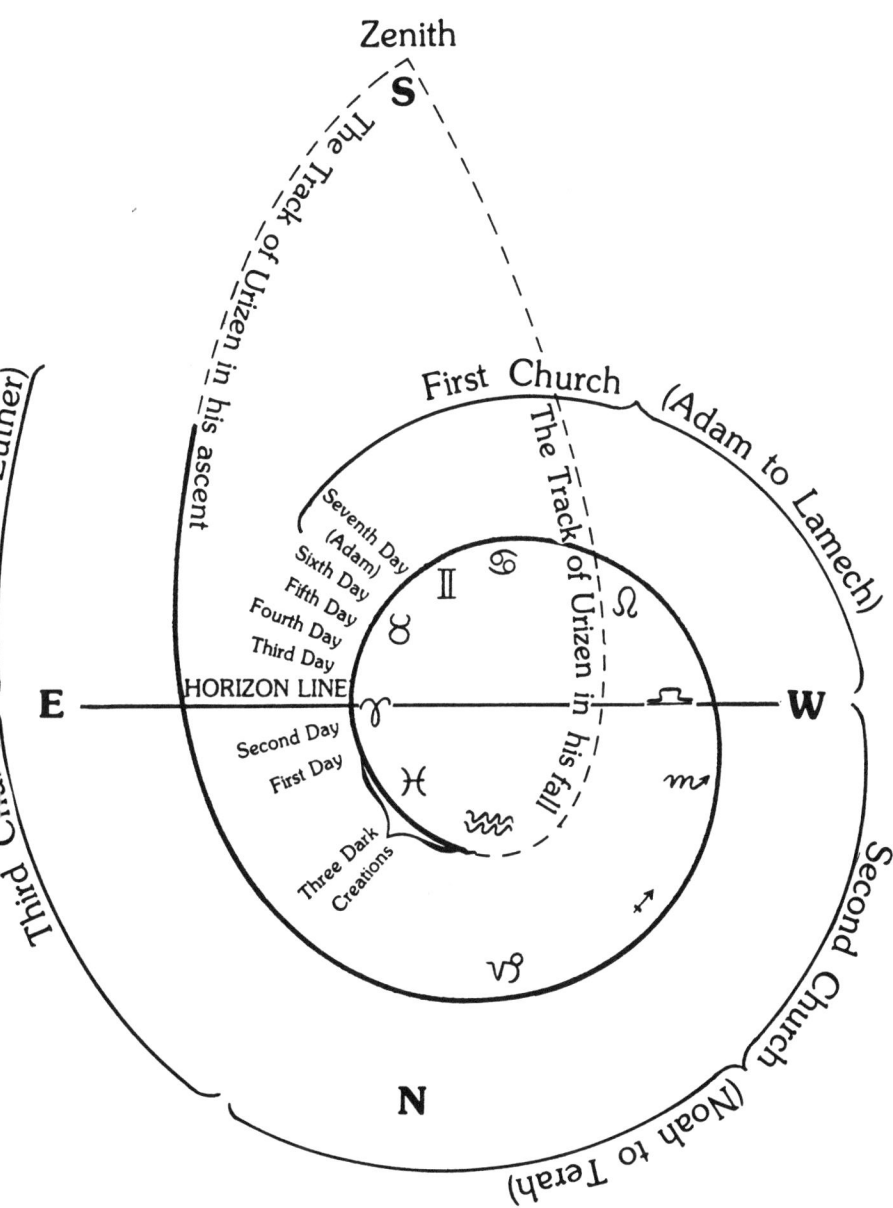

CHART OF THE DESCENDING AND ASCENDING REASON (*Works of Blake*, 1:305).

The interpretation, never conclusively argued, recalls Yeats's remark in the 1937 *Vision* that once the central symbol of his system was clearly in mind, it "appeared everywhere."[119]

As the issue finally appears in *A Vision*, however, Yeats's proof that Blake's system implied the presence of gyres is not convincing[120] and seems simply to reflect his desire to have *A Vision* bolstered by the work of other writers. Significantly, he disclaims a strong connection between his system and Blake's in 1937: "There was nothing in Blake, Swedenborg, Boehme or the Cabala to help me now."[121] Thus, it seems reasonable to conclude that the symbol of the gyre that became the core of his own system was in Yeats's mind in an embryonic form as early as the Blake book and that he toyed then with applying it to Blake. When the symbol firmly established itself in the automatic writing, Yeats applied it to "The Mental Traveller," a poem that had always fascinated him and, by association, to Blake's system as a whole. By 1937, however, he recognized the confusion between his own system and Blake's and abandoned the argument that the systems were closely connected.

The fact that Blake's presence persists in 1937 in various notes and comments points out one of Yeats's central problems in writing about the occult: He intuits associations that he cannot prove. Yeats was aware of this problem and is, therefore, ordinarily scrupulous in signaling whether a statement is intellectual fact or fancy, as when he writes in *Per Amica*, "Then my imagination runs from Daimon to sweetheart, and I divine an analogy that evades the intellect" (*M.*, p. 336). Undoubtedly, these intuitions initially started him on his quest for scientific proof, and Harper and Kelly have traced how Yeats's need for certainty led him into spiritual research and produced the essay, "Preliminary Examination of the Script of E[lizabeth] R[adcliffe]."[122]

Yeats's first occult essay after the Blake book is "Magic," an odd mixture of attitudes and styles that was first published in 1901. It opens with a somewhat self-conscious credo: "I believe in the practice and philosophy of what we have agreed to call magic" (*E. & I*, p. 28). Yeats then recounts his own visionary experiences with Mathers and the story of Joseph Glanvil's Scholar-Gipsy, the personal experiences and poetic legends that were, to him, his strongest evidence. The Society for Psychical Research is lurking in the background, however (*E. & I.*, p. 48), and though Yeats claims to have evidence that would convince their scientific minds, he vows to keep the record shut: "After all, one can but bear witness less to convince him who won't believe than to protect him who does, as Blake puts it, enduring unbelief and misbelief and ridicule as best one may" (*E. & I.*, p. 38). There is some slight posturing in the essay and some frank evasion. Yeats is aware of the scientific arguments against spiritualism, but he cannot combat them. Instead, he simply argues, in metaphor, for the importance of the topic (*E. &*

I., p. 52). As Harper and Kelly remark of Yeats's occult essays in general, there is confidence in the theories, but no detailed exposition; instead Yeats falls back on "vague if picturesque archaisms,"[123] and what began as a precisely worded defense of magic eventually retreats into the more comfortable area of poetic symbol.

"Magic" is typical of Yeats's essays in general and of his occult essays in particular, where his customary method was simply to affirm his beliefs and support them with "beautiful or striking illustrations."[124] As he grew older, however, he was haunted by the fear that his whole philosophy of life might be based on error.[125] If spiritual phenomena could be explained simply as deception or unconscious memory, his beliefs had no solidity. A medium might produce biographical details from the life of her dead "contact," details that she herself could not know, as proof that a Spirit was speaking through her, but a skeptic could still argue that, however improbable it might seem, the medium had acquired the knowledge by some everyday earthly means. Yeats was aware of the problem as early as "Magic," but there he simply dismissed it: "One cannot go on believing in improbable knowledge for ever" (*E. & I.*, p. 45). About 1912, however, in order finally to prove his convictions, Yeats began rigorous spiritualistic research, and a series of occult essays followed.

Yeats met many of the famous mediums of his time, including Elizabeth Radcliffe, whom he consulted regarding a personal problem, very likely his mistress's false pregnancy of May 1913.[126] During the summer of that year, Miss Radcliffe, via automatic writing, demonstrated contact with various dead men and women who communicated details of their lives in several languages. Yeats was convinced that here at last was solid scientific evidence to discredit the "unconscious memory" theory of mediumship and began an essay based on the Radcliffe manuscripts. At the same time—May 1914—he was investigating the miraculous bleeding oleograph of the Sacred Heart in Mirebeau, an adventure that produced yet another unpublished essay, and in October 1914, he completed "Swedenborg, Mediums, and the Desolate Places."[127] These essays eventually funneled into *Per Amica Silentia Lunae* (1917), the immediate forerunner of *A Vision*.

Harper and Kelly have presented a detailed account of the history of the unpublished essays in *Yeats and the Occult*, and Arnold Goldman, in the same volume, has discussed the nature of Yeats's spiritualistic research. For the purpose of this study, the importance of these essays lies in the fact that they demonstrate a vacillation in Yeats's mind as to how this material should be presented. In "Magic," whether from vows of secrecy or fear of ridicule, Yeats had decided to keep the record of his early experiments in occultism closed. The essay on the Mirebeau phenomenon reads like a short story or an innocuous first-person magazine piece, probably because, although Yeats appreciated the poetic value of the miracle, he was not convinced of its authenticity. The Radcliffe essay, on the other hand, was meant to convince the skeptic. Yeats's more scientific approach had a serious purpose: "I am looking for some theory that will recover our belief in spirits, in whom I believe, with evidence as to deception."[128]

Harper and Kelly postulate three reasons that the Radcliffe article was never published. First, it was, Yeats came to see, exploratory rather than definitive; it was titled a "preliminary" investigation, after all.[129] Second, after more careful consideration, the evidence may not have seemed so conclusive as Yeats originally thought; it did not really eliminate the unconscious-memory theory. Finally, and most important, the "scientific manner" was not natural to Yeats.[130] It was just such material as might convince the intellect, but leave the imagination untouched. There was little that could be done with it artistically. Thus, in "Swedenborg, Mediums, and the Desolate Places," written immediately after the Radcliffe essay, one sees Yeats renouncing "evidence of the kind the Society for Psychical Research would value."[131]

In comparing spiritualistic data with folklore— the stories of Galway and Aran that had originally sparked Yeats's interest in the occult—he was not only changing methods, he was changing goals. He was not now simply attempting to prove the existence of the Spirits; he was "discovering a philosophy."[132] The problem had been enlarged and, therefore, neatly evaded. Yeats had returned to the position of "Magic," the position of faith that he held both early and late in his career. It is essentially an artistic stance, a promise to protect the believer, to reinforce the tradition rather than to convince the skeptic. In *Per Amica Silentia Lunae*, Yeats writes of his choice of the artistic stance as quite deliberate:

> At one time I thought to prove my conclusions by quoting from diaries where I have recorded certain strange events the moment they happened, but now I have changed my mind—I will but say, like the Arab boy that became Vizier: "O brother, I have taken stock in the desert sand and of the sayings of antiquity." (*M.*, p. 343)

This same artistic and personal stance—Yeats's strongest—eventually furnished the unifying tone of the final version of *A Vision* where, once again, imagination, not intellect, is the ultimate means of knowing.

The new goal of a total philosophy adds a tighter sense of organization to *Per Amica* than Yeats had shown in his earlier essays. "Magic" begins with a sense of definition and purpose but seems to ramble toward the end; "Swedenborg, Mediums, and the Desolate Places" presents a loose catalog of mystics and their ideas. In *Per Amica*, however, one senses the strong dualistic pattern, following from the occult doctrine of correspondence, the first postulate of mystics, which will later inform *A Vision*. The essay has two major divisions: "Anima Hominis," man and the world of matter, and "Anima

Mundi," the spiritual world. This contrast, cast in terms of Yeats's personal experience, is established in the first section: On the one hand is man in himself, self-doubting, struggling with impure motives; on the other, that "heroic condition" man knows from dreams and art (*M.*, pp. 325–26). Section 2 begins the essay proper, which is focused largely on art, as is the 1925 *Vision* to a lesser extent. In the 1937 version, as will be seen, the philosophy specifically as it relates to history overtakes the more immediate concern with aesthetic theory, and Yeats there dramatizes with his own life the implications of the philosophy for the artist.

Although the concept of the Mask has not yet been introduced at this point, it is clear from Yeats's remarks that art acts as a Mask in two ways: as an "opposing virtue," in such cases as Lady Gregory and Florence Farr, and as a "compensation for some accident of health or circumstance," as in the case of Synge (*M.*, p. 327). Section 3 summarizes: "The work is the man's flight from his entire horoscope" (*M.*, p. 328). This leads to a subdivision between happy and tragic art that hinges on the degree to which the struggle of man and art-mask is evident in the work. Keats, whose art is happy, gives us only "his dream of luxury" (*M.*, p. 329), but Dante fought a "double war" against himself and the world, and this makes his art tragic (*M.*, p. 330).

What is emerging here, it seems, is the embryonic concept of the Four Faculties, and in section 5 Yeats makes the famous remark, "We make out of the quarrel with others, rhetoric, but of the quarrel with ourselves, poetry" (*M.*, p. 331). This seems to imply the division between primary and antithetical natures, for the rhetoricians are men of the crowd, the poets solitary men. For a poet to choose the art-mask of the rhetorician would be to become a sentimentalist. Instead he must choose the "anti-self or antithetical self" (*M.*, p. 331), the Daimon of *A Vision*.

Although Yeats introduces the term *Daimon* later in the essay, it is associated throughout *Per Amica* more firmly with the Mask than it is in *A Vision*. The term *antithetical* is also already in use in this essay, but tied to the concept of the Daimon and with no "primary" to balance it. This is because, in the terminology of *A Vision*, the essay deals only with antithetical types, not with all of mankind, although the saint, later a primary type, comes into the discussion as a foil to the artist. Obviously, all these concepts are reconsidered extensively before they find their place in *A Vision*.

This anti-self, the "wing-footed wanderer," as Yeats calls the Daimon here (*M.*, p. 332), is defined in terms that are reserved in *A Vision* for the Mask: "He is of all things not impossible the most difficult" (*M.*, p. 332). In the next section, section 6, he represents an "impossible perfection" (*M.*, p. 333); and Yeats makes the distinction between the saint and the hero, who would both live the life of the anti-self, if that were possible, and the artist who seeks perfection in his work but not in his life (*M.*, p. 333). A culture may also have a Mask, and the Middle Ages and Renaissance found theirs in imitation of Christ, making the age gentle and passive (*M.*, p. 333). Later in the essay he mentions Christ as the "antithetical self of the classic world" (*M.*, p. 337), and this is one of the first examples of Yeats's expanding his early philosophy beyond aesthetic theory and into historical thought.

In the same passage he relates the doctrine of the Mask to morality, which he conceives of as "theatrical":

> If we cannot imagine ourselves as different from what we are, and try to assume that second self, we cannot impose a discipline upon ourselves though we may accept one from others. Active virtue, as distinguished from the passive acceptance of a code, is therefore theatrical, consciously dramatic, the wearing of a mask. (*M.*, p. 334)

It is important to note that Yeats, like Blake, binds morality closely to the imagination and thinks of it as active. One thinks again of the criticism that Yeats lacks a vision of evil or that *A Vision* is morally neutral. Because Yeats, in his discussion of the twenty-eight incarnations, chooses chiefly artists to illustrate the false and true Masks (simply, perhaps, because they were the biographies he knew best), one tends to forget that the doctrine of the Mask represents a moral as well as an aesthetic theory. The world is conflict, drama. Had Yeats elaborated his moral position, it would have been, like Blake's, active and imaginative, set in opposition to the passive Christian code.

The Daimon comes to a man through the Mask and is his opposite and his destiny (*M.*, p. 336). The saint wears his Mask as he finds it, but the artist and hero (the hero is linked in different ways with both the saint and the artist) "change its lineaments" (*M.*, p. 337) by virtue of this same power of imagination. Here the concept of morality seems to divide into passive and active, and here again is the embryonic form of primary and antithetical classification: those who serve from a sense of duty and those who create. Applying the terminology of the Christian Cabala, Yeats finds the saint upon the straight upward path leading from matter to spirit, while the artist follows the "winding movement of Nature" (*M.*, p. 340), the path of the serpent. Again, one recalls O'Donnell's discussion of Yeats's choice between the life of an adept and that of an artist; the poet must be rooted in nature:

> I think that we who are poets and artists, not being permitted to shoot beyond the tangible, must go from desire to weariness and so to desire again, and live but for the moment when vision comes to our weariness like terrible lightning, in the humility of the brutes. (*M.*, p. 340)

Yeats remarks in the 1937 version of *A Vision* that the instructors came, in part, to answer a question raised in *Per Amica*.[133] In fact, it seems not to have been a question but more an expression of faith that invited the instructors:

I do not doubt those heaving circles, those winding arcs, whether in one man's life or in that of an age, are mathematical, and that some in the world, or beyond the world, have foreknown the event and pricked upon the calendar the life-span of a Christ, a Buddha, a Napoleon: that every movement, in feeling or in thought, prepares in the dark by its own increasing clarity and confidence its own executioner. We seek reality with the slow toil of our weakness and are smitten from the boundless and the unforeseen. (*M.*, p. 340)

Yeats seems here to be predicting the vision that is to come, and the final sections of part 1 discuss this third Cabala path. As Kathleen Raine explains it, "Divine energy flows continually from the uncreated source through the ten divine names, numerations or powers,"[134] the ten Sephiroth as symbolized on the Cabala Tree of Life diagram. The saint can travel straight upward and so, beyond matter, while the poet must wander in nature through the connections between Sephiroth until he completes the path and is united with the spiritual. The third way to achieve a union with the spiritual world is by a zigzag path, the sudden illumination from above, the lightning of vision. This is the reward of those who keep to the winding path.

Having brought the essay to the discovery of vision as a means of uniting natural man and the spiritual, Yeats pauses at the conclusion of part 1 to consider his future. Now that he is growing old, having found vision and the Mask, he perhaps need never wake from visionary dreams. His struggles and suffering over, he might, in the words of the conclusion of the 1937 *Vision*, "find everything in the symbol."[135] But, as in 1937, there is no rest. Remembering Wordsworth, "honoured and empty-witted" in old age, he will instead "climb to some waste room" to resume his study and life of struggle (*M.*, p. 342). This deliberate dramatizing of his own personal situation as an artist is a technique Yeats will use again in *A Vision*.

In the opening of part 2, as mentioned before, Yeats formally abandons any scientific approach in favor of a personal artistic stance (*M.*, p. 343). Since vision is the means of making contact with Anima Mundi, the subject of part 2, Yeats begins by explaining various methods of obtaining vision, his early training under Mathers, and his own method of directing the course of his sleeping dreams. What he has discovered in dreams has convinced him of the existence of the Great Memory. Further, since the images arising from this memory show "intention and choice" (*M.*, p. 345), he theorizes the existence of a Great Mind as well. These ideas go back to "Magic," but it is not until *Per Amica* that Yeats makes clear the distinction between the spiritual world both as a well of images, the Great Memory, and as the active directing power of spirits, the Great Mind. It was because Yeats was convinced of the existence of this mind and memory by his own experience and the testimony of folklore that he began the study of spiritism (*M.*, p. 348).

If the first postulate of mysticism is the doctrine of correspondence—the distinction between matter and spirit—the first postulate of spiritism is that all souls have a "vehicle or body" (*M.*, p. 348), a "plastic power" that allows the soul, after death or during life, to leave the material body and take any shape by an act of imagination (*M.*, p. 349). This vehicle is what Yeats calls (in "Swedenborg, Mediums, and the Desolate Places") the animal spirits and is the individualization of the general soul—a neutral, unconscious power pervading the universe (*M.*, p. 351). In this sense, each individual soul is organically united with the world soul, Anima Mundi:

> Our animal spirits or vehicles are but, as it were, a condensation of the vehicle of *Anima Mundi*, and give substance to its images in the faint materialisation of our common thought, or more grossly when a ghost is our visitor. (*M.*, p. 350)

Once the vehicle is understood, as Yeats writes, "many crooked things are made straight" (*M.*, p. 352). Since our vehicle mirrors forms existing in the Anima Mundi, thought, in effect, has body. Séance materializations are explained in that the disembodied forms "borrow" material substance from the body of the medium or from water vapor.[136] The implications for art are explored in "The Symbolism of Poetry," where Yeats claims one can "call down" the "disembodied powers" or moods from Anima Mundi by creating the perfect symbolic form for them to inhabit (*E. & I.*, pp. 156–57).

In beginning his study of spiritism, Yeats was forced to break with his "masters," probably Madame Blavatsky among them, who denied him license to seek knowledge among the dead (*M.*, p. 348). Yet, being a poet and so, almost by definition, committed to earthly life and process, he could not accept an abstract or idealized other world:

> The poet must not seek for what is still and fixed, for that has no life for him; and if he did, his style would become cold and monotonous, and his sense of beauty faint and sickly. (*E. & I.*, p. 287)

He must seek among the dead, for Anima Mundi must be human, linked in a larger pattern of process to the life of the living, not the memory of some ideal stage before the fall into matter, but a pool of the memories of actual individual dead men and women, memories of material life. This is why the disembodied state of Meditation so fascinated him, why so many of the poems and plays are derived from it, and why it occupies so central a place in *Per Amica*. It is the core of the complex of ideas regarding life between death and birth in *A Vision*.

Since the discarnate life will be discussed in its final *Vision* form in chapter 2, little needs to be said here regarding part 2, sections 7 through 15; all of the ideas there turn up again in "The Soul in Judgment." Yeats has not, at this point, divided the discarnate life into six separate stages; most of his remarks concern the Meditation, with some slight discussion as well of Beatitude or Marriage. The basic pattern is the same in both works: a working through the events of life back to a basic simplicity, followed by a working forward to an acceptance of the next incarnation. Only the *Vision* terminology and a precise separation of the six stages is lacking. The "condition of fire," a concept that does not appear prominently in *A Vision*, is likely the Thirteenth Cone, which is also glimpsed in Beatitude. What Yeats calls here the "condition of air" is probably the discarnate struggle between lives, Meditation:

> There are two realities, the terrestrial and the condition of fire. All power is from the terrestrial condition, for there all opposites meet and there only is the extreme of choice possible, full freedom. And there the heterogeneous is, and evil, for evil is the strain one upon another of opposites; but in the condition of fire is all music and all rest. Between is the condition of air where images have but a borrowed life, that of memory or that reflected upon them when they symbolise colours and intensities of fire. (*M.*, pp. 356–57)

As one can see, most of the concepts that would later be incorporated into "The Soul in Judgment" are in place but lack precise definition. The Cabala symbolism, which will be abandoned in *A Vision*, still has a strong pull on Yeats's mind; but since this symbolism, as Yeats uses it in *Per Amica*, is threefold, and the oppositions of living and dead, man and Daimon, or more to the point, the struggle of the artist with himself and with the world, illustrated by Dante, are dualistic or fourfold, there is a failure of the old learning and the new philosophy to mesh. This is particularly obvious when Yeats speaks of the Daimon as the third path, the lightning of the Cabala (*M.*, p. 361). Daimon and artist form a strong dualistic bond, paralleling spirit and matter, the lightning and the winding path, vision and art. The Cabala, however, calls for an extra path, that of the saint. Because this path is part of the Cabala symbolism, it must be included, but it certainly confuses the organizational unity of the essay. Yeats does not give this path the equal weight it should have, instead using the saint simply as a foil for the artist, while the concept of the hero never finds its proper place. Further, the conjunction of Daimon and lightning makes the Daimon seem much more distant and divine than she eventually becomes in *A Vision*.

Part 2 ends as did part 1 with personal reflection. Yeats recalls those moments when the Anima Mundi seemed close:

> It seems as if the vehicle had suddenly grown pure and far extended and so luminous that the images from *Anima Mundi*, embodied there and drunk with that sweetness, would, like a country drunkard who has thrown a wisp into his own thatch, burn up time. (*M.*, p. 365)

Yet, this state of being is extraordinary; the common condition of life is hatred. In order to find this sweetness again, he must court the Daimon and "begin to make a new personality" through a deliberate Mask (*M.*, p. 365). Like *A Vision*, *Per Amica* ends with a choice that reminds one of the endings of the 1890s stories: Shall he take to his "barbarous words" again or to some "simple piety"? (*M.*, p. 366). This personal tone, a self-dramatization with the growing force of Yeats's career behind it, is ultimately his strongest voice. The weight of his life and work do more to persuade one to his convictions than any scientific proof he might have found. Not surprisingly, it is the style he eventually adopts for *A Vision*.

2
Circuits of Sun and Moon: A Comparison of the Systems

1925 Book 1. "What the Caliph Partly Learned," and 1937 Book 1. "The Great Wheel"

THERE can be little doubt that *A Vision*, 1925, was simply premature. Yeats himself realized it. "I could I daresay make the book richer, perhaps immeasurably so, if I were to keep it by me for another year," he writes in the dedication," but I am longing to put if out of reach that I may write the poetry it seems to have made possible."[1] Though this passage seems to indicate that the decision to produce the first book in 1925 was Yeats's personal choice, in actuality, his instructors commanded it:

> And then, though I had mastered nothing but the twenty-eight phases and the historical scheme, I was told that I must write, that I must seize the moment between ripe and rotten—there was a metaphor of apples about to fall and just fallen.[2]

The book was published with Yeats's prediction that he would one day complete what he had begun, and no sooner was the book in the hands of the printer than he began to read philosophy, seeking confirmation and clarification of what he had been taught. Later, the Spirits returned to complete their instruction (*Vision*, 1962, p. 21).

When he returned to the work, he realized that books 1 and 2 needed the greatest amount of revision. He had not fully understood the system and, in 1937, he confesses:

> During the first months of instruction I had the Great Wheel of the lunar phases as printed at the end of this paragraph, but knew nothing of the cones that explain it, and though I had abundant definitions and descriptions of the *Faculties* at their different stations, did not know why they passed one another at certain points, nor why two moved from left to right like the sun's daily course, two from right to left like the moon in the

Zodiac. Even when I wrote the first edition of this book I thought the geometrical symbolism so difficult, I understood it so little, that I put it off to a later section; and as I had at that time, for a reason I have explained, to use a romantic setting, I described the Great Wheel as danced on the desert sands by mysterious dancers who left the traces of their feet to puzzle the Caliph of Bagdad and his learned men. I tried to interest my readers in an unexplained rule of thumb that somehow explained the world. (*Vision*, 1962, pp. 80–81)

The postponement to which Yeats refers reads: "In Book II is described the geometrical foundation of this symbolism and of the other characters of the wheel" (*Vision*, 1925, p. 12).

The implication of this passage and of the revision itself is that, in order for the system to be fully intelligible, the two symbols—wheel and cone—which were analyzed separately in books 1 and 2 in 1925, must be integrated. In 1937, book 1 deals with both symbols, book 2 with the relationship between the cones and the Principles that Yeats also misunderstood in the earlier version. The 1937 version, then, is an intellectual clarification of the 1925 text, but it is also a refinement of concepts, a reaching after an almost elusive subtlety, sometimes at the cost of clarity. The 1925 version is compartmental, each section of the work is titled and self-contained. In 1937, *A Vision* has more the appearance and feel of a meditation; there is much more poetic statement. In the years between the two works Yeats's purpose had changed, so it makes little sense to say that the later book is the better one. In fact, in some ways, the 1925 version is preferable, particularly book 1, which contains the most familiar and readily understood facets of the system. Though both versions use the same material, it is more accessible in the early book 1, as a comparative tracing of the ideas will show.

Following the prefatory poem, "The Wheel and the Phases of the Moon," and Owen Aherne's "The Dance of the Four Royal Persons," Yeats begins, in part 1, section 3, with a straightforward presentation of the wheel as an "arbitrary" classification of personality types (*Vision*, 1925, p. 12), although he refutes the term *arbitrary* later (*Vision*, 1925, p. 139). He defines the distinction in the wheel of the Faculties between Sun (or primary, objective man) and Moon (the antithetical, subjective man), using as in 1937, definitions from Murray's dictionary. He explains that man has a series of embodiments corresponding to these twenty-eight fundamental types and concludes that "all men are characterised upon a first analysis by the proportion in which these two characters or *Tinctures*, the objective or *primary*, the subjective or *antithetical*, are combined" (*Vision*, 1925, p. 14).

The discussion of the tinctures leads logically into section 2, "The Four Faculties," where Yeats defines Will, Mask, Creative Mind, and Body of Fate, the first two of which are antithetical and the second two primary. These two sets constitute the tinctures. Since, as with many of Yeats's major terms, the Faculties are redefined in the later version, it might be well to quote the entire passage as it appears in the original:

> By *Will* is understood feeling that has not become desire because there is no object to desire; a bias by which the soul is classified and its phase fixed but which as yet is without result in action; an energy as yet uninfluenced by thought, action, or emotion; the first matter of a certain personality—choice. If a man's *Will* is at say Phase 17 we say that he is a man of Phase 17, and so on. By *Mask* is understood the image of what we wish to become, or of that to which we give our reverence. Under certain circumstances it is called the *Image*. By *Creative Mind* is meant intellect, as intellect was understood before the close of the seventeenth century—all the mind that is consciously constructive. By *Body of Fate* is understood the physical and mental environment, the changing human body, the stream of Phenomena as this affects a particular individual, all that is forced upon us from without, Time as it affects sensation. The *Will* when represented in the diagram is always opposite the *Mask*, the *Creative Mind* always opposite the *Body of Fate*. (*Vision*, 1925, pp. 14–15)

In comparison, in the 1937 version, Image has disappeared and a moral sense (ought) is faintly implied as well as a division between natural and reasonable Faculties not stressed in the earlier version. As is typical of the later version, the prose and the definitions themselves are greatly simplified:

> It will be enough until I have explained the geometrical diagrams in detail to describe *Will* and *Mask* as the will and its object, or the Is and the Ought (or that which should be), *Creative Mind* and *Body of Fate* as thought and its object, or the Knower and the Known, and to say that the first two are lunar or *antithetical* or natural, the second two solar or *primary* or reasonable. A particular man is classified according to the place of *Will*, or choice, in the diagram. (*Vision*, 1962, p. 73)

As in 1937, Yeats describes the Will as looking into a painted picture, the Creative Mind as looking into a photograph, and defines the sensuous, as opposed to the concrete, as that which one relates to one's self (*Vision*, 1925, pp. 15–16).

Section 3, "The Place of the Four Faculties on the Wheel," is a bit confused. The placement is explained by the use of examples rather than by theoretical statement, but if one follows the examples, it seems to be the case that Will and Creative Mind move around the wheel in opposite directions: Will from Phase I to Phase 28, or counterclockwise, and Creative Mind from Phase 28 to Phase I, or clockwise. Likewise, Mask moves counterclockwise, Body of Fate clockwise, but they begin from Phase 15, while Will and Creative Mind begin at Phase I. Will and Creative Mind meet a Phase 15, Will and Body of Fate at Phase 22, and Creative Mind and Mask at Phase 8 (*Vision*, 1925, pp. 16–17).

This movement in two directions is what Yeats means in 1937 when he writes, "These pairs of opposites whirl in contrary directions, *Will* and *Mask* from right to left, *Creative Mind* and *Body of Fate* like the hands of a clock, from left to right" (*Vision*, 1962, p. 74); but the revision has obscured the meaning, and one needs the detailed examples from 1925 to understand the general statement of 1937. *Right* and *left* are relative terms and it is difficult to relate them to the gyre, especially since, as Yeats says, "the forms of geometry can have but a symbolic relation to spaceless reality" (*Vision*, 1962, p. 69). In keeping with his principle of revision, that is the integration of wheel and cone, Yeats is here obviously trying to relate the movement to the gyre rather than, as in 1925, to the wheel, which is an abstract and somewhat arbitrary schematization from the gyre; but the omission of the necessary theoretical basics in this instance gives rise to some confusion in charting the Faculties.

Yeats also notes in this section the four cardinal signs—Head, Heart, Loins, and Fall—which mark a point on the wheel where the Four Faculties are at equal distances from one another, and he makes the distinction between Oppositions or contrasts (relations between Will and Mask, Creative Mind and Body of Fate) and Discords (relations between Will and Creative Mind, Mask and Body of Fate) (*Vision*, 1925, pp. 16–17; 1962, p. 93). The opening and closing of the tinctures is touched upon briefly, but again Yeats promises to explain the geometrical reasons for the interchange in book 2 (*Vision*, 1925, p. 17).

Section 4, "Drama of the Faculties and of the Tinctures, etc.," contains the familiar Commedia dell'Arte analogy to the Four Faculties much as it appears in the 1937 version. The significance of conceiving of the interaction of the Faculties as "drama" has, of course, much to do with Yeats's plays and poetry, and with the personal artisitc stance he adopts in 1937 where this drama is actualized. Here again, in Yeats's definitions of major terms, particularly *primary* and *antithetical*, one finds a convenient point of comparison for the two versions. The 1925 definitions, quoted below, give a specific individual reference, while in the 1937 text, and typical throughout it, the definitions have a more social import:

> By being is understood that which divides into *Four Faculties*, by individual the *Will* analysed in relation to itself, by personality the *Will* analysed in relation to the *Mask*. It is because of the antithesis between *Will* and *Mask* that subjective natures are called *antithetical*, while those in whom individuality and *Creative Mind* predominate, and who are content with things as they find them, are called *primary*. (*Vision*, 1925, p. 20)

The implication here seems to be that *antithetical* refers to a personality's inner conflict (Will versus Mask), primary to an individual's sense of contentment, perhaps with his given Body of Fate. In 1937, this conflict is societal, man against the mass of men:

> In what I call the cone of the *Four Faculties* which are what man has made in a past or present life—I shall speak late of what makes man—the subjective cone is called that of the *antithetical tincture* because it is achieved and defended by continual conflict with its opposite; the objective cone is called that of the *primary tincture* because whereas subjectivity—in Empedocles "Discord" as I think—tends to separate man from man, objectivity brings us back to the mass where we begin. (*Vision*, 1962, pp. 71–72)

Both definitions are contained in the terms; the important thing to note is that by 1937, Yeats saw the terms and the system as a whole from the perspective of society and history rather than from that of the individual.

What follows of the 1925 *Vision*, book 1 (that is, section 5 through the "Table of the Four Faculties") is, in the 1937 version, simply a textual revision of the original book 1. A notable exception, however, is part 11, "The Daimon, the Sexes, Unity of Being, Natural and Supernatural Unity," a section omitted from the 1937 version—unfortunately, since it explicates quite directly several key concepts, particularly that of the Daimon, which cause confusion in the later version. What Yeats seems to be suggesting here, in symbolic language, is a duality of the mind similar to the distinction between the conscious and unconscious of popular contemporary psychology. The mind divides into light and dark: Will and Creative Mind are in the light, Body of Fate (because it works through accident) in the dark. Mask or Image "is a form selected instinctively for those emotional associations which come out of the dark, and this form is itself set before us by accident, or swims up from the dark portion of the mind" (*Vision*, 1925, p. 27).

One recognizes immediately the affinity between these forms, presented philosophically, and some of Yeats's more poetically stated theories regarding the source of creative power. In the essay of 1900, "The Symbolism of Poetry," Yeats writes:

> All sounds, all colours, all forms, either because of their preordained energies or because of long association, evoke indefinable and yet precise emotions, or, as I prefer to think, call down among us certain disembodied powers, whose footsteps over our hearts we call emotions; and when sound, and colour, and form are in a musical relation, a beautiful relation to one another, they become, as it were, one sound, one colour, one form, and evoke an emotion that is made out of their distinct evocations and yet is one emotion.[3]

One remembers that the Sidhe often choose to inhabit a beautiful body and that the dancers of "Rosa Alchemica" urged all men "into the dance! that the gods may make them bodies out of the substance of our hearts."[4] There the vitalizing powers that descend to inhabit man-made forms are called moods, and by them men's minds are changed and great events accomplished. In another place the powers may be called emotions, but though details differ, the essential statement remains the same. The belief in a nonhuman, or at least nonrational, source of beauty and power permeates Yeats's work, and one should not be surprised that it turns up, disguised as the unconscious, in *A Vision*, nor that Yeats, the love poet, should populate the dark of the mind with a member of the opposite sex, a sort of anima figure, whose relationship to the mind in light is like the sexual love of man and woman. This brand of sexual aesthetics is a central preoccupation of the 1925 edition, particularly in "The Gates of Pluto."

This section is so seminal, not only to an understanding of the system itself, but to an understanding of Yeats as a poet involved in what Harold Bloom has called the "antithetical quest," a kind of self-exploration for the sake of art,[5] that it deserves a more minute examination. These two minds—light and dark—make up man and Daimon, the Will of one being the Mask of the other, the Creative Mind of one being the Body of Fate of the other. In other words, the Daimon is the reverse of the wheel of man as women are the reverse of the wheel of men and "man and Daimon face each other in a perpetual conflict or embrace" (*Vision*, 1925, p. 27). Demon est Deus Inversus, Yeats's Cabalistic name, is thus a code for his concept of mind and, by implication, of the creative process, a precarious balance achieved out of the struggle of opposites. A man's Daimon has complete control of the dark of the mind, her Creative Mind comes to him, in a dream for example, as his Body of Fate, the given; her Will or "bias" is his desired object or Mask (*Vision*, 1925, p. 27). One can, therefore, as Yeats writes, "think of man as *Will* and *Creative Mind* alone, perpetually face to face with another being who is also but *Will* and *Creative Mind*, though these appear to man as the object of desire, or beauty, and as fate in all its forms" (*Vision*, 1925, p. 28).

Yeats here is using a figure of speech, but there are other parts of the 1925 *Vision*, particularly "The Gates of Pluto," in which one is almost forced to think of the Daimon as literally a separate being. More will be said of the Daimon later; but though Yeats, and others, write of it extensively, the concept, which sometimes suggests the Christian soul, sometimes the Jungian unconscious, remains shadowy in both versions of *A Vision*. For example, the 1937 text uses a negative definition:

> Memory is a series of judgments and such judgments imply a reference to something that is not memory; that something is the *Daimon*, which contains within it, co-existing in its eternal moment, all the events of our life, all that we have known of other lives, or that it can discover within itself of other *Daimons*. (*Vision*, 1962, p. 192)

If a man seeks to live only in the light, the Daimon will quench the light, and Mask and Body of Fate will become evil; "when however in *antithetical* man the *Daimonic* mind is permitted to flow through the events of his life (the *Daimonic Creative Mind*) and so to animate his *Creative Mind*, without putting out its light, there is Unity of Being" (*Vision*, 1925, p. 28). This seems to be, on one level at least, simply a poetically stated argument against the practice of what a psychologist would call repression, a plea for the integration of the conscious and unconscious life, much like D. H. Lawrence's in *Psychoanalysis and the Unconscious*. Further, it seems to argue strongly against Harold Bloom's charge of fatalism in Yeats and, in fact, places the poet solidly within the "diminished but authentic Romanticism" that Bloom grants to Freud and Wallace Stevens, men who do not "quest after a cure that cannot be found," but recognize poetry as a discipline like psychoanalysis that has as its aim self-knowledge and self-control. What could be more Yeatsian than the "balance of opposites" that Bloom finds in Freud? Unity of Being, which Bloom scorns as an ultimate "beyond knowledge"[6] seems, in this passage, to be simply mental health achieved by an introspective effort to come to terms with all sides of the personality, its potential and its limitations:

> He who attains Unity of Being is some man, who, while struggling with his fate and his destiny until every energy of his being has been roused, is content that he should so struggle with no final conquest. For him fate and freedom are not to be distinguished; he is no longer bitter, he may even love tragedy like those "who love the gods and withstand them"; such men are able to bring all that happens, as well as all that they desire, into an emotional or intellectual synthesis and so to possess not the Vision of Good only but that of Evil. (*Vision*, 1925, pp. 28–29)

Obviously, the passage is more complicated than this explanation would make it seem, but there may be a reading problem here, a tendency to overread Yeats, even as he himself often tended to overwrite. One should be on guard not to make Yeats more occult, and therefore more difficult, than he actually is; and from a purely critical point of view, if it is legitimate to seek subtle symbolic meanings in matter-of-fact writers, might it not also be legitimate to search out the realistic, commonsense core in Yeats's often elaborate ideas and prose?

A second problem exists in regard to the term, "Unity of Being," for critics often equate it with the disembodied state of ideal beauty, Phase 15. Yeats is very careful to distinguish between the two in 1925:

> In the phases between Phase 12 and Phase 18, the unity sought is Unity of Being, which is not to be confused with the complete subjectivity of Phase 15, for it implies a harmony of *antithetical* and *primary* life, and Phase 15 has no *primary*. Between Phase 12 and Phase 18 the struggle for this unity becomes conscious and its attainment possible. (*Vision*, 1925, p. 60)

Unity of Being is possible because of the relative positions of the Four Faculties on the wheel, not because the Will is near to Phase 15.

Since Yeats is now attempting to unite the two symbols that he segregated in the earlier version, book 1 of the 1937 version begins with passages taken from book 2 of 1925. His reworking of the sections that give historical evidence in support of the system's wisdom show the effects of his philosophical reading since 1925—he corrects Birkett to Burnet, for example, and Heraclitus to Empedocles (*Vision*, 1925, p. 132; 1962, p. 67). Flaubert and Blake are again mentioned, but the emphasis is on an initial grounding of the system within the tradition of the ancient philosophers Empedocles and Heraclitus, and upon Swedenborg and Berkeley.

As opposed to 1925, the tendency in 1937 is to begin with large concepts, overall views, and historical background and to work down to the smaller details of the system. Thus, he begins by drawing from the vortex of Empedocles the "fundamental symbol" of his instructors (*Vision*, 1962, p. 68), the two opposing cones that are constantly expanding and contracting, "dying each other's life, living each other's death" (*Vision*, 1962, p. 68). This is followed by evidence from various sources of the prevalence of gyres in ancient and modern thought. Section 3 explains the metaphysical basis for the single gyre in terms of time symbolized by a line, and space by a plane intersecting it at a right angle. With reference to Berkeley and Kant, time is identified with subjectivity, space with objectivity. "Line and plane," Yeats explains, "are combined in a gyre which must expand or contract according to whether mind grows in objectivity or subjectivity" (*Vision*, 1962, p. 70).

Section 4 states simply that Yeats's instructors soon abandoned the single cone in favor of a double cone, "preferring to consider subjectivity and objectivity as intersecting states struggling one against the other" (*Vision*, 1962, p. 71). The subjective cone is, of course, antithetical, the objective cone, primary. These cones "mirror" reality, "but are in themselves pursuit and illusion.... The sphere is reality" (*Vision*, 1962, p. 73). More is said of the puzzling sphere in the early edition (book 2) than the later one, but it seems a hazy concept throughout the long history of *A Vision*. Subjective and objective are defined according to Murray's dictionary and the Four Faculties are introduced and defined at the conclusion of this section.

Section 5 relates the movement of the Faculties through the gyres rather than (as in book 1, section 3 of the 1925 edition) their movement around the wheel. In 1937, Yeats is very nearly reversing his approach; rather than beginning with the given diagram of the wheel as in 1925, which furnishes a much less formidable introduction into the system, and explaining in book 2 the origin of the wheel in the cones, Yeats here deduces the wheel from the cones by simply rounding the double-cone diagram into a circle and adding the numbers to devise the personality classification system (*Vision*, 1962, pp. 78, 80).

This shift in approach raises one of many problems in visualizing the diagrams of the system. Here, in rounding out the cones, for example, one is directed to interpret the wheel as a stylized *side view* of the interpenetrating cones; while elsewhere, notably in the diagram that prefaces "Dove or Swan" with its layers of historical time, one gets the idea that the wheel is a *cross section* of the interpenetrating cones. Part of the problem is terminology. In 1925, Yeats writes that the wheel is "a single gyre of a great cone containing, as we shall see presently, twelve cycles of embodiment. Every gyre of every cone is in the same way equal to an entire cone revolving through twenty-eight phases or their equivalent" (*Vision*, 1925, p. 139). Since *gyre* can mean both a circle described by a moving body (that is, a revolution) and a spiral form or vortex, it seems impossible to say definitely how one is to visualize the spatial relationship of cone and wheel. Is the wheel one revolution, one gyre, of the cone, or—since one knows vaguely that systems of cones lie at right angles to each other, and Yeats says here that the gyre is equal to a cone—is the wheel an abstract representation of two interpenetrating spiral forms (gyres) lying at a right angle to what Yeats here calls a cone? The spatial or "spaceless" relationships Yeats postulates are difficult to grasp. The diagrams are symbolic of his "vision" and thus may not fall within the realm of ordinary spatial comprehension. A vision is, by definition, a glimpse at a different world where the laws of matter may not apply; a mystical or visionary work may be characterized by a subject matter that outdistances any discursive means of expressing it.

Part 2, section 1, is Yeats's confession of his earlier ignorance of the cones that explain the wheel, followed in section 2 by a more complete definition of the Four Faculties. Section 3 is the Commedia dell'Arte comparison and ideas taken from book 1, section 4, of the 1925 edition, which is titled "Drama of the Faculties and of the Tinctures, etc." and explains the movement from primary to antithetical to primary. Section 4 is the picture-and-photograph analogy and the definition of *sensuous*, while section 5 describes the opening and closing of the tinctures and their interchange. In 1925, this discussion of the tinctures was placed within the discussion of phase types. The opening of the tinctures makes Unity of Being possible (*Vision*, 1962, p. 88) since all Four Faculties become reflected inward toward the making of "personality" as opposed to the primary "character." The Four Qualities (Will as instinct or race, Mask as emotion, Creative Mind as reason, and Body of Fate as desire) have been dropped from the later version as have the definitions of love and hate. In general, the 1925 version shows more interest in love and sexuality than the 1937 version.

Since the table of the Four Faculties and the twenty-eight incarnations were among the first information given to or composed by Yeats, were immediately understood by him, and remained essentially unchanged (*Vision*, 1962, p. 19) throughout the process of automatic writing and editing, the remainder of book 1 is rewritten for purely stylistic reasons. The only exception occurs in section 17 where "Enforced and Free Faculties," "The Two Conditions," "The Two Directions," "Relations," "Objectivities," and "Consciousness" are new additions to the text.

1925 Book 2. "What the Caliph Refused to Learn," and 1937 Book 2. "The Completed Symbol"

The abstract symbolism of the cones and their relationship to the Principles, which the Caliph, perhaps wisely, refused to learn, were for Yeats the most difficult parts of the system. He apologizes for his misunderstanding of them in 1937 (*Vision*, 1962, pp. 80–81, 187), and in 1925 he confesses that "these few pages have taken me many months of exhausting labour" (*Vision*, 1925, p. 170). Yet, despite this labor, the 1925 book 2 lacks a sense of mastery over the material. The step-by-step, linear structure of book 1, made possible admittedly only by putting off the difficult parts of the system, is missing, and Yeats presents instead a confused hodgepodge of fragments and digressions.

A quick glance at the book's section headings will help to diagnose the problem: Yeats was attempting in this book to deal with three major facets of the system—the cones, the Principles, and the concept of the Great Year. Difficult enough to master in themselves, the interrelationship of these three concepts in the system was a puzzle that, by his own admission, seemed beyond Yeats in 1925.

As has been shown, Yeats's motive in revising book 1 was to integrate the two symbols, wheel and cone. Likewise, in revising book 2, he strives for a closer integration of the cones and the Principles; but he has discovered here, too, that much of the material of book 2 can be either cut altogether or placed elsewhere in the work. The bulk of the material that explains the cones has been incorporated into book 1 of 1937. Another obvious example of cutting is the material on the Great Year, notably section 10, "The Great Year in Classical Antiquity," which becomes the separate new book 4 of 1937, "The Great Year of the Ancients." Since the concept of the Great Year is necessary to an understanding of the cones, Yeats makes mention of it in the 1937 book 2, sections 8 and 9, but the creation of the new book 4 allows him to treat the long history of this topic in support of the system as a whole without marring, as in 1925, the unity of book 2.

The proper theme of book 2, as Yeats comes to see in revision, is the relationship of the cone of the Principles to that of the Faculties and the general implications of the cones themselves. It is, one assumes, partially to highlight this central theme that extraneous material is omitted from the later version or reduced in prominence and transferred to another part of the work. Section 20 of 1925, "The Cones of Sexual Love," and section 18, "The Three Fountains and the Cycles of Embodiment," for example, do not appear in the 1937 version since neither is essential to understanding. Further, the 1937 *Vision* as a whole is focused less on the sexual, personal, or individual (including the fascination with the seemingly unique phenomenon of Christ in section 18) and more upon the larger implications of the system in regard to society and history. A comparison of *Calvary* (1920) and *The Resurrection* (1931) shows a similar shift in focus. The earlier interest in the mystery of Christ (Was He Victim or Sage?) is replaced with an interest in the event of the Resurrection in terms of the history of the world and various modes of thought or character types of the wheel.

This tendency toward a wider scope is also perhaps a part of the reason that the two major sections on William Blake—section 3, "Blake's Use of the Gyres," and section 5, "Blake and the Great Wheel"—become, in 1937, only scattered references (*Vision*, 1962, pp. 189, 213, 262). In the years between the works, Yeats has moved further away from the singular influence of Blake, who in 1937 is just one of many who preceded Yeats in his interest in the gyres.

Other portions of the 1925 edition shift position in the later work. It is known that Yeats has taken the introductory references to Flaubert's "La Spirale" and Swedenborg from the 1925 book 2, section 1, and used them in the 1937 book 1, section 2. Likewise, the origin of the symbol of the gyre in the intersecting lines of time and space, a basic introductory concept, has been moved from the 1925 book 2, section 2, to the 1937 book 1, section 3. "The Fool by the Roadside," which introduces "The Gates of Pluto," is also omitted; having dropped, in 1937, the cover story of the Robartes manuscript and having decided to report the true origins of his documents, Yeats has no need to include the somewhat coy and contrived poem, "Desert Geometry or The Gift of Harun Al-Raschid," one of the half dozen he was "fool enough to write" in conjunction with the Robartes cover story (*Vision*, 1962, p. 19). "Complementary Dreams," section 21 of book 2 in 1925, appears as a personal narrative in the 1937 section 12 of "A Packet for Ezra Pound." Material from "Life After Death," section 14, book 2, 1925, more properly belongs in the 1937 book 3, "The Soul in Judgment," a fact of which Yeats was aware in 1925 when he wrote in that section:

> I have touched upon these things to set them in their place in the system and touched upon them only, for I shall describe them in detail later on. (*Vision*, 1925, p. 161)

A corresponding passage in 1937 reads: "I shall write little of the *Principles* except when writing of the life after death" (*Vision*, 1962, p. 207), and here, as elsewhere in the two works, one can sense the difficulty of writing *A Vision*. Yeats needs the Principles to explain the cones and "complete" the symbolism of the Faculties, but he cannot say too much about them in book 2 lest an overabundance of data confuse the reader. The system, by definition, is incomprehensible except as a whole, an integrated unity of separate aspects but still one symbol. No single aspect makes sense by itself. Yet, in setting down the system, it must be broken apart, analyzed. When this is done the unity is lost; the absorption in the one symbol that provides the motivation for the work dissolves in the explanation of the system piece by piece.

Yeats noticed the same problem in mystical writing when he studied Blake's system: "Things we have to give in *succession* in our explanatory prose are set forth *simultaneously* in Blake's verse."[7] Any system, when analyzed in fragments, must seem partial, for there is only one symbol, that of the universe itself:

> Sometimes the mystical student, bewildered by the different systems, forgets for a moment that the history of moods is the history of the universe, and asks where is the final statement—the complete doctrine. The universe is itself that doctrine and statement. All others are partial, for it alone is the symbol of the infinite thought which is in turn symbolic of the universal mood we name God.[8]

Thus, both versions of *A Vision*, but that of 1937 particularly, vacillate between Yeats's poetic, emotional response to the system as one symbol and his frustration, disappointment often, with the flat, mathematical terms he must use to explain it. This characteristic of the work is significant, for Yeats's organizational problems illustrate once again that the system is mysticism, not philosophy as it has come to be thought of since the empiricists. At some point in understanding, a leap is made from what is actually understood and capable of being discursively explained to an intuition or poetic perception of the system as symbol.

A similar problem must have existed regarding terminology. Many terms that would seem to be major are sketchily defined in 1925 and all but omitted in 1937. Of Anima Mundi and Anima Hominis, for example, Yeats writes in 1925:

> Sometimes this cone respresents the individual soul, and that soul's history—these things are inseparable—sometimes general life. When general life, we give to its narrow end, to its unexpanded gyre, the name of *Anima Hominis*, and to its broad end, or its expanded gyre, *Anima Mundi*. (*Vision*, 1925, p. 129)

Only Anima Mundi, which Yeats identifies as the "Soul of the World," is specifically further defined, late in book 2, as "the receptacle of emotional images when purified from whatever unites them to one man rather than to another" (*Vision*, 1925, p. 176), and one imagines from this that Anima Hominis is a like receptacle, but of emotions united to a particular individual. Anima Hominis may be what Yeats calls elsewhere the Record. The terms are ignored in the 1937 version, and it seems reasonable to conclude, considering their prominence in Yeats's poetry and prose, that he came to consider them as having more poetic than conceptual value.

The original documents must have contained an abundance of terms, almost too many to handle coherently. Some must have been imprecise or repetitive. In 1925, for example, Yeats speaks of Destiny and Fate as Faculties and defines the Faculties as follows: "*Will* is *Will*, Mind is *Creative Mind*, *Destiny* is *Mask*, Fate is *Body of Fate*" (*A Vision*, 1925, p. 138). Yet in an earlier passage, he writes of the two cones, which the 1937 version called primary and antithetical, that one is "the contact of the mind with *Fate*, and the other the contact of the mind with *Destiny*" (*Vision*, 1925, p. 130). If Destiny is Mask, then according to the 1937 version, it is the Will, not the Mind, that makes contact with it. Either Yeats has simply been careless with terms here, as in another place where he substitutes "energy" for what should properly read "Will" (*Vision*, 1925, pp. 135–36), or the Faculties, particularly the dual nature of the individual (Will and Creative Mind), are still vague in his total understanding of the system as it would finally appear in 1937. In still another place he calls Destiny beauty and Fate truth (*Vision*, 1925, p. 135).

A Vision, 1937, in general shows a paring down of terminology that in turn emphasizes a few selected major terms and makes the skeleton of the system easier to discern. There seems to be as well a new sense of mastery over these terms, particularly the Four Principles. In 1925, they are really only named, their function only hinted at. For example, in "The Cones of the Lunar and Solar Year," Yeats writes:

> When the Lunar and Solar cones are considered separately, we call the first the cone of the *Faculties* and the second the cone of the *Principles*; and we divide that of the *Faculties* into two cones, the one Solar and the other Lunar; and divide the cone of the *Principles* in the same way. The Four Principles are *Spirit, Celestial Body, Husk* and *Passionate Body*—we shall describe each presently—and they correspond to *Creative Mind, Body of Fate, Will* and *Mask* respectively. (*Vision*, 1925, p. 146)

He goes on to say that, in the diagram of the Great Wheel, the words *Head, Heart, Loins,* and *Fall* correspond to Spirit, Passionate Body, Husk, and Celestial Body at the opening of the next civilization (*Vision*, 1925, p. 147).

To say that one abstract term corresponds with another abstract term does little in the way of explaining either term, however, and Yeats himself admits that the terms are "confusing" (*Vision*, 1925, p. 147). In 1937, Yeats will define the Principles as nonmaterial aspects of being that, unlike the Faculties, operate during both incarnate and discarnate existence; but when the terms are at last defined toward the end of the 1925 book 2 (section 13, "The Four Principles"), the definitions again consist of vague correspondences between abstractions:

> The *Husk* is sensuous and instinctive, almost the physical body during life, and after death its record.
> The *Passionate Body* is passion, but unlike the *Mask*—which if permitted to govern the mind is isolating passion,—is without solitude.
> The *Celestial Body* is the portion of Eternal Life which can be separated away.
> The *Spirit* is almost abstract mind, for it has neither substance nor life unless united to the *Passionate Body* or *Celestial Body*.
> Unlike the *Faculties* they do not create separated or abstracted form. (*Vision*, 1925, p. 160)

Yeats's reluctance to confront these terms is evident throughout the 1925 edition. He opens book 2 of 1937 by confessing, "I knew nothing of the *Four Principles* when I wrote the last Book: a script had been lost through frustration, or through my own carelessness" (*Vision*, 1962, p. 187). The liberation of his new understanding of this part of the system manifests itself in a burst of lucid, fairly straightforward statements. As it will be necessary to have these terms in discussing "The Gates of Pluto," Yeat's 1937 definitions are quoted here:

> The *Principles* are the *Faculties* transferred, as it were, from a concave to a convex mirror, or vice versa. They are *Husk, Passionate Body, Spirit* and *Celestial Body. Spirit* and *Celestial Body* are mind and its object (the Divine Ideas in their unity), while *Husk* and *Passionate Body*, which correspond to *Will* and *Mask*, are sense (impulse, images; hearing, seeing, etc., images that we associate with ourselves—the ear, the eye, etc.) and the objects of sense. *Husk* is symbolically the human body. The *Principles* through their conflict reveal reality but create nothing. They find their unity in the *Celestial Body*. The *Faculties* find theirs in the Mask. (*Vision*, 1962, pp. 187–88)

One gets a much better sense of the Principles here, and their relationship to the Faculties emerges as, very roughly, that of the eternal to the temporal or the divine to the human. In describing what must be the lost script of the Principles that the instructors returned to teach again, Yeats equates the distinction between the Faculties and the Principles with that "between experience and revelation, between understanding and reason, between the higher and lower mind, which has engaged the thought of saints and philosophers from the time of Buddha" (*Vision*, 1962, p. 22). They are the "innate ground" of the Faculties and represent a larger field of influence than the Faculties alone:

> The wheel or cone of the *Faculties* may be considered to complete its movement between birth and death, that of the *Principles* to include the period between lives as well. (*Vision*, 1962, p. 188)

The concept of larger and larger fields of influence, each containing smaller cones, and in turn contained by a larger one, is central to the system and may, in fact, be an organizational principle of the later work. In 1925, "Dove or Swan," book 3, precedes "The Gates of Pluto," book 4. In 1937, the order is: book 3, "The Soul in Judgment" (a revision of "The Gates of Pluto"); book 4, "The Great Year of the Ancients"; and book 5, "Dove or Swan." Books 1 and 2 of both editions deal with the wheel and the twenty-eight embodiments, a cycle symbolized by days of the month, and the basic concept of the cone from which that and all cycles are derived. In introducing the Principles in book 2 of 1937—and he is simply introducing them there, not fully explicating them (*Vision*, 1962, p. 207)—Yeats is making a transition into the next larger field of influence, that of the wheel of the Principles with its larger divisions into months of the year (*Vision*, 1962, p. 188). The logical book to follow then is "The Soul in Judgment," which discusses the Principles more fully and on a more eternal level, not as in 1925, "Dove or Swan," which is a temporal application of the system to history.

In 1925, Yeats may have been structuring on a temporal progression from days (the wheel of the Faculties) to months (the wheel of the Principles) to years; hence, "Dove or Swan" with its consideration of historical time (years) as book 3 and "The Gates of Pluto," the timeless, as book 4. When Yeats himself discusses time, the information he relates has simply been given to him as fact, and he quarrels mildly with it. According to the documents, each Faculty and each Principle has a time designation. But, since Husk and Passionate Body disappear after death, and Spirit and Celestial Body unite, one is dealing really with only one Principle, the Celestial Body, which Yeats interprets as timeless (*Vision*, 1962, p. 192). Thus, it seems reasonable to say that "The Soul in Judgment" and "The Gates of Pluto" deal with the realm of the timeless, despite the fact that all the Principles (with their various time designations) are theoretically involved after death. In other words, the wheel of the Faculties is temporal; the wheel of the Principles is nontemporal.

Yeats, being a disciple of Berkeley, had always thought of time and space as "abstract creations of the human mind" (*Vision*, 1925, p. 129), and thus, in a sense, all time and all space are coexistent. But the 1925 arrangement of books does not show this; there is a confusion of real ("Dove or Swan") and symbolic (the cones of the Principles) time designations. The 1937 arrangement has the feel of integrating time and the timeless, an addition that the system—both by logic and mood—seems to demand. The implication is of a deeper acceptance of the endless progression of the cycles and less concern with escape, what might be called a more mature romanticism.

The 1925 arrangement breaks the mood, structurally, by interjecting this consideration of history between two books dealing with the timeless and the abstract. Structurally, the 1937 version makes a smooth arch from the individual temporal (the wheel of the Faculties) through eternal considerations ("The Soul in Judgment") and back to the temporal, collective man in history ("The Great Year of the Ancients") with "Dove or Swan" serving as a kind of coda or denouement. In one sense, this is simple classical plotting, with "The Soul in Judgment" occupying the climactic position, or it is simple discursive logic. In the context of Yeats's other work, however, one can sense that the structure is also meant to convey a poetic emotion. The moment of vision, achieved by the transcendence that begins in time and matter and returns to them again, marks most of Yeats's work as romantic and mystical. A striving for the same effect is apparent in the later version of *A Vision* and is further evidence that the book as a whole is a work of art and not philosophy.

Although "The Completed Symbol" introduces many side issues, its main intent, as the title suggests, is to show the entire scope of the symbolic system, in a sense, to invest the somewhat mathematical schema of book 1 with the emotional power that the system had for Yeats as one symbol. To be sure, the diagrams are still there, placed to show the relationship of the wheels of the Faculties and the Principles, the first of which is charted according to the twenty-eight lunar phases, the second according to the solar months of the zodiac. What should be noted, however, is not only the precise explication of the system, but the tone of the 1937 book 2. It is much more meditative than the largely expository book 1. The intent is to show the power of the symbol, and one gets in places the same sense of personal reverie that closes the work as a whole. For example, toward the end of book 2, 1937, Yeats writes:

> I have now described many symbols which seem mechanical because united in a single structure, and of which the greater number, precisely because they tell always the same story, may seem unnecessary. Yet every symbol, except where it lies in vast periods of time and so beyond our experience, has evoked for me some form of human destiny, and that form, once evoked, has appeared everywhere, as if there were but one destiny, as my own form might appear in a room full of mirrors. (*Vision*, 1962, pp. 213–14)

It is interesting to note the mood of confidence in this passage and to compare it to "The End of the Cycle," the conluding section of the work. The mock despair of the system there and the concluding upswing of faith are again evidence that the work is emotionally orchestrated.

1925 Book 2, Section 10. "The Great Year in Classical Antiquity," and 1937 Book 4. "The Great Year of the Ancients"

Yeats, like any symbolist, has a vested interest in tracing his symbols back to antiquity. A symbol's diversity of cultural origin gave it authority of itself, proved its validity of meaning, and for the poet's use, divested it of personal eccentricity. And so, he writes in 1925's book 2, section 10: "Before further explaining these cones which the reader must have found very troublesome, I would discover if Antiquity had similar measures" (*Vision*, 1925, p. 149).

It was, perhaps, a sense of the audacity of what he was proposing to the twentieth century that prompted Yeats to interject section 10, "The Great Year in Classical Antiquity," into a book that was otherwise abstract and somewhat obscure, as though, having gone so far in the explanation of the cones, he needed, at that point, to prop up the system's credibility with objective historical parallels. Certainly, a great many authorities are quoted in that section and in "The Great Year of the Ancients" in the 1937 version, and a comparison of these parallel authorities in the two versions may be helpful in charting the growth of *A Vision*.

A major difference is that in 1937 Yeats gives much more attention to the Great Year as defined by Plato. Plato, of course, is mentioned in 1925, but only as one of many in the densely packed catalog of Yeats's predecessors in section 10. In 1937, he is perhaps the major source, along with Cicero, who is also most conspicuous in 1925. Vico, an important source for other writers of the period, notably Joyce, is mentioned for the first time in 1937. Heraclitus and Empedocles, central in both works but absent from section 10, 1925, are mentioned as the originators of "the symbol expounded in this book of a phaseless sphere that becomes phasal in our thought" (*Vision*, 1962, p. 247). This inclusion illustrates the more speculative, slow-paced approach to the material that Yeats took in 1937. The Upanishads, a late influence, are mentioned for the first time in 1937, and the names of Spinoza, Leibnitz, and Newton show the effects of Yeats's later reading in philosophy. Other names are taken from Yeats's reading in anthropology, history, and other disciplines: Marx, Sorel, Croce, Gerald Heard, Henry Adams, Petrie, Spengler, Josef Strzygowski (mentioned in 1925 in "The Gates of Pluto"), Frobenius, Nicholas of Cusa, Pierre Duhem, and Francis Thompson. Plotinus, an important later source, Socrates, Hermes, and Anaximander are cited in 1937; Dante becomes more important, and Virgil retains his prominence.

In 1925, the names are Plato, Virgil, Cicero, Plutarch, Hipparchus, Tacitus, Macrobius, Milton, Syncellus, M. Cumont, E. M. Plunkett, Dr. Alfred Jeremias, Dr. Fritz Homell, Savonarola, Kepler, Machiavelli, and Salomon Reinach. The implications of all this are, perhaps, obvious: Yeats had read more and better sources by 1937 and was better able to recognize the most powerful evidence among them, for example, the increased stress on Plato, the choice of Dante over Milton. Further, since the sources vary, it seems clear, as Yeats himself often repeats, that once he understood the system, he could see its implications everywhere.

A full, book-length treatment could contain all this scholarship, especially tempered with speculation as the 1937 text is, but the 1925 section 10, only nine pages in length, is overloaded with theories and scholars. It is as though Yeats were uncertain himself about the meaning of the Robartes documents or their acceptability to his readers and sought authorities to support the system. He even writes at one point, "However I but suggest and wait judgment, being no scholar; and it may be, but seek a background for my thought, a painted scene" (*Vision*, 1925, p. 157). Morton Irving Seiden, whose pioneering work, *William Butler Yeats: The Poet as a Mythmaker, 1865–1939*, opened the way for further comparative studies such as this one, feels that it was to elaborate upon this "painted scene" that Yeats attempted the second edition of *A Vision*. Seiden writes:

> He wanted more authorities—as many as possible—who might help him both to clarify and further to substantiate what he already believed. Between the publication of *A Vision* in 1925 and his death in 1939, indeed, he read and studied more than he had read, perhaps, in all the preceding years of his life.[9]

Though Seiden's extensive exploration of Yeats's philosophical background and thought does much to help the reader understand the almost overwhelming wealth of ideas in *A Vision*, Yeats's stated reason for revision was that he simply did not understand the system when he wrote the first edition (*Vision*, 1962, pp. 18, 187). True, Yeats did add considerable new material in 1937, but the main purpose of this painted scene was to relate the geometry of the cones to the process of time and the rise and fall of civilizations and so to find, like the Caliph, a rule of thumb that explains both individuals and nations.

Astrology is such a map but, as the "Mythology" section at the end of the 1925 edition notes, it is more. By welding his own system to the early astrologer's "Book of Life" (*Vision*, 1925, p. 150), Yeats could invest the mathematical structure with the "present vivid experience" of mythology (*Vision*, 1925, p. 252)—could make it contain a wealth of vital symbolism. His system, being modern, was a composite of various ancient sources, but he was, of course, particularly interested in theories that reinforced his own. Of Plato, for example, he writes:

> Our interest in Plato's comment is precisely that he does use it as we use the lunar phases, as if it were the moving hands upon a vast clock, or a picturesque symbolism that helped him to make more vivid, and perhaps date, developments of the human mind that can be proved dialectically. (*Vision*, 1925, p. 155)

In other words, Plato used the Great Year in the same way that Yeats did. In another place he remarks that "the alternation of *antithetical* and *primary* months is certainly Platonic" (*Vision*, 1925, p. 157).

As has been shown, book 2 as a whole required extensive reorganization. Section 10, in itself, needed to be almost totally reworked into "The Great Year of the Ancients." Its major fault, of course, is that there is simply too much material; the section is dense and hard to follow. By 1937, Yeats had acquired even more information, but he had also sorted out the relative importance of each source. Further, bearing in mind the changes Yeats made in structure—the rearrangement of the order of the books—the function of "The Great Year of the Ancients" had changed from that of section 10 of 1925. The random remark regarding the attempt to provide a painted scene became the aesthetic principle behind book 4. Thus, in revising, Yeats becomes more selective and strives to make the book as a whole a half-speculative, half-factual reinforcement of the system.

The book begins, then, in speculation, and no one can be quite so speculative as Yeats. Rhetorical question after rhetorical question in sections 1 and 2 ease the reader into a mood of meditation. "Caesar and Christ always stand face to face in our imagination" (*Vision*, 1962, p. 244), Yeats writes, and from that thematic identification of opposing symbols, he proceeds to draw forth a detailed and orderly history of thought upon the topic. As in 1925, he begins with Cicero and his definition of the Great Year, but now he has the confidence to control the facts according to his own poetic perception of the system. The history of the idea given in 1937 is a selection from a multitude of thoughts and interpretations, and the selection is made from the perspective of Yeats the artist, striving both to be clear and orderly in his presentation of fact and to shape those facts into an aesthetic experience. Thus, by artistic choice, he derives from Cicero, or more properly from the concept of the mind working on the natural year, the idea of antinomies that he needs for his own work: "Perhaps at the start a mere magnification of the natural year, it [the Great Year] grew more complicated with the spread of Greek astronomy, but it is always the simpler, more symbolic form, with its conflict of light and dark, heat and cold, that concerns me most" (*Vision*, 1962, p. 246).

Likewise, in section 4 he begins to draw out the central dichotomy between the individual and the type: "So far the Ideas had been everything, the individual nothing; beauty and truth alone had mattered to Plato and Socrates, but Plotinus thought that every individual had his Idea, his eternal counterpart; the Greatest Year and the Great Years that were its Months became a stream of souls" (*Vision*, 1962, p. 247).

In section 5, he notes the shift from Cancer (the Greek concept) to Aries (the Persian) as the beginning of the year. Applying the doctrines of Empedocles this means a shift "from the extremes where the world was destroyed to the midway point where it was restored, where Love began to prevail over Discord, Day over Night" (*Vision*, 1962, p. 249). When Christ's resurrection is placed in Aries (sections 5 and 6), the implication is that the world, according to the system, is constantly regenerating, that a periodic "world restorer" is as much a part of the plan as the destruction symbolized by Caesar's death in the same sign.

What follows is a history of the calculation of the Great Year. Hipparchus's discovery that the zodiacal constellations were moving and Ptolemy's fixing of the rate of movement led to the 36,000-year Platonic Year. At the same time, it necessitated the concept of an abstract fixed zodiac, the ninth sphere of fixed stars. Ptolemy's discovery cast doubt upon the idea that the stars themselves determined human destiny; now they became rather a system of calculating the condition of the universe at a given time. Thus was born the idea of the fixed type coexisting with the unique individual. Because the constellations are in motion, each individual born is somehow different from all others; but because the constellations move so slowly, the general zodiac types persist as valid references. The same laws operate in regard to nations. Ptolemy's dating is problematical, but it is close enough to the assassination of Caesar and to the birth of Christ to make both seem miraculous (section 9), taking one back to section 2 where the original antinomy of Caesar and Christ was set up as a poetic postulate.

In section 6, Yeats begins to incorporate his own system of cones into the concepts from this history of thought regarding the Great Year. In section 10, by again linking ancient systems with his own, he is able to realize a major aim of any such system: the prediction of the coming age. Aries on the map of the twenty-eight incarnations marks the position of the vernal equinox (the phase of Will in the wheel of 26,000 years) at the beginning of the next antithetical era: "It is the Aries or solar east of the double cone of its particular era set within the circuit of the Great Year" (*Vision*, 1962, pp. 254–55). This next influx, at Phase 17, will be characterized by "the greatest possible intellectual power because it is the centre of that quarter of the Wheel symbolical of the logical intellect, and because it is one of the four moments where the *Faculties* are at equal distance from one another: conflict, and therefore intensity of consciousness, apportioned out through the whole being" (*Vision*, 1962, p. 255).

Such large schematizations are, as Yeats realized, "too theoretical, too arbitrary, to serve any practical purpose" (*A Vision*, 1962, p. 255); and so, in section 11, he narrows his focus to a consideration of his own era as mapped on the historical diagram prefacing "Dove or Swan." Here he discovers the conflict between religious and secular thought that foreshadows the coming antithetical dispensation (*Vision*, 1962, p. 257). This prediction arises from a reading of the diagram as a simple visual metaphor showing one gyre contracting as the other expands. If one reads, as Yeats's instructors do, the numbers printed in black—that is, the dates, not the phases (for example, at the horizontal line: 250, 900, 1180, and 1927)—one discovers that these four periods present the position of the Four Faculties on the cone of the era and are, as Yeats says, "eternally co-existent" (*Vision*, 1962, p. 257). When "seen in time," Yeats explains, the spirits of these periods, which "seem to us past," are present, though unseen, and affect the present (*Vision*, 1962, p. 257). That Yeats, as though for simplicity's sake, can so casually speak of these periods as "seen in time," and does in fact seem to prefer to call them "four co-existent acts" (*Vision*, 1962, p. 257), shows what a thoroughgoing Berkeleian he was. Time and timelessness, space and spacelessness, are two ways of looking at the same reality, but as Yeats illustrated in his rearrangement of the books, it is more accurate to think of them as coexistent.

The structural line of book 4 seems to break up somewhat in sections 12 and 13. Abruptly, Yeats introduces archaeological evidence in support of the symbolism of the system and finds, like a true symbolist, that Strzygowski's data, for example, will mesh with his own: "If I translate his geographical symbolism into the language of the system I say that South and East are human form and intellectual authority, whereas North and West are superhuman form and emotional freedom" (*Vision*, 1962, p. 258). Likewise, Frobenius's Altar and Cavern are Yeats's space and time (*Vision*, 1962, pp. 259–60) and represent, by an extension that goes back to the line and plane of book 1, another theoretical basis of the gyre in space and time (*Vision*, 1962, pp. 70–71), "the first distinction between *primary* and *antithetical* civilisations" (*Vision*, 1962, p. 261). Petrie, Spengler, Marx, Sorel, and finally, Vico, in whom these other theories had their origin, are introduced as though, having given evidence of the validity of the system's symbols, he must now support its claim to be as modern a myth as the scientific myth of progress:

> Certainly my instructors have chosen a theme that has deeply stirred men's minds though the newspapers are silent about it; the newspapers have the happy countermyth of progress; a theme as important perhaps as Henry Adams thought when he told the Boston Historical Association that were it turned into a science powerful interests would prevent its publication. (*Vision*, 1962, pp. 261–62)

Section 16 refutes a possible misconception, that the coming antithetical age will be primitive and barbaric, referring one back to section 10, where the future dispensation is discussed in full. Section 17 has a sure sense of conclusion: Yeats summarizes the interchange of the tinctures and the symbolic value of terms, especially primary and antithetical, and points up in dramatic prose the purpose of book 4, which is to show how the approaching antithetical influx coincides with the intellectual climax of the Great Year (*Vision*, 1962, p. 263). He concludes:

> Something of what I have said it must be, the myth declares, for it must reverse our era and resume past eras in itself; what else it must be no man can say, for always at the critical moment the *Thirteenth Cone*, the sphere,

the unique intervenes. (*Vision*, 1962, p. 263)

1925 Book 4. "The Gates of Pluto," and
1937 Book 3. "The Soul in Judgment"

This study has thus far ignored "Dove or Swan," which follows "What the Caliph Refused to Learn" in 1925, because except for the conclusion, which was later omitted, it is essentially the same in 1937 as in 1925. The significance of this omission will be discussed in another chapter. Except for "Dove or Swan," "The Soul in Judgment" shows the least structural revision of all the books of the 1937 *Vision*. The pattern, as in "The Gates of Pluto," is simply a tracing, in sequence, of the stages of existence between death and birth. The 1937 version is considerably shorter, approximately two-thirds the length of the 1925 book. In some ways, it is clearer and easier to read, partly because the material is better understood by Yeats and better expressed, partly because much of the earlier clutter of detail and terminology has been dropped. Yet, there are themes in the 1925 version that one wishes Yeats had retained and expanded: the discussion of the nature of evil, for example, which is slighted in 1937, and the discussion of the Arcon, which might have developed into a full aesthetic theory, or at least greatly supplemented Yeats's essays on art.

Although "The Soul in Judgment," unlike books 1 and 2, contains no apologies for earlier misunderstandings, there is ample evidence in "The Gates of Pluto" to suggest that Yeats was far from sure of his material in 1925. "Much in this chapter belongs to a part of the system that requires a more detailed study than I can at present give" (*Vision*, 1925, p. 241), Yeats writes in a footnote. In another place he writes that the documents here are "more than usually obscure and strange," and that he is "afraid of unconsciously perverting their meaning" (*Vision*, 1925, p. 229). According to Aherne, even Robartes's notes are confused and inadequate on the topic of existence between death and birth because he, like Kusta ben Luka, had been the victim of the Frustrators (*Vision*, 1925, p. 238); Aherne himself on four occasions feels obliged to make parenthetical additions to Yeats's text. Yeats's own coy remark toward the end of the book—"Have I found a good net for a herring fisher?" (*Vision*, 1925, p. 251)—seems to be an attempt, and not an infrequent one in Yeats, to make an image do service for genuine explication. One remembers his remark in regard to the 1925 work as a whole: "I tried to interest my readers in an unexplained rule of thumb that somehow explained the world" (*Vision*, 1962, p. 81).

The stages between death and birth, six in all, are roughly the same in both versions, although their treatment is greatly simplified in 1937. Two exceptions, the Going Forth and the Vision of the Friends, both of which are omitted in 1937, will be discussed later. The versions agree in regard to The Vision of the Blood Kindred, the first state, which is simply the newly dead man's vision of all those persons who were bound to him in life.[10] The accompanying Separation of the Four Principles—which in its detailed form, section 3, so bored Edmund Wilson[11]—is in 1937 merely a footnote, although the point of the states between death and birth remains, in essence, to effect this separation. The same footnote mentions the effects that the burial service can have on the quality of the Meditation. Yeats leaves this out of the text in 1937 because it seems to him now not "a necessary deduction from the symbol," but "an unverifiable statement of experience" (*Vision*, 1962, pp. 223–24). The 1925 version as a whole stresses the interaction of living and dead more strongly; Yeats's insistence on the importance of symbolism in the burial ritual there calls to mind section 6 of "Under Ben Bulben" where, perhaps because of the persistence of this belief, he dictates his own burial service.

The greatest amount of confusion in the book centers on the second stage, partly because its description is overloaded with terminology (the Meditation, the Teaching, the Return, the Dreaming Back, the Phantasmagoria, the Waking and Sleeping States) and partly because terms are often used in a double sense. *Meditation* seems to be the generic term, encompassing the others, but Yeats also writes in 1925 that Meditation "ends with burial" (*Vision*, 1925, p. 223). In 1937, however, he says that the dreaming of Meditation may last for centuries if there has been great egotism and tragedy (*Vision*, 1962, p. 224). Such minor contradictions are abundant in both versions and make these books very frustrating reading; one is forced, often, to guess, and it is most accurate to guess here that Meditation (which is capitalized in 1937 but not in 1925) is not one of the six states (Vision of the Blood Kindred, the Return, the Shiftings, the Beatitude, the Purification, the Foreknowledge—according to the 1937 text). Yeats in fact says in 1937 that the true name of the second stage is the Return, although even that term seems confused with the Dreaming Back (*Vision*, 1962, pp. 225–26).

The second stage contains three facets: the Return, which traces events in reverse chronological order to their cause; the Dreaming Back, which traces events backward in the order of their intensity to their full consequences; and the Phantasmagoria (capitalized in 1937 but not in 1925), which seems in the earlier edition to be simply this procession of events, but which in 1937 is equal to the Return and the Dreaming Back. Yeats writes of it there: "The second stage contains in addition to the *Dreaming Back* and the *Return* what is called the *Phantasmagoria*, which exists to exhaust, not nature, not pain and pleasure, but emotion, and is the work of *Teaching Spirits*. The physical and moral life is completed, without the addition of any new element that the objects of hope may be completed, for only that which is completed can be known and dismissed" (*Vision*, 1962, p. 230).

This seems to be a statement made more for the sake of symmetry than real explication. The terms are not fully explained. Emotion seems to differ from pleasure and pain in that it represents hope or future plans rather than the past, but what place has nature in a disembodied state? The 1925 version states that the Return exists to exhaust pleasure and pain (*Vision*, 1925, p. 225), but the association of the Dreaming Back with nature is, in 1925, largely inferred as the dream of the Passionate Body (*Vision*, 1925, p. 226). If Passionate Body is Passion, as it is in 1925 (*Vision*, 1925, p. 160), it is a bit difficult to see how a dream of passion can exhaust nature, especially since the Passionate Body corresponds to Mask, which is an antithetical image and is nonmaterial.

It is well to bear in mind here, however, that existence from death to birth, the realm of the Principles, does not correspond to existence from birth to death, the Faculties. If the two realms were opposite, like the natural world of man and the spiritual fairy world of Irish folklore, the antithetical Mask in the wheel of the Faculties could be the primary object of sense, the Passionate Body, in the wheel of the Principles, as Yeats says it is in 1937. But Yeats's theory shows the wheels, not reversed but lying at right angles to each other (*Vision*, 1962, p. 188). This seems to be yet another example of Yeats's poetic perceptions in conflict with the dogma of the documents.

In the 1937 version, where Husk is sense, Passionate Body the object of sense—that is, the material world (*Vision*, 1962, pp. 187–88)—it seems reasonable to write as Yeats does that the Return (and since Yeats uses *Return* in 1937 both as a general term for stage 2 and as a specific minor term for one of three facets of stage 2, one can take him here to mean the facets, the Dreaming Back and the Return respectively) "has for its object the *Spirit's* separation from the *Passionate Body*, considered as nature, and from the *Husk* considered as pleasure and pain" (*Vision*, 1962, p. 226). The point is trivial, but it illustrates how opaque the system can be, and how Yeats's lack of understanding of the Principles, discussed earlier in regard to Book 2, spills over into "The Gates of Pluto" and confuses matters there as well.

Another problem exists in considering the Waking and Sleeping States that occur in stages 2 and 3, the Return and the Shiftings, and possibly in the Vision of the Blood Kindred, but not in the Beatitude or later stages (*Vision*, 1925, p. 238). In the Waking State, also called the Teaching, images of sense are imposed on the Spirit by other beings. This state corresponds, in a way that Yeats does not make clear, with the Sage and, during this stage, the gyre moves. In the Sleeping State, images are recovered from the Record, another vague concept that can be equated roughly with the unconscious; this stage corresponds to the Victim, and during this stage the gyre is stationary (*Vision*, 1925, pp. 224–25). (This is, by the way, the only reference to a stationary gyre; the system would seem to demand that the gyre be constantly in motion.) At any rate, the Waking State is apparently a dream of the

Celestial Body, the Sleeping State a dream of the Passionate Body; the states alternate and the objective of the states is to separate the Spirit from both the Husk and the Passionate Body through respectively the Return and the Dreaming Back (*Vision*, 1925, pp. 224–26). "Every event so dreamed," Yeats writes of this process, "is the expression of some knot, some concentration of feeling separating off a period of time, or portion of the being, from the being as a whole and the life as a whole, and the dream is as it were a smoothing out or an unwinding" (*Vision*, 1925, p. 227). Teaching Spirits, which Yeats identifies for the first time in 1937 as Spirits of the Thirteenth Cone "who substitute for *Husk* and *Passionate Body* supersensual emotion and imagery; the 'unconscious' or unapparent for that which has *disappeared*" (*Vision*, 1962, p. 229), assist the Spirit in this symbolic learning process.

The problem occurs in the alternation of these two states. Yeats writes: "After its imprisonment by some event in the *Dreaming Back*, the *Spirit* relives that event in the *Return* and turns it into knowledge, and then falls into the *Dreaming Back* once more" (*Vision*, 1962, p. 226). How can an event recovered from the Dreaming Back order of intensity be interjected into the Return's chronological order of events without forcing the Return to assume that same order of intensity, in violation of its own definition? If the Dreaming Back seeks to know consequences, why does it relive the event in the Return that is concerned with causes? If the Teaching Spirits substitute images for sense and the objects of sense, why do the Spirits need the help of incarnate minds, as Yeats says they do (*Vision*, 1962, pp. 226–27; 1925, p. 228), to assist the second stage?

The intention here is not so much to quarrel with Yeats's logic as to point up how frustrating the text can be. The subject matter in itself is intensely interesting, not to mention its obvious relevance to the plays and poetry. One wishes, and undoubtedly Yeats wished, that the explanation could be clearer, for the poetic value of the material of stage 2 is high. In fact, most poems and plays that can be said to have been drawn from the system are centered on this vaguely defined state or on the concept of the interchange of the tinctures; oddly enough, almost no artistic use is made of the parts of the system that Yeats understood well, the twenty-eight embodiments, for example, or the Foreknowledge. "The Dance of the Four Royal Persons" shows no artistic commitment, nor does "The Phases of the Moon." It is almost as though intellectual understanding numbed the imagination, invalidated the material for artistic use. Or, inversely, the complexity of certain sections accounts for both their incomprehensibility and their artistic fascination.

Certainly, the presence of "knots" in the incarnate life and the necessity of unraveling these knots after death, which are the core of the second stage, have this fascination; and the fascination is prolonged and heightened by its seeming infinitude, the gradual perfecting of the self through a series of incarnations. The escape, like the romantic ideal of transcendence, while it exists, is held so distant that it can encompass both hope and sorrow. Although there is a realm of "Those who wait," that is, those who have completed the cycles (*Vision*, 1925, p. 237), there is no immediate reward or paradise. "Neither between death and birth nor between birth and death can the soul find more than momentary happiness," Yeats writes. "Its object is to pass rapidly round its circle and find freedom from that circle" (*Vision*, 1962, p. 236).

The remaining states, while they are less intriguing, are much more readily understood. At the end of the second state, the events of the past life are whole and can be dismissed; the moral life, however, is only whole in respect to the moral code that the being accepted during life. A man who did good without knowing evil or evil without knowing good cannot be said to be either good or evil; he lacks full understanding and must enter the Shiftings where the Spirit is purified of good and evil. This is accomplished by the Spirit's living a good life in the knowledge of, or in conquest of, evil—or vice versa. If his motives were good, his surroundings evil in life, these conditions will be reversed in the Shiftings (*Vision*, 1962, pp. 231–32; 1925, pp. 229–30). Although Yeats comments that the documents are obscure here and quotes them directly (*Vision*, 1925, p. 229; 1962, pp. 231–32), the ideas are fairly straightforward, and only one paragraph is devoted to the Shiftings in 1937. The concept of evil in the later text is somewhat neutral. Yeats says only that "cruelty and ignorance, which echo the *Sage* and *Victim* of Book I, constitute evil as my instructors see it, and are that which makes possible the conscious union of the *Daimons* of man and woman or that of the *Daimon* of the living and a *Spirit* of the *Thirteenth Core*, which is the deliverance from birth and death" (*Vision*, 1962, p. 240).

One implication of this passage seems to be that in love one partner must always be Victim, one Sage or tyrant, as Yeats says elsewhere. It is difficult to see, at this point, how evil can effect deliverance from the cycle as this passage implies, but the 1937 discussion of Victimage for the Ghostly Self seems relevant. In 1925, the discussion of evil is much more interesting and elaborate. Yeats says, for example, that good is only good as a "conquest" of evil and that evil or good is generally done in ignorance. Thus, the Daimon, which is here roughly the intellect, seeks the knowledge of good and evil that was hidden in life, not by the necessity of an external law, but by the necessity of its own nature, in order to be "satisfied" (*Vision*, 1925, p. 230). It is interesting that although this seeking for the knowledge of good and evil was the cause of the Christian Fall, Yeats attaches no real moral significance to it, and is in fact eager to reassure the reader that there is no suffering involved in acquiring such knowledge.

What is more interesting is the implied connection between evil and sexual love: "Evil is that which opposes Unity of Being and seeing that man seeks his *primary* in woman, and woman her *antithetical* in man, a relationship of sex displays good and evil in their most subtle and overpowering form" (*Vision*, 1925, p. 230). Thus, in the Shiftings, men and women relive their loves to "expiate," often with the help of the living, the "cruelty and deceit" that all strong passions contain (*Vision*, 1925, p. 233). To say that man seeks his primary in woman and woman her antithetical in man implies that men are always antithetical, women always primary, and in fact Yeats defines antithetical as masculine, primary as feminine (*Vision*, 1962, p. 263). But this, taken logically, contradicts the system in general and 1925, book 1, section 11, directly where men and women equally share the Four Faculties (*Vision*, 1925, pp. 27–28). Theoretically, a woman could seek the primary in a man, or a man the antithetical in a woman, depending upon their phases.

The distortion is minor, however, and, one senses, personal—an example of Yeats's using the system both to acquire a muse and as a balm for the knot of his own unhappy love. He writes, almost wishfully: "Strong love given in ignorance may be relived again and again, though not with suffering, for all now is intellect and he is all *Daimon*, and tragic and happy circumstance alike offer an intellectual ecstasy at the revelation of truth, and the most horrible tragedy in the end can but seem a figure in a dance" (*Vision*, 1925, p. 231). In 1937, the connection between sex and evil is only subtly implied but the emotion is still strong beneath the surface and elicits from Yeats almost the only moral judgment he makes in regard to the system. Speaking of the expiation that lovers must endure, he writes, "This is just, for there had been no need of expiation had they seen in one another that other and not something else" (*Vision*, 1962, p. 238). This failure to find the Daimon of the other is the cause of expiation, which may last through many lifetimes and may impose the image of the beloved upon a new living man or woman. "Expiation is a harmonisation of being, and we seek out the image, reflected in some living man or woman, of that other being, that we may achieve it in action" (*Vision*, 1925, p. 233).

In writing of the fourth state, Marriage or the Beatitude, Yeats again in 1937 cuts a full section down to one paragraph. Beatitude in 1937 is "a moment of consciousness" or "complete equilibrium after the conflict of the *Shiftings*" (*Vision*, 1962, p. 232). In 1925, the description is much less abstract and clinical, and more in keeping with the connotation of blessedness. Yeats's description is self-explanatory:

> In life, seeing that the *Four Faculties* and the *Husk* and *Passionate Body* constrain all, we are in accident and passion; but now *Spirit* and *Celestial Body* constrain all, the one calling up all concrete universal quality and idea, and the other closing it in the unique image. Nor can I consider the *Beatitude* as any state beyond man's comprehension, but as the presence before the soul in some settled order, which has arisen out of the soul's past, of all those events or works of men which have expressed some quality of wisdom or of beauty or of power within the compass of that soul, and as more

completely human and actual than any life lived in a particular body. It is the momentary union of the *Spirit* and the *Celestial Body* with the *Ghostly Self* and fades into or is preceded by what is called the *Vision of the Clarified Body*, which is indeed a Vision of our own *Celestial Body* as that body will be when all cycles end. (*Vision*, 1925, p. 235)

The Vision of the Clarified Body, which sounds much like the Christian resurrection of the body, has been dropped from the later version, as has the description of the "works of men," which suggests, particularly in the conjunction of the universal idea and the unique image, the ultimate work of art or some sort of Byzantium.

The Christian implications, which receive considerable attention in 1925, are limited in 1937, although Yeats does again quote the passage, "The *Celestial Body* is the Divine Cloak lent to all, it falls away at the consummation and Christ is revealed" (*Vision*, 1962, p. 232). In 1925, this commentary was given to Owen Aherne in a parenthetical note, a necessary rhetorical maneuver, perhaps, since Yeats had so firmly set up the polarity of himself as sympathetic to the antithetical and Aherne to the Christian primary. Christian associations with the system are made throughout *A Vision* in 1925, but Yeats apparently did not wish to speak directly of these matters and thus invented the ruse of being "indulgent to Christian or *primary* prejudice" in Aherne (*Vision*, 1925, p. 235). This may have been wise, for Aherne does make rather radical statements, as when he writes that "the *Beatitude* and the two states that follow correspond to the 13th, 14th and 15th Cycles which correspond in their turn to Holy Ghost, Son and Father" (*Vision*, 1925, p. 236). If the Thirteenth Cycle corresponds to the Holy Ghost, the coming era would, perhaps, be the same Kingdom of the Spirit that Aherne sought in Joachim's book in "The Tables of the Law." One does not see how this three-part Christian scheme could merge with the dualistic system of *A Vision*, however, and the line of thought involving the Fourteenth and Fifteenth Cycles is not pursued in 1937.

The two final stages are again troublesome. Purification, the fifth stage in 1937, does not appear in 1925, but it is likely that the Going Forth, sketched briefly in 1925 and absent in 1937, is the same state as Purification. There is no internal evidence to suggest why this change was made, but the two states are too much alike not to make this identification. Both involve a forgetting of thoughts and images drawn from the Faculties, both last for centuries; in fact, next to the Return, the Going Forth is the longest state (*Vision*, 1925, p. 239). The stated purpose of the Spirit during this stage in both editions is to seek a new Husk (*Vision*, 1925, p. 237; 1962, p. 233), and during the state it is "free and in relation to *Spirits* free like itself" (*Vision*, 1962, p. 233), or as the earlier text puts it, is "in the presence of all those activities whose *Complementary Dream* is in our art, or music or literature, and of those men and women who have finished all their cycles and are called 'Those who wait'" (*Vision*, 1925, p. 237).

The Spirit in the Beatitude would remain there, the 1925 text says, except for its "terror of what seems to be the loss of its own being" (*Vision*, 1925, p. 236), which forces it to rebirth. As the Purification progresses, the Spirit substitutes for the perception of the Celestial Body seen as a whole its own personal aim and becomes self-directing; the name of the state apparently is derived from the Spirit's attempt to purify that aim (*Vision*, 1962, p. 233). Such purification may require the assistance of the living, "into whose 'unconsciousness' or incarnate *Daimon*, some affinity of aim, or the command of the *Thirteenth Cone*, permits it to enter" (*Vision*, 1962, p. 234).

The idea that disembodied Spirits make use of the minds of the living to achieve the passage from death to birth is extremely pervasive in 1925 and has implications for Yeats's theories of art. In 1937, the discussion of the relationship of art and the dead is much more circumscribed but the theoretical basis is still apparent. "Those who taught me this system did so, not for my sake, but their own," Yeats writes; in a footnote he adds: "They say that only the words spoken in trance or written in the automatic script assist them. They belong to the 'unconscious' and what comes from them alone serves. My interpretations do not concern them" (*Vision*, 1962, p. 234). It is quite possible that *A Vision* and other works of art are the result of discarnate Spirits' attempts to rid themselves of a former life in order to be reborn into the next. In 1925, Yeats writes of the Spirits in the Shiftings, where the Celestial Body is in contact with the Thirteenth Cycle, that they "may carry to the living messages concerned with purposes that transcend individual life" (*Vision*, 1925, pp. 231–32). They make themselves known, as did Yeats's communicators, by various scents and sounds, and take on the same mental condition as their living contact. One remembers a remark the communicators once made to Yeats: "You have said what we wanted to have said" (*Vision*, 1962, p. 17).

The final state before rebirth is, in 1925, called the Foreknowing; in 1937, the Foreknowledge. Yeats describes it in 1925 as that state in which the Spirit, having substituted a new Husk and Passionate Body for the vision of the Celestial Body, begins again to crave pleasure and pain. In the Foreknowledge, a reversal of the Dreaming Back, "it sees events and people that shall influence its coming life upon earth, and as it can see that influence, as can no living man, it is possessed with violent love and hate, a wilful passion comparable to the fated passion of the *Dreaming Back*" (*Vision*, 1925, p. 237). Spirits in this state may attempt to prevent what they foresee and become Frustrators—or as Yeats says in 1937, in one of his few references to modern psychology, the "censor" (*Vision*, 1962, p. 235). In 1925, Yeats mentions the Vision of the Friends, a parallel state to the Vision of the Blood Kindred, which occurs during the sleep in the womb (*Vision*, 1925, p. 238);

but in 1937, he says simply, "During its sleep in the womb the *Spirit* accepts its future life, declares it just" (*Vision*, 1962, p. 235).

Following the descriptions of the six stages, the remainder of "The Soul in Judgment" is devoted to incidental information (section 10, which concerns the appearance of the Spirit in the various states, the length and purpose of expiation) and to a rather-too-brief discussion of Victimage and bonds in sections 11 and 13. The 1937 book as a whole has a feeling of reticence in regard to life after death; the 1925 version is much more stimulating. There, the concluding sections, 11 through 16, are a mixture of theory and poetic speculation. The 1925 section 11, "Funeral Images, Works of Art, and the Dead," which contains anecdotes of relationships between the dead and the living, serves as introductory material in the 1937 section 3, in keeping with Yeats's later tendency to begin the books with anecdote and speculation.

Of particular interest is section 12, "The Spirits at Fifteen and at One," a discussion of the aesthetic concept of the Arcon that was, unfortunately, omitted in 1937, perhaps because by that time Yeats no longer saw the stages between death and birth as related to the twenty-eight-phase wheel or perhaps, having written out the concept's implications in his own art, he no longer needed such discussion. In 1925, he seems to have seen the period between embodiments in terms much like those of the wheel of the Faculties; the Spirits have phases and a relationship to man much like that of his own Daimon. They also have a great influence on the works of living man, for Yeats writes:

> The Spirits at 15 need help that, before entering upon their embodied state, they may rid themselves of all traces of the *primary Tincture*, and this they gain by imposing upon a man or woman's mind an *antithetical* image which requires *primary* expression. It is this expression, which may be an action or a work of art, which sets them free, and the image imposed is an ideal form, an image of themselves, a type of emotion which expresses them, and this they can do but upon one man or woman's mind; their coming life depending upon their choice of that mind. They suffer from terror of solitude, and can only free themselves from terror by becoming entirely *antithetical* and so self-sufficing, and till that moment comes each must, if a woman, give some one man her love, and though he cannot, unless out of phase and obsessed to the creation of a succuba know that his muse exists, he returns this love through the intermediary of an idol. This idol he creates out of an image imposed upon his imagination by the Spirit. (*Vision*, 1925, pp. 241–42)

The relationship between man and Spirit here seems to echo strongly the relationship in book 1, section 11, between man and Daimon, particularly in the love relationship of their opposing sexes, the opposition of primary and antithetical phases, and the aesthetic implications of these oppositions. Yeats never says directly that the Daimon is a disembodied Spirit, but he does say, in 1937, that "all spirits inhabit our unconsciousness or, as Swedenborg said, are the Dramatis Personae of our dreams" (*Vision*, 1962, p. 227), and the sense of interaction between incarnate men and women and Spirits, though stronger in 1925, is present in both versions.

The Spirit at 15 presents to the man's imagination an antithetical image that requires primary expression; this expression, which frees the Spirit from terror and the man from desire, is called an antithetical Arcon (*Vision*, 1925, p. 242). One assumes that the man chosen is primary. On the other hand, the Spirit at Phase 1 must reverse the process through a primary Arcon, that is, antithetical expression with an antithetical man, and *A Vision* may be just such a primary Arcon. These Arcons represent a form of expiation for bonds made in former lives; any opposition of antithetical and primary—lovers, master and slave, or mother and child—may become such a bond: "Any relation that is deeper than the intellect may become such a bond" (*Vision*, 1962, p. 239). A strong bond may form a separate gyre that cannot be broken by the influence of a stronger gyre until it first exhausts itself (*Vision*, 1962, p. 237).

Expiation may take two forms: Victimage for the Dead, which arises because union between incarnate Daimons (that is, a particular experience) was prevented and is an expiation of passion exorcised on some living person; and Victimage for the Ghostly Self, which is brought about by a denial of experience itself and is characterized by spirituality (*Vision*, 1962, p. 239). Christ, Dante, and Yeats's own Deirdre and Naisi are all examples of Victimage for the Ghostly Self (*Vision*, 1925, pp. 243–44); they tend to choose goals or loves in life that cannot prosper. In 1937, Yeats also calls this state Victimage for a Spirit of the Thirteenth Cone because the Daimon seeks supernatural experience and may even take the place of the Spirit (*Vision*, 1962, p. 239). Though Yeats does not doctrinally connect Victimage for the Ghostly Self with the primary Arcon and in that way make it the province of the antithetical man exclusively, he is, as Aherne points out in the introduction, prejudiced toward the antithetical. The implication here seems to be that antithetical man, "man alone" he may be called, is the more vitally concerned with his Ghostly Self, that element which is unique in man and his fate (*Vision*, 1925, p. 243) and which Aherne associates with the Holy Ghost, the spark of divinity in each individual man (*Vision*, 1925, p. 236). It is possible, too, that Victimage for the Ghostly Self and Victimage for the Dead may coincide and "produce lives tortured throughout by spirituality and passion" (*Vision*, 1962, p. 240). One thinks in this connection of the protagonist of "The Tables of the Law" and of the "Tragic Generation"—particularly Lionel Johnson, who had always a fascination for Yeats.

This Victimage for the Ghostly Self represents "the moment of the greatest genius possible to that man or woman" (*Vision*, 1925, p. 243), presumably when the Ghostly Self comes to that man or woman by symbol. The point is that Victimage marks the intermingling of natural and supernatural elements that is central in Yeats's metaphysics. When the Arcon is present, one has a rationale for extending the implications of such thought to Yeats's art:

> In every supernatural communication or influence which has a public object there is such an *Arcon* that its supernatural body may give stability and continuity. These beings begotten in tragedy may be brought forth in joy; and all works which are new creation, and so not from desire which can but repeat that which is already known, are brought forth under their influence or under that of beings, born from men and from the spirits at Phase 15. (*Vision*, 1925, p. 244)

Certainly there are ideas within this passage that are similar to those in "The Symbolism of Poetry" and "Rosa Alchemica," and to the concept of tragic joy. It may not be farfetched to suggest also that the concept of the Arcon, omitted in 1937, informs the opening section of "The Soul in Judgment."

"The Soul in Judgment" begins by setting up two symbols in opposition: Paul Valéry, who in *Cimetière Marin* "rejoices that human life must pass," and the singing girl, who cries, "O Lord, let something remain" (*Vision*, 1962, pp. 219–20). Again, as in much of the revision, this introductory symbolism is meant to induce a mood of speculation in the reader; but unlike the opposition of Caesar and Christ in "The Great Year of the Ancients," the symbolism here points to a moral. Valéry is wrong, not only in his joy, but more fundamentally in his failure to see himself as light; for the Spirit is light (*Vision*, 1962, p. 220). That Valéry was a poet adds a further dimension to the argument; for as moving as Yeats finds the poem, he cannot include it among his sacred books. Perhaps it is Valéry's eschatological shortsightedness that spoils his art, his failure to see the causal relationship between death (or the realm between death and birth) and art. Yeats claimed for his own poetry a new "self-possession and power" due to his experience of the system (*Vision*, 1962, p. 8).

There remain two concepts to discuss in the 1925 version, that of the Record and that of the Automatic Faculty. The second concept, which does much to explain, in Yeats's own view, his experience of automatic writing, is omitted in 1937, likely because there he relates this experience directly. It is known that the dead have Waking and Sleeping States and that they use the incarnate mind to expiate events in their former lives. When incarnate man dreams in sleep, he communicates with the dead in their Waking State; but the dreams do not end even when the man wakes, although he ceases to be aware of his dream. This continuing dream is the Automatic Faculty that, on the one hand, seems to be simply the unconscious mechanism of the brain that perpetuates physiological functions like breathing. Yeats describes it as an "element of personality" that corresponds to the Spirits at Phase I and "prolongs, when we walk or breathe, an act which was in the first instance voluntary" (*Vision*, 1925, p. 246). This Automatic Faculty may, under an impulse from the Spirit, create "an automatic personality which resembles the spirit" (*Vision*, 1925, p. 246). Again, one assumes that this would be an unconscious personality and still an element of the incarnate personality.

But here the concept becomes unclear. Aherne, in one of his several footnotes in this section, relates a story of Robartes's having contacted the automatic personality of an Arab boy, which strongly suggests that the boy was possessed by the Spirit. In the next paragraph, Yeats refers to the Spirit that "created" the automatic personality and notes that the Spirit's expression often reveals a mind superior to that of the incarnate man (*Vision*, 1925, pp. 246–47). Thus, the contradiction: Does the Automatic Faculty properly belong to the incarnate man or the Spirit? Yeats mentions the poltergeist phenomenon and "*Daimonic* domination" (*Vision*, 1925, p. 248), but since the concept of the Daimon is itself shadowy—it seems sometimes to be the unconscious, sometimes a disembodied Spirit making use of the Faculties of an incarnate man—this contradiction remains unresolved.

A primary man can, through abstinence, keep his Automatic Faculty from desire and fear and so "be both vehicle and questioner. His mind has but a single direct movement which may be wholly dominated" (*Vision* 1925, p. 248). This can be taken to mean dominated by his own conscious personality. The antithetical man, however (Yeats writes "antithetical *inspiration*"), may demand a separation of vehicle and questioner, a relationship like that between Priest and Sybil. Such a demand among many may create a clairvoyant coven and, one imagines, develop into the situation of mutal inspiration that Yeats experienced with Mathers and records in "Swedenborg, Mediums, and the Desolate Places." Where the bond is between two people only, the mind of one displays such an intense need for truth that "the *Automatic Faculty* of the other grows as it were hollow to receive that truth" (*Vision*, 1925, p. 248). If the man wishes only to impose belief on others, the automatic personalities will practice deception, "but if the man desires truth itself that which comes will be the most profound truth possible to his fate" (*Vision*, 1925, p. 249). This can be taken to be an almost autobiographical account of the experience of Yeats and his wife as he saw it.

The Waking Spirits that make this experience possible continue to influence man's destiny "by their control of his automatic movements during ordinary life" (*Vision*, 1925, p. 249). This may account for luck in certain individuals. In addition, waking man may also commune with Sleeping Spirits, and this is the situation during expiation and during the creation of the work of art. Yeats's comments here will, perhaps, shed light on his aesthetics:

Self-exhaustion of man's creative power can make his *Automatic Faculty* plastic to the *Waking* Spirits but it can only be roused into that extremity of creation and so of exhaustion, by conflict. Exhaustion and creation should follow one another like day and night, his creation bringing contact with one form of the *spiritual primary*, his exhaustion with another, and this can only come from a choice forced by conflict with the *physical primary*. (*Vision*, 1925, p. 249)

Although almost none of the aesthetic implications of the system appear in 1937, the idea of a superhuman source of art, a muse, which here responds to the artist's exhaustion, is not a new one in Yeats. One is reminded of the passage in *The Celtic Twilight* in which Yeats remarks: "Images form themselves in our minds perpetually as if they were reflected in some pool. We gave ourselves up in old times to mythology, and saw the gods everywhere.... We can make our minds so like still water that beings gather about us that they may see, it may be, their own images, and so live for a moment with a clearer, perhaps even with a fiercer life because of our quiet."[12]

The Record is another vague concept. Early in the book Yeats equates it with "the unconscious memories of the living," or "all those things which have been seen but have not been noticed or accepted by the intellect" (*Vision*, 1925, p. 222). Later, he seems to equate it with Anima Hominis, "images of *Anima Mundi* which have some personal link with ourselves" (*Vision*, 1925, p. 245), but the contorted prose in these passages makes a clear definition difficult. Section 14, "The Record and the Memory," does little to clarify the concept. The Record seems to consist of concrete images, the sound of wind or sea to use Yeats's examples, rather than ideas or language and is associated with the Husk, but Yeats also says that a Spirit may, with difficulty, recover a foreign language from the Record of another Husk although that language was unknown to that Spirit in its own life (*Vision*, 1925, pp. 250–51). In "The Soul in Judgment," it is mentioned only once as the "concrete memory" as distinct from the "abstract memory" (*Vision*, 1962, p. 229).

The best definition of the Record appears in book 2 of 1937. The complete passage is quoted here not only to catch the definition, but also to illustrate how elusive, if not absolutely deceptive, the system's terminology can be. Part of the problem is that one is asked to look at the system from both a temporal and a nontemporal viewpoint, from within and without, and so to apply two sets of terminology. Further, as in Yeats's diagrams, his instructors' attempts to simplify often add to the confusion:

The ultimate reality, because neither one nor many, concord nor discord, is symbolised as a phaseless sphere, but as all things fall into a series of antinomies in human experience it becomes, the moment it is thought of, what I shall presently describe as the thirteenth cone. All things are present as an eternal instant to our *Daimon* (or *Ghostly Self* as it is called, when it inhabits the sphere), but that instant is of necessity unintelligible to all bound to the antinomies. My instructors have therefore followed tradition by substituting for it a *Record* where the images of all past events remain for ever "thinking the thought and doing the deed." They are in popular mysticism called "the pictures in the astral light," a term that became current in the middle of the nineteenth century, and what Blake called "the bright sculptures of Los's Hall." We may describe them as the *Passionate Body* lifted out of time. (*Vision*, 1962, p. 193)

First, it seems to do little toward explanation to substitute the Record, where all past actions are forever immediate, if that is what Yeats's remark means, for an "eternal instant," where all things are present. They seem to be the same thing. A further, and admittedly somewhat cranky, point is that in order to get at this nebulous definition of the Record, one must, in one short paragraph, wade through three equally precise terms (*Daimon, Ghostly Self, Passionate Body*), three more general terms of the system (*sphere, antinomies, Thirteenth Cone*), four major philosophical considerations (reality, the one and the many, eternal instant, time), and three quotations.

Yeats's 1925 concluding section, "Mythology," is a capsule statement of the essential aspiration of the work as a whole. As is typical of Yeats's policy of revision, it appears in 1937 early in the book and serves as a speculative introduction. There, drawing from *The Mandookya Upanishad*, he describes a state of pure light where the soul is united to the blessed dead, possibly like Beatitude in his own system. Comparing Eastern and Western cultures, a contrast prevalent in 1937, or perhaps the modern world with antiquity, he remarks:

Because we no longer discover the still unpurified dead through our own and others' dreams, and those in freedom through contemplation, religion cannot answer the atheist, and philosophy talks about a first cause or a final purpose, when we would know what we were a little before conception, what we shall be a little after burial. (*Vision*, 1962, p. 223)

The focus here, as in the original 1925 statement, is an insistence upon the immediacy of our philosophical perceptions. The discipline of philosophy may prove that we are immortal, but our imaginations remain unmoved, "subjected to nature as before" (*Vision*, 1925, p. 251). In contrast, the ancient philosopher's thought was reinforced by "present vivid experience" that is, by mythology (*Vision*, 1925, p. 252).

Yeats's concluding argument is not logically strong. Everyone shares the natural faculties of great men, the argument runs, because everyone can appreciate some few lines of Milton or Shakespeare. True, but the concluding statement regarding supernatural faculties is not analogous, as the parallelism of the prose might seduce one into believing. "That we may believe that all men possess the supernatural faculties I would restore to the philosopher his mythology" (*Vision*, 1925, p. 252) means, in very rough paraphrase, that if philosophers wrote of the supernatural, or reinforced their thought with mythology, everyone would believe it and—what is more to the point—live it. This rather harsh restatement points to a central issue of the work. To Yeats, mythology is not, as it is to most moderns, archaeological or fictional; it is a vital life-style. Modern philosophers will not begin to write mythologically, assuming that Yeats wants to start such a trend, because their culture does not give them the "present vivid experience" with which to begin. If they did, it would not convince us of our supernatural faculties and for the same reason.

Further, the artist cannot now, if he ever could, dictate belief. Yeats's early political period, when he attempted to raise public taste, and his late desire for an "aristocratic" theatre, reflect a lesson learned: It is not an aesthetic or a mythological age, and no artist, single or in concert, can make it so. Hence, the modern artist's "alienation." The same problem exists in Yeats's so-called ritual drama. A ritual is a formalization, a giving form to, the "present vivid experience" of a people; the experience cannot be imposed by the artist. In 1937, as will be shown, Yeats is intensely aware that "grease" is not "flame" (*Vision*, 1962, p. 55). Still, he clings to the system, and the tension between his allegiance to that system and the manner in which a modern man must present it becomes an absorbing drama in itself.

3
Unnatural Stories: A Comparison of the Fiction in the Two Versions of *A Vision*

Aherne and Robartes

LOOKING back on the early *Vision*, Yeats was filled with "shame." He had "misinterpreted the geometry," and "failed to understand distinctions upon which the coherence of the whole depended."[1] This strong sense of having failed with the material is pervasive in the prefatory parts of the 1937 version, and self-doubt in regard to the system is never fully exorcised from the work.

Yet, while the confused interpretation of the system itself is the main source of Yeats's dissatisfaction, neither is he happy with the 1925 covering story of Michael Robartes's discovery:

> As my wife was unwilling that her share should be known, and I to seem sole author, I had invented an unnatural story of an Arabian traveller which I must amend and find a place for some day because I was fool enough to write half a dozen poems that are unintelligible without it. (*Vision*, 1962, p. 19)

Yeats is referring, of course, to the 1925 deception that Michael Robartes discovered the book of Giraldus and the Judwali tribe, and that he and Yeats and Aherne quarreled, first about "Rosa Alchemica" and later about the 1925 *Vision*,[2] a deception he alludes to elsewhere as, for example, in "A People's Theatre"[3] and in the notes to "Michael Robartes and the Dancer."[4] He tells us, in a note, that "Michael Robartes and His Friends" is the amended version of the unnatural Arabian story, but this remark hardly dispels all questions about the fiction. Why, for example, does the deception continue in John Aherne's letter in 1937? Why are the later stories, with all their improbable events, considered to be more "natural" than the earlier one in which a traveler discovers a tribe with a strange philosophy? Why, finally, are the stories necessary at all? What do they contribute to the book as a whole?

In fact, as George Mills Harper has discovered in examining the automatic script, the instructors were not pleased when Yeats spoke or wrote too freely of spirits, and it may well have been they, not George Yeats, who wanted to conceal their role in the making of *A Vision*.[5] Thus, the stories may have been written, initially, to conceal the book's true origins. Once in motion, however, the fiction took on a certain vitality of its own and provided an additional imaginative dimension to the bare mathematical system.

In view of the fact that the stories and prefatory material are so conspicuous and extensive, it is odd that they have received so little critical attention. Hazard Adams, who first explored this area, sees the fiction in *A Vision* as a half-satirical, half-serious "explication of the structure of symbolism" in the book, especially as that symbolism applies to history. Unfortunately, however, Adams has a tendency to see *all* the prefatory material, including Yeats's straightforward account of the process of automatic writing itself, as comedy. (Yeats did sometimes wear a "doltish mask"[6]—that is, the likeness of a bumbling, superrational modern man blundering through a complex intellectual search—but not always.) Although Adams does not explicate the stories in detail, he is right to insist on their significance and to see in them the linkage between Yeats's personality and the vast tradition of myth and magic within which he worked.

Few other critics have looked beyond the system. Harold Bloom says only that "we must be wary of Yeats when he shows his own uneasiness by grotesque self-referential ironies in the introductory parts of the book, and even more when he has the Instructors say that they have come primarily to give him metaphors for poetry."[7] Helen Vendler gives the material one paragraph:

> The tales which preface *A Vision*—the "Stories of Michael Robartes and His Friends"—now have a faded antiquarian savor in their remoteness, their rather perverse and precious humor, and their artificial tone. They serve as a fictional frame for the system, linking it to that elusive compilation of Giraldus, the *Speculum Angelorum et Hominum*, which it so mysteriously resembles. Yeats must have enjoyed the elaborateness of his stage scenery, and the tales hint at the spirit in which the book is to be taken.[8]

Unfortunately, Vendler does not elaborate on the relationship between the stories and the system, but her instinct is sound. The stories do determine how one must interpret the work as a whole. In order to understand this fictional frame, however, it is first necessary to go back to the roots of the two main characters, Aherne and Robartes.

Yeats first used paired characters, the Reverend William Howard and John Sherman, in *John Sherman* (1891). Sherman is the dreamer and, ultimately, the more important if not the more powerful of the two. Of Howard, the worldly man, Yeats writes:

He could think carefully and cleverly, and even with originality, but never in such a way as to make his thoughts an allusion to something deeper than themselves. In this he was the reverse of poetical, for poetry is essentially a touch from behind a curtain.[9]

In this early work, the tension of the pairing seems to be that between Howard's ambition and competence and Sherman's "helplessness that needed protection,"[10] a helplessness that is a correlation to his dreamy, poetic nature. In this, Sherman seems to represent the young Yeats in conflict with the sense of duty or social pressure represented by Howard, the ambitious man. It is interesting to note that, even this early, Yeats is contrasting what will later be called antithetical and primary character types and extracting the dramatic possibilities of thus setting them in opposition.

The paired characters in a later book, *The Speckled Bird*, are more skillfully drawn figures, but they are still strongly autobiographical. Michael Hearne, the Yeats figure, and Maclagan, who is modeled upon MacGregor Mathers, occupy center stage; but the novel is also populated with faintly disguised portraits of Maud Gonne, John Butler Yeats, and Olivia Shakespear.[11] The conflict here is between Maclagan's magic and the poetic inspiration of Hearne, and again, the pair represent an internal conflict within Yeats himself. Now, however, the conflict is not between adolescent dreaminess and the pull of the world, but between Yeats's equally strong attractions to magic and poetry from 1897 to 1903.

William H. O'Donnell, the book's editor, writes of the theme as "the incompatibility of the spiritual and natural worlds" (*S. B.*, p. xxvii), a conflict common to many of Yeats's poems and stories. George Mills Harper, however, writing specifically about *The Speckled Bird* in *Yeats's Golden Dawn*, enlarges this idea to show how the question evolves into a less personal one, a difference of opinion about the proper kind of symbolism. Maclagan is working in simple correspondences as dictated by the tradition, but, as Yeats's notes indicate, Michael wants the "introduction of such a symbolism as will continue and make more precise the implicit symbolism in modern art and poetry. The antagonism must be made the antagonism between the poet and magician" (*S. B.*, p. 226). The focus is not so much upon contrasting types of characters as upon the contrasting aims of poetry and magic.

Thus, while the technique of contrast persists in *The Speckled Bird*, more attention is focused on the central character, Michael Hearne. Maclagan is, like Howard, initially the figure of power; Hearne is the isolated poetic figure. Early in book 1, as Hearne walks home from the sea, he sees a large bird on the shore with several noisy smaller birds following it. It is a moment like that in Joyce when Stephen realizes the significance of his name and his isolating destiny as a poet:

He thought: "It is an owl. That is what the Bible means when it says,

'Mine inheritance is as the speckled bird, all the birds of the heavens are against it.' I wonder why the other birds are so angry." (*S. B.*, p. 2)

The concept of duty, more central in *John Sherman*, now becomes a subplot: the conflict between John Hearne, Michael's painter-father, modeled on Yeats's own father, and his friend, Henderson. John has been shot at by his own tenants in a land dispute, and his coachman has been killed, but John has refused to identify the murderer. Thus, claims Henderson, the figure of duty, he has gained popularity with the peasants by betraying his duty to his class. John, however, feels an allegiance only to art and the dictates of his own life (*S. B.*, p. 5).

John, like Yeats's own father, feeds Michael's poetic imagination, as does a tinker who reappears throughout the story, telling the tales of fairy legend Yeats himself loved to hear. These influences, and Michael's reading in medieval romance, reinforce the young poet's discontent: "Michael went about now in a continual disappointment with the world he lived in. Nothing there seemed beautiful or strange or magnificent" (*S. B.*, p. 10). Fascinated by the tinker's stories, Michael begins the discipline necessary to visionary experience.

Now fifteen years of age, Michael has become totally preoccupied with his visions, and the local doctor has pronounced him morbid and unhealthy. He is taken away to Italy, then to France where he meets Maclagan, whose description suggests both MacGregor Mathers and Robartes:

> He had a dark clean-shaven clearly cut many-lined face, and might have been of any age from thirty to fifty, and of almost any nation. He was well made, and wore an old brown velvet coat, and talked in a deep voice and with a certain air of mystery, that either repelled or attracted one. (*S. B.*, p. 19)

Yeats's description of Mathers from "The Trembling of the Veil" also indicates the identification of Mathers and Maclagan:

> At the British Museum Reading-Room I often saw a man of thirty-six or thirty-seven, in a brown velveteen coat, with a gaunt resolute face, and an athletic body, who seemed, before I heard his name, or knew the nature of his studies, a figure of romance.[12]

In "Rosa Alchemica" the coloring becomes red rather than dark, a coloring suggesting the traditional Irish figure of rough-cut wisdom, like Owen Roe O'Sullivan, or one especially called by the other world, like Yeats's Red Hanrahan; but the sense of the mysterious remains the same:

> I found before me Michael Robartes, whom I had not seen for years, and

whose wild red hair, fierce eyes, sensitive, tremulous lips and rough clothes, made him look now, just as they used to do fifteen years before, something between a debauchee, a saint, and a peasant.[13]

Later in the same story, Robartes's face appears to the narrator to be a mask (*M.*, p. 279), and he dreams that he, himself, is a mask that persons who are "more than human" try on and discard (*M.*, pp. 286–87). The use of the idea of Mask here seems to point to a further significance of this concept in Yeats's theories of personality and art. The narrator is possessed by the thought that Robartes is dead, has been dead for ten or twenty years, and that the seemingly human gestures he makes are done "at the bidding of beings greater or less than man" (*M.*, p. 279). Mask, in the poet, then, may suggest the intervention of Spirits who actually create the work. This seems to be the idea behind Yeats's discussion of the Arcon in 1925.

In *A Vision* of 1925 and 1937, this eerie, ghostlike quality is presented less ominously as a strange, ageless health that defies time. Aherne's 1925 introduction describes Robartes after thirty-years' absence:

His athletic body, and his skin that had seemed, even when I first met him, sundried and sun-darkened, his hawk-like profile, could belong to no other man. I wish the thirty years had changed me as little, for I saw no change in that erect body except that the hair that had been some kind of red, was grey, and in places, fading into white. (*Vision*, 1925, p. xv)

In 1937, Yeats has John Duddon describe both Robartes and Aherne:

Presently Aherne came in with a big old man. Aherne, now that I saw him in a good light, was stout and sedentary-looking, bearded and dull of eye, but this other was lank, brown, muscular, clean-shaven, with an alert, ironical eye. (*Vision*, 1962, p. 37)

The "fierce" eyes of Robartes in "Rosa Alchemica" are now, significantly, "ironical"; but he is the same strangely ageless, sunburned traveler, and even more powerful than ever.

Maclagan was, like Mathers, largely a scholar of the occult. Although seemingly powerful at first, he lacks the assurance of Robartes. Instead of having power, power is exercised upon him. He is poor and unrecognized, a writer of the popular sixpenny astrology books read by servant girls; but he still believes that the great "Adepts," some of whom still live on earth, have brought Michael and him together for the "great work," a sketching out of the "Eleusinian rites" (*S. B.*, p. 62). Later in the book, he behaves as Mathers did, claiming authority from direct communication with the great Adepts themselves (*S. B.*, p. 92). When the break between Maclagan and Hearne finally comes, it is a separation of magic and art; Maclagan writes to Michael:

> I have come to recognise that you are not a magician, but some kind of an artist, and that the *summum bonum* itself, the potable gold of our masters, [is] less to you than some charm of color, or some charm of words. (*S. B.*, p. 92)

Michael, unlike Yeats, has no part in the ousting of Maclagan and the takeover of the order they have founded together. He seems relatively unaffected by the affair and, in fact, is himself surprised to learn how little the fall of Maclagan distresses him (*S. B.*, p. 93). Later, however, he is able to see the crumbling of Maclagan's ambitions as a parallel to the tragic outcome of his own unhappy love affair (*S. B.*, p. 105).

In writing so coldly of this business, Yeats is clearly attempting to distance himself from the material; in fact, *The Speckled Bird*, in general, shows a great deal of perspective on the occult world Yeats knew. For example, the scene at Mrs. Allingham's in book 2, where the mystics gather to found the new order, is full of satire much like that in *The Words upon the Window-pane*, although both works, of course, also reveal a more serious purpose. Each person present is a partisan for a particular occult phenomenon, like the young man who supports his preference for fasting by saying that it is "not really disagreeable except at meal-times" (*S. B.*, p. 70). And, each mocks the others' methods for reaching the spiritual realm. There is a great deal of humor in this passage, but Yeats's notes for unwritten scenes are harsher. One describes a room used for a ritual: "Whitewashed walls, ugly chairs, dirt, etc., etc." (*S. B.*, p. 226). Another says: "Describe the way modern boots show under the robes. The way robes part in the middle, [showing] the modern clothes" (*S. B.*, p. 227). George Mills Harper confirms that the "motley crew" at Mrs. Allingham's included a number of people Yeats knew and that the scene represents a satiric dismissal of the sects and ideologies he had already explored and abandoned.[14] Not even Maclagan himself escapes Yeats's critical eye. He seems a bit overzealous and more than a little paranoiac. Robartes, on the other hand, and to a certain extent Aherne, are powerful figures with great dignity, at least in 1925.

Yet, for all Yeats's open-eyed criticism of the movement, it affected him deeply and permanently. Mathers particularly, despite his fall, was to persist as a character in Yeats's fiction to the end. Kathleen Raine writes of him:

> Mathers's continued hold over Yeats's imagination surely helped to create the figure of Robartes as the mysterious wanderer in whose power it lies to appear to whom he pleases, or to summon to him those whom he wishes in a manner which appears the work of chance but is in reality through magical power.[15]

Although the chain from Mathers through Maclagan to Robartes seems to be a clear-cut development, one should, perhaps, also nominate A.E. as a model for the magician. The three 1897 stories are dedicated to him, and the narrator speaks of "our student years in Paris" and the "magnetic power he had once possessed over me" (*M.*, p. 271). Although Mathers, of course, also had an influence, Yeats seems to have seen him fairly objectively, as *The Speckled Bird* illustrates; "magnetic power" suggests A.E. Further, there is a qualitative difference between Maclagan (who, as the name suggests, is MacGregor Mathers) and Robartes. The absence of pettiness, the new calm and sense of sorrow in Robartes, qualities that could not have been derived from Mathers, suggest that A. E.'s personality has tempered the character of Maclagan.[16] The Irish bard, suggested by the red coloring, also comes into the character and, of course, Yeats himself, the "uncompromising Pre-Raphaelite" (*Vision*, 1925, p. xv).

Virginia Moore, in researching the early history of the Order, has turned up an interesting parallel to Robartes. A certain Dr. Felkin, an Order member, split from Mathers because he wanted to get closer to the Third Order. In his travels, he acquired an Arab teacher, Ara ben Shemesh, who may have suggested Kusta ben Luka to Yeats, and eventually met in Germany a Dr. Rudolf Steiner, a Rosicrucian whom Felkin considered to be an incarnate member of the Third Order.[17] Dr. Steiner, who predicted the Second Coming of Christ, was briefly famous in occult circles, and Yeats certainly would have heard of him through his wife, who joined a group of Steiner theosophists in 1914.[18] Although Dr. Steiner's fame arrived too late (1908) to influence the early stories, Felkin and Steiner's biographies could have determined the later development of Robartes. Another parallel is Leo Africanus, Yeats's spiritual counterpart, who appeared in a séance in 1911 and was, like Robartes, a traveler in Arabia, familiar with Arab physicians and medicine.[19]. Clarence Mangan, an early hero of Yeats's, had the same brown jacket and haunting features as Robartes, and a look about him of the poet and magician.[20]

All of these possible models shared an interest in magic and vision, and this spiritual power is the source of their fascination. Mathers and Robartes are, at the least, magicians, and possibly Secret Chiefs of the Order. The Golden Dawn assumed the existence of Adepts, magi either incarnate or discarnate who had superior knowledge and power. They were said to make up the Third Order of Masters.[21] Mathers, Chief of the Second Order, claimed his authority from communication with them; he writes of them in a letter to Florence Farr Emery in 1900:

> I again reiterate that *every atom* of the knowledge of the Order has come *through me alone* from 0-0 to 5-6 inclusive, and that it is I alone who have been and am in communication with the Secret Chiefs of the Order.[22]

Mrs. Mathers makes a similar statement in the preface to the 1926 edition of

The Kabbalah Unveiled.[23]

While other Order members may have been skeptical about the Secret Chiefs or Third Order Adepts, Mathers was not. In a manifesto dated October 1896, and quoted by Kathleen Raine, he writes of his meetings with them:

> When such a *rendezvous* has been in a much frequented place, there has been nothing in their personal appearance or dress to mark them out as differing in any way from ordinary people except the appearance and sensation of transcendent health and physical vigour (whether they seemed persons in youth or age) which was their invariable accompaniment: in other words, the physical appearance which the possession of the Elixir of Life has traditionally been supposed to confer. On the other hand, when the rendezvous has been a place free from easy access by the Outer World they have usually been in symbolic robes and insignia.[24]

Robartes certainly has all the characteristics of an Adept of the Third Order, and Kathleen Raine points out other associations that would have appealed to Yeats, notably the wise-old-man figure of Jungian psychology who appears also in Shelley's poetry.[25] Robartes also has affinities with the figures of the tarot. Raine recounts that when Arland Ussher, a student of the tarot, attempted to equate the tarot symbols with Yeats's *Vision*, he received little help from Mrs. Yeats. Mr. Ussher's opinion was that, although both Yeats and his wife owned tarot packs and told fortunes from them, either they did not consider the tarot a system of thought or they refrained from discussing it because of vows of secrecy taken in the Order[26] where it was used in ritual and meditation. According to Eliphas Lévi, the tarot represented the central Golden Dawn symbol, the Tree of Life, in pictorial form.[27] Mathers certainly placed great emphasis on the cards; his pamphlet, *The Tarot*, quoted in part by Raine, assigns an allegorical equivalent to each card and arranges the cards in sequence to tell a general or ideological fortune.[28]

Yeats never wrote directly of the tarot, but its symbolic influence is pervasive. The "Stories of Red Hanrahan," which Raine discusses in full, merge the four sacred objects of Ireland with the four sacred weapons of the magician: the lotus-headed wand of fire, the cup of water, the dagger for air, and the pentacle for earth.[29] The original woodcut illustrations for the 1904 edition, executed by Robert Gregory and reproduced by Raine, show a stylized landscape with a flowing river and the four suit designations from the modern pack, which are of course derived from the tarot. Hanrahan himself is symbolized by the tarot fool, the prince of the otherworld who must travel, ragged and beset by dogs, through this world. He carries a wand, the symbol of his otherworldly royalty, and a wallet full of subconscious memories of his royal past. The dogs are passions that attack him.[30] He is a dreamer, like the wise fool of Shakespeare or the beggars of Yeats's works. He appears also in

The Speckled Bird as the tinker, "an old ragged man with something fastened to his back resting beside a very twisted thorn tree' (*S. B.*, p. 53).

Robartes, while a traveler, is not the fool. In Raine's interpretation, he is the hermit, the figure of wisdom. Also a traveler, he carries a lantern half concealed in the folds of his cloak and a staff to help him on his journey; but, unlike the fool, the hermit is a venerable figure.[31] The figure of the magician is, itself, a tarot symbol, as are the tower, the wheel, and the chariot, all used by Yeats in his poetry and plays.[32] Raine discounts the idea that the tarot embodies Egyptian mythology, but the Golden Dawn was eclectic and might have accepted such an association. Certainly Madame Blavatsky had a strong interest in Egyptian wisdom and might have provided Yeats's introduction to the "golden-eyed hawk of the sun," "the moon-ruled cat," "the great cackler" (the hern?), the egg, the lotus, and the donkey—all Egyptian symbols that, according to Raine, "enabled Yeats to mask esoteric themes in forms acceptable in their own right."[33] Robartes, like Yeats, was a devoted student of these esoteric themes and symbols as well as of modern philosophy, and he may be, in the final analysis, primarily modeled on Yeats himself.

Yet, as fascinating as Robartes is, Aherne is in many ways the more interesting character. Certainly he is the more accessible, for Robartes, despite his immense knowledge, his power, his strong sense of purpose, despite even his suffering in love, seems distant and cold. Aherne is one of us; like Holmes's Dr. Watson, he is the commonsense human link between the reader and the remote magus. In the 1937 version, he is nothing like Robartes; he is, in fact, even a little dull: "stout and sedentary-looking, bearded and dull of eye" (*Vision*, 1962, p. 37). One of Daniel O'Leary's remarks points up the ideological contrast between Aherne and Robartes:

> "Robartes," said O'Leary, "sees what is going to happen, between sleeping and waking at night, or in the morning before they bring him his early cup of tea. Aherne is a pious Catholic, thinks it Pagan or something of the kind and hates it, but he has to do what Robartes tells him, always had to from childhood up." (*Vision*, 1962, p. 35)

One gets the picture of a highly conservative, even stuffy, old curmudgeon, petulantly correcting Robartes on the one hand (*Vision*, 1962, pp. 50–51), yet on the other, compelled to do his bidding. And there is a slightly condescending tone in O'Leary's remark that there will be plenty of time for them to tell their stories before Aherne returns because "as I left the study Michael Robartes called the universe a great egg that turns inside-out perpetually without breaking its shell, and a thing like that always sets Owen off" (*Vision*, 1962, p. 33). Had the stories' setting been less mysterious, and the plot less condensed, Aherne might have provided the comic relief for the relentless solemnity of Robartes. Stopping just short of this, Yeats uses him both to provide the conservative perspective and to run errands in the plot, a role obviously not appropriate for Robartes, who must remain isolated from the everyday world.

Yet, this 1937 Aherne represents an extensive alteration of the original character as he appears in "The Tables of the Law." Though never identical because of Aherne's preoccupation with Christianity, Aherne and Robartes were originally much more alike. Even as late as "The Phases of the Moon," published in 1919, both Robartes and Aherne seem to be initiates in the system of *A Vision*, and it is Aherne who begs Robartes to sing the changes of the moon.[34] Aherne has no primary scruples there. It was only as the material was reworked over the years that Yeats saw the need to polarize the two characters, allowing Aherne to assume some of the qualities of the narrator of the early stories: "Rosa Alchemica," "The Tables of the Law," and "The Adoration of the Magi."

Robartes develops in a straight line, becoming more intensely the magus he always potentially was. In "Rosa Alchemica," he is able to hypnotize the narrator with the aid of a powerful, perhaps magical, incense; by 1937, he is able to foresee events, has located the lost egg of Leda and has become at the least a prophet, if not an Adept of the Third Order. Aherne, on the other hand, has a more checkered past.

In 1937, Yeats has John Aherne write that Robartes "had founded a society, with the unwilling help of my brother Owen, for the study of the *Kabbala Denudata* and similar books "(*Vision*, 1962, p. 54), but there is no evidence in the original stories to suggest that Aherne had anything to do with the Order of the Alchemical Rose. His preoccupation with mystical Christianity and his difference, temperamentally, from Robartes instead suggest that Yeats did not intend to imply his involvement in the Order of the Rose. Yeats, in fact, writes in his 1909 journal:

> I now see what is wrong with "Tables of the Law." The hero must not seem for a moment a shadow of the hero of "Rosa Alchemica." He is not the mask but the face.[35]

This change in Aherne's character goes largely unnoticed because the reader familiar with him from the 1937 *Vision*, and thus accustomed to seeing him in ideological conflict with Robartes, naturally associates him with the now somewhat comic voteen of the 1897 stories who clutches his rosary close to his heart, his mind shut tight against occult contamination (*M.*, p. 292). This man is not Aherne, as a close examination of the next shows, but a nameless observer whose initial purpose is to make the exotic material more accessible to the average reader. Eventually, however, he comes to illustrate what so many critics have missed in Yeats's various treatments of occult themes and sources: The realm of the Spirits is real, powerful, and dangerous.

The narrator in "Rosa Alchemica" lives in a lavishly furnished house in Dublin, the outstanding feature of which is a cloistering tapestry, "full of the blue and bronze of peacocks" (*M.*, p. 268). It is he who witnesses the "tragic end" of Robartes (*M.*, p. 267) and escapes the temple to tell the story ten years later. It should be noted, incidentally, that the narrator never actually sees Robartes dead. He is still alive and sighs faintly when the narrator attempts to wake him, just before he himself flees the angry fishermen (*M.*, p. 291). Thus, Yeats's resurrection of the character later is not so improbable as it at first might seem. The narrator only assumes there was a tragic end.

"The Tables of the Law" begins with dialogue: "Will you permit me, Aherne,' I said, 'to ask you a question?'" (*M.*, p. 293). The narrator had been a fellow student of Aherne's in Paris (*M.*, p. 294), as well as of Robartes's (*M.*, p. 271). There are a few engravings and photographs of the Jesuits in his family's past, but Aherne is not wealthy and his house is monastic (*M.*, p. 294), certainly not the lavish abode of the narrator himself. The issue of wealth and material possessions, always a symbolic point of reference for Yeats in drawing characters, contrasts the two perspectives: mask and face, narrator and Aherne. Notice that the narrator has removed his historical family portraits—which are of politicians, not churchmen—to make room for his expensive art treasures (*M.*, pp. 267–68). Yet the narrator, too, as a later remark shows, is involved in occult entanglements and suffers like Aherne and Robartes. Caught, like Aherne, halfway to fulfillment via the occult, he considers himself even less fortunate than the suffering friends he observes because he is but "half initiated into the Order of the Alchemical Rose" (*M.*, p. 306).

In "The Adoration of the Magi," the narrator relates a story that, he claims, took place "a little after my last meeting with Aherne" (*M.*, p. 308). Three old men who have heard of the supposed death of Robartes visit the narrator and, he relates, "I brought them into my study, and when the peacock curtains had closed behind us, I set their chairs for them close to the fire" (*M.*, p. 308). The mention of the curtains tells the reader that this is the same narrator as in the first and, by implication, the second story. The deliberateness with which Yeats includes these details seems to indicate that he wanted the narrator's continuity through the stories firmly established in the reader's mind. Toward the end of the stories, one sees why.

The three stories are meant to be taken together,[36] not only because of the similarity of their content, but because, in the order they are presented, they represent the history of a man humbled and made wiser by his brush with the occult: "I have turned into a pathway which will lead me from them and from the Order of the Alchemical Rose. I no longer live the elaborate and haughty life, but seek to lose myself among the prayers and the sorrows of the multitude" (*M.*, p. 315). Although the stories can be read separately, taken together the three stories reveal a fourth, that of the narrator who grows in significance. The ending of "Rosa Alchemica" may seem to be a demonstration of simple, blind faith. The reader's allegiance is still with Robartes. One may even think of the narrator as a coward, little better than the ignorant fishermen, who fear what they cannot understand in society's terms. By the end of the final story, however, having watched the narrator in his further exploration of the occult, having seen through his eyes the tragic example of Aherne, one recognizes that faith is now a desperate need and a genuine salvation. The narrator's initial position in "Rosa Alchemica" was wrong; one must not dabble in occult matters. Alchemy is no innocuous metaphor. The "demons of the air" are real and dangerous. One can lose one's soul.

Aherne's discovery of the lost book of Joachim of Flora, which predicts "a complete triumph of the Spirit" (*M.*, p. 296), not Robartes's later discovery of Giraldus's book, is the first use Yeats makes of the real-life discovery of the Cypher MSS by the Reverend A. F. A. Woodford in a London bookstall in 1884. This manuscript, seemingly destined to fall into the proper hands, furnished the foundations for the Isis-Urania Temple of the Golden Dawn.[37] Another possible source of the "discovered book" motif is the traditional Smaragdine (Emerald) Tablet, supposedly found on the dead body of Hermes Trismegistus, which constitutes the prime document of the hermetic doctrine of correspondence, and which Yeats would have learned of in Madame Blavatsky's *Isis Unveiled*.[38]

Although "The Tables of the Law" is too early, perhaps, to be legitimately interpreted in terms of *A Vision*, what Joachim's book seems to be predicting is the antithetical dispensation, which is described in the story as a total freedom in which the old laws and commandments of Christianity are swept away (*M.*, p. 298). Later, as Yeats looked back on the stories of 1897, he saw them in terms of *A Vision*; writing in the "Introduction to 'The Resurrection,'" he says:

> Presently Oisin and his island faded and the sort of images that come into *Rosa Alchemica* and *The Adoration of the Magi* took their place. Our civilisation was about to reverse itself, or some new civilisation about to be born from all that our age had rejected, from all that my stories symbolised as a harlot, and take after its mother; because we had worshipped a single god it would worship many or receive from Joachim de Flora's Holy Spirit a multitudinous influx.[39]

Joachim's book also establishes the idea of the two societies that will be formed just before the annunciation: the mass the mankind, completely primary, mechanical, and undifferentiated: and the small, secret groups of antithetical individuals, schooled in occult doctrine and prepared for the coming age:

> He [Joachim] considered that those whose work was to live and not to reveal were children and that the Pope was their father; but he taught in secret that certain others, and in always increasing numbers, were elected, not to live, but to reveal that hidden substance of God which is colour and music and softness and a sweet odour; and that these have no father but the Holy Spirit. Just as poets and painters and musicians labour at their works, building them with lawless and lawful things alike, so long as they embody the beauty that is beyond the grave, these children of the Holy Spirit labour at their moments with eyes upon the shinning substance on which Time has heaped the refuse of creation; for the world only exists to be a tale in the ears of coming generations; and terror and content, birth and death, love and hatred, and the fruit of the Tree, are but instruments for that supreme art which is to win us from life and gather us into eternity like doves into their dove-cots. (*M.*, pp. 300–301)

One can see how this passage relates to Michael Hearne's ambitions and how it would have attracted the young Joyce, putting, as it does, art above the law, the creative spirit above the institution of the Church. It also says a great deal about Yeats's theory of creation as spiritual intervention, and it anticipates *A Vision*. For Aherne, Joachim's teachings represent a higher Christianity, perhaps the only Christianity possible for a man of his temperament and times. Yeats describes Aherne as "the supreme type of our race," who, escaping the half-education of the times, turns away "towards desires so unbounded that no human vessel can contain them" (*M.*, pp. 293–94). There is good reason to assume that Aherne is a portrait of Yeats's early friend, Lionel Johnson, who shared a similar fate to that of Aherne and of whom Yeats wrote in his memoirs:

> In him more than all others one can study the tragedy of that generation. When the soul turns from practical ends and becomes contemplative, when it ceases to be a wheel spun by the whole machine, it is responsible for itself, an unendurable burden. Not yet ready for the impression of the divine will, it floats in the unnatural emptiness between the natural and the supernatural orders.[40]

Like Robartes and the narrator, Aherne has been a student of alchemy and mysticism, but he was always more "orthodox" than Robartes and "had suppassed him in a fanciful hatred of all life" (*M.*, p. 294). This hatred is in fact a tortured knowledge, shared by the narrator, that the beauty one can imagine can never be actualized; art, then, is a rebel's weapon, sent into the world to overthrow life itself by "sowing everywhere unlimited desires" (*M.*, p. 294). This is the same emotion that so attracted Yeats in *Axel*, which he had read before 1894 and which he described as "part of a religious rite, the ceremony perhaps of some secret Order wherein my generation had been initiated."[41] The play is based upon the bitter knowledge that the world can never fulfill the splendor of our dreams. In a scene that Villiers has titled

"The Supreme Choice," Axel speaks the words that Yeats was to repeat so often afterward: "Live? Our servants will do that for us!"[42] Sara, in love with Axel, is tempted by the world of action that "calls" to them, the place where dreams can be realized, but Axel knows that one can never live up to the beauty one can imagine: "They are so beautiful!—why should we realize them?"[43]

To Aherne, half monk, half soldier of fortune, Joachim's teachings offer escape from Axel's paradox, the possibility of turning dreams into action, action into dreams (*M.*, p. 294), a unity in spirit with God, a sharing of divine essence on earth, without the penalty of death. Aherne's tragedy is that he learns that earth *is* separation from God; life is sin, the Church's doctrine of original sin. Being so distanced from life and so thoroughly understanding that this distance is the law of his being, his tragedy is greater even than Axel's. He can neither sin and live, nor like the proud, romantic Axel, scorn life and die. He knows too much: "It was revealed to me that man can only come to that Heart through the sense of separation from it which we call sin, and I understood that I could not sin, because I had discovered the law of my being, and could only express or fail to express my being, and I understood that God has made a simple and an arbitrary law that we may sin and repent!" (*M.*, p. 305).

On a more cosmic level, Aherne is the man caught at the moment of historical change: too Christian to accept the antithetical influx, too antithetical to live content in the primary law. His Catholicism, as the narrator notes, can only "hold him on the margin" (*M.*, p. 305). The drama of that moment is a theme Yeats treats often throughout his work. In the early stories, the conflict is between the conventional man and the artist or saint, the rational man and the man outside society who follows his vision; but the primary-antithetical tension, even before the terms are invented, forms the backbone of these stories. In "The Old Men of the Twilight," for example, the old Druid, like many of the heroes of *The Secret Rose*, has put himself apart from the mass of men, and his curse is uncertainly and the twilight existence of neither life nor death:

> Because you have lived where the feet of the angels cannot touch your heads, nor the hair of the demons sweep your feet-soles, I shall make you an example for ever and ever; you shall become grey herons and stand pondering in grey pools and flit over the world in that hour when it is most full of sighs; and your deaths shall come by chance and unforeseen, for you shall not be certain about anything for ever and ever. (*M.*, p. 194–95)

The heron, neither land nor sea bird, seems always for Yeats the symbol of that twilight existence, of longing and the loneliness of wisdom, outside the rational law of sin and redemption. "God has not died for the white heron."[44] Michael Hearne is such as outsider; so, apparently, was Owen

Aherne originally intended to be. The name suggests the two characters' affinity. But by 1937, Aherne is a servile man of reason; Robartes is the tragic dreamer. Aherne's tragic line—"I am not among those for whom Christ died" (*M.*, p. 305)—now belongs to Robartes:

> One night, between three and four in the morning, as I lay sleepless, it came into my head to go pray at the Holy Sepulchre. I went, prayed, grew somewhat calmer, until I said to myself, "Jesus Christ does not understand my despair, He belongs to order and reason." (*Vision*, 1962, p. 41)

What has happened is that Aherne and Robartes have substantially changed personalities. Of course, Aherne is still the Christian, Robartes still the magician; but their emotional natures and the degree to which Yeats exposes these natures have switched. Aherne and the narrator are tragic in 1897, while Robartes, though he may meet a tragic end, is certainly no tragic figure in "Rosa Alchemica." In the 1925 edition of *A Vision*, his "gloom" over the loss of his beggar maid is minimized (*Vision*, 1925, p. xviii). There is no tragic dimension given to his love life as in 1937 (*Vision*, 1962, p. 40); of the end of his affair with the ballet dancer in 1925, he says only that he "forgot [his] sorrow in wine" and went on to Cracow (*Vision*, 1925, p. xvii). If, on the other hand, one did not have "The Tables of the Law," it would be easy to surmise from the two versions of *A Vision* that Aherne was a creature incapable of anything but pedantry and petty spite.

It has been suggested here that, as Yeats worked on the material, he saw the structural value of contrasting the pair more strongly, an inspiration probably suggested by the system's two terms—*primary* and *antithetical*—and by his work on the personality types of the twenty-eight incarnations. If he created a symbolic, even allegoric, character to represent each tincture, he could dramatize their interaction in fiction and so present the material in a more immediate manner. It was logical to return to the early stories because there he had already treated the themes of contrast that now reemerged in the system: the isolated man against the man in society, the dreamer and the rationalist, the pagan and the Christian world view, and the interaction between the living and the dead. *A Vision* must, indeed, have seemed the fulfillment of what he, Mathers, and the others had sought in the Order; and so, again, it was logical to resurrect Robartes, the occult seeker who embodied them all. Robartes reinforced the thread of friendship and scholarship that bound the past to the present. No other Yeats character, except the now-discredited Maclagan, had the scholarship, the dogmatism, and the single-minded dedication to occult matters to credibly discover the book of Giraldus; Robartes had the final advantage of being linked with Aherne, who was associated with primary Christianity. There were only two problems: resurrecting the dead Robartes, and reconstructing Aherne, who because Robartes could not change, must recover from his early despair and assume the dull role of primary man.

Yeats's remark that he must "amend and find a place for" the Robartes story (*Vision*, 1962, p. 19) and the 1937 letter from John Aherne, which in effect repudiates "Rosa Alchemica" and tries to set the tangled history of the matter straight, are indications of his struggle to make the early stories and poems conform to his purpose in the final version. In addition to poems, there are also references to the Robartes material elsewhere in Yeats's work, for example, in "A People's Theatre," first published in 1919:

> Are we approaching a supreme moment of self-consciousness, the two halves of the soul separate and face to face? A certain friend of mine has written upon this subject a couple of intricate poems called *The Phases of the Moon* and *The Double Vision* respectively, which are my continual study, and I must refer the reader to these poems for the necessary mathematical calculations.[45]

The "friend" here is of course Robartes himself, and there is even evidence that Yeats thought of having his two characters claim some authorship of *A Vision* and other related works as well. An early working title was *The Discoveries of Michael Robartes*, which Allan Wade assumes was an early version of *A Vision*.[46] Such a title would seem to focus more attention on Robartes than the completed book did but, of course, does not indicate that Robartes would have "written" it. In the preface to *Michael Robartes and the Dancer* (1921), Yeats writes of editing Robartes's letters, "I hope that my selection from the great mass of his letters and table talk, which I owe to his friend John Aherne, may be published before, or at any rate but soon after this little book."[47] As late as 1933, however, Yeats writes to Olivia Shakespear that he is thinking of making Robartes write an annotation on "Louis Lambert,"[48] an essay that Yeats published in 1934. Aherne supposedly refused any portion of the profits from the 1925 *Vision* because, he wrote, "later on I may publish my own commentary" (*Vision*, 1925, p. xxii).

The story was slow to jell. In the preface to *The Wild Swans at Coole*, 1919, Yeats writes: "Michael Robartes and John Aherne, whose names occur in one or other of these, are characters in some stories I wrote years ago, who have once again become a part of the phantasmagoria through which I can alone express my convictions about the world."[49] Yet, the phantasmagoria was far from clear. In a note from *Collected Poems*, dated 1922, Yeats remarks that Robartes "partly found and partly thought out"[50] the philosophy, yet in the 1925 *Vision*, there is no suggestion that the system owes anything to Robartes's original thought. When Yeats writes to Allan Wade in the same year, he repeats the story of Robartes's discovery much as it appears in the 1925 edition, but here the names are again Michael Robartes and John Aherne.[51] It seems improbable that this is a slip of the pen. Did Yeats intend to avoid the difficulties of Owen's early personality, as seen in "The Tables of the Law" and "The Phases of the Moon," by inventing a more orthodox brother? In the preface to *The Wild Swans at Coole*, Yeats remarks, "I have the fancy that I read the name John Aherne among those of men prosecuted for making a disturbance at the first production of 'The Play Boy,' which may account for his animosity to myself."[52] In a 1922 note, the confusion of the two characters is still unresolved: "John Aherne is either the original Owen Aherne or some near relation of the man."[53]

In the editorial introduction to their critical edition of *A Vision*, 1925, George Mills Harper and Walter Kelly Hood discuss the evolution of the early *Vision* manuscripts in detail, including Yeats's initial effort to cast the material in the form of a dialogue between Robartes and Aherne. The number of "false starts," the conceptual confusion within the system, and the admonitions of secrecy from both George Yeats and the instructors show clearly why the problem of how to present this exotic material so absorbed Yeats. He seems finally to have settled on a piecemeal tactic whereby he would first seed the ground with advance poems and sly hints within his prose work. As he wrote to Allan Wade in 1922, "I am giving it to the world in fragments, poems, notes, and a Cuala volume."[54]

At one time, Yeats even intended to match Robartes's manuscript with a like system of his own; Allan Wade furnishes the abandoned introduction, written by Aherne, in his collection of Yeats's letters:

> He [Robartes] called upon me the next day, made some kind of an apology, and said that I must come to see Mr. Yeats and that he had made an appointment for us. At Woburn Buildings he told of his Arabian discoveries and spread out upon the table his diagrams, his notes, my written commentary without even explaining that it was mine; and after a couple of hours' exposition, and answering many questions, asked Mr. Yeats to undertake the editorship.
> Mr. Yeats opened a large gilded Moorish wedding chest, took out a number of copybooks full of notes and diagrams; showed that our diagrams and his were almost exactly the same; that our notes only differed from his because our examples were Arabian whereas his were drawn from European history and literature.
> "You can only have found that all out," said Robartes, who was pale and excited, "through the inspiration of God."
> "Is not that a rather obsolete term?" said Mr. Yeats. "It came in the first instance quite suddenly. I was looking at my canary, which was darting about the cage in rather brilliant light, when I found myself in a strangely still and silent state and in that state I saw with the mind's eye symbols streaming before me. That still and silent state always recurs in some degree when I fix my mind upon the canary."[55]

The process described is called scrying (also spelled *skrying*), a kind of astral projection, or out-of-body travel, induced by self-hypnosis. Dr. Dee, a figure from hermetic tradition, had practiced it in Cracow, which is one of the reasons Robartes is attracted to that city (*Vision*, 1925, p. xvii). The scryer stares intently at some object (Yeats kept a glass of water on his table at Woburn Buildings for the purpose) until vision occurs.[56] The purpose of Yeats's having a matching manuscript is, presumably, to give the material more authenticity by supplying numerous origins, a tactic kept up in the 1925 edition where alternate sources for the material are suggested (*Vision*, 1925, p. xix).

This search for a proper format seems linked to Yeats's concern that the material be taken seriously. Ireland in the early 1920s seemed to him to be the chaos predicted by the system. In 1921, he wrote of leaving Ireland and England altogether[57] and of the "return of evil."[58] Foreshadowing Robartes's comments on war fifteen years later, he wrote to a friend in 1922: "The one enlivening Truth that starts out of it all is that we may learn charity after mutual contempt. There is no longer a virtuous nation and the best of us live by candle light."[59] Powerless in himself, he felt that the system had truth to give. In 1921, he wrote to A.E., urging him to write "that essay," as "practical advice in simple words given to some young man." The topic, clearly one that had been discussed often between the two men, is vaguely defined as "unity and culture." Notice how sensitive Yeats is here to his own public image and the probable response to *A Vision*, and yet how stubbornly faithful he is to his conception of it as truth:

> This conception of unity and culture has become a cardinal principle in all exposition of the future in my system. My friends who are not with me at the moment insist upon it constantly. I am most anxious not to appropriate the idea or seem to do so. If I only express it it will seem but a deduction from one man's unpopular system. They will say "O that is Yeats" and pass it by. ... We writers are not politicians, the present is not in our charge but some part of the future is.[60]

Michael Robartes's Discovery

It may have been this concern over the book's reception that convinced Yeats to devise the elaborate cover story of the 1925 edition. If the story were believed, the book would seem to contain, as Yeats thought it did, the wisdom of antiquity, not one man's eccentric philosophy. But, to what extent did Yeats think he could fool his public? Literary deceptions were common, and Yeats's audience was sophisticated. He had already revealed his plan in the note to *Michael Robartes and the Dancer*, and the portrait of Giraldus, printed in both versions, looks strikingly like Yeats. The story is improbable, but, on the other hand, no more so than those of the Cypher MSS or the Emerald Tablet. Robartes was no more improbable a personage than

Mathers himself.

Still, Yeats could not have expected the story to seem credible. It is, rather, a romance calculated to gain the book a hearing in terms of an intellectual adventure. The very improbability of the tale in the context of the time and the audience for whom Yeats was writing may even have, backhandedly, implied the truth of a system that, like the doctrines of the various orders, was too powerful to be revealed directly. Certainly one senses in the poems and notes and other oblique references to the system, in the seamless fictional framework, and in Aherne's authorship a deliberate fogging of the material and an attempt to keep it mysterious.

A part of this mystery was the dual source of the material: Giraldus, the sixteenth-century author of the *Speculum*, and Kusta ben Luka, the founder of the Judwali tribe who, according to Yeats's poem about him, was attached to the court of Harun Al-Raschid and received his knowledge from his wife. In 1925, Kusta ben Luka's part in the development of the system is equal to Giraldus's; although Yeats and Robartes are, of course, working from Giraldus's book, the oral, or "choreographic," tradition is equally important. There are, in fact, two stories in 1925: the one about Robartes's discovery of Giraldus's book, and another, "The Dance of the Four Royal Persons," in which ben Luka, as an old man, instructs Harun Al-Raschid's successor. The separate book titles, "What the Caliph Partly Learned" and "What the Caliph Refused to Learn," further reinforce ben Luka's importance in the earlier version. Michael J. Sidnell has called "The Dance of the Four Royal Persons" a "parable of artistic and intellectual sincerity" and suggested that the tale illustrates Yeats's belief that the system must be lived in order to attain any real validity.[61]

The motif of the dance was, of course, a favorite of Yeats's, not only in sense of the dancer merged with the dance (artist with art form) as in "Among School Children," but in the more subtle sense of dance as evocation. The idea of dancing to or tracing out a pattern, an idea implied in the "Marbles of the dancing floor" in "Byzantium,"[62] was fully developed in 'Rosa Alchemica," where the dancers traced the pattern of the rose overhead upon the dance floor in order to "trouble" or "break" the conventional mundane life and call down the moods among men (*M.*, p. 288). The dance of the Judwali, although it is specifically a teaching device, seems also to hint at this type of ritual.

The source of the dance motif, again, is tied up with Mathers. In *The Speckled Bird*, Mrs. Maclagan—Moina Bergson Mathers, the Vestigia of the 1925 *Vision*—performs an old Egyptian fire dance:

> It was a hymn in praise of Isis and as she sang it she moved hither and thither over the floor, weaving, Maclagan whispered, symbols in honour of the divinity; the old symbols, he said, were made upon the temple floors by the feet of dancers. (*S. B.*, p. 103)

To the Yeats figure, Michael, the performance is reminiscent of something from a London stage; clearly, Yeats's ironical eye is still focused on the distance between ritualistic art and masquerade. Michael can praise, however, the "idea" of combining words and gestures and of tracing out symbols on the floor; and Yeats, of course, would make better use of that idea later.

In 1937, ben Luka is mentioned only in John Aherne's letter. It seems likely that Yeats himself, here for the first time revealing a true source of the material in his wife's automatic writing, has taken over the role of the Four Royal Persons, the original Judwali. The Giraldus story is again the parallel scholastic written tradition. The idea of Yeats as Kusta ben Luka is reinforced by John Aherne's remark that, according to the legend he has heard, ben Luka was a young man when Harun Al-Raschid died (*Vision*, 1962, p. 54). By calling attention to the contradiction, Yeats forces the reader to ask why ben Luka is deliberately made old. The answer is, of course, that Yeats himself is old and wants to suggest the identity of himself and ben Luka, as he does also in "The Gift of Harun Al-Raschid," a concealed account of the automatic writing.

The ben Luka–Giraldus counterpointing also seems to parallel Robartes and Aherne, the contrast of antithetical and primary man. Yeats, of course, is also identified with ben Luka because each had a psychic wife, but in the same passage he reveals that Duddon has discovered the resemblance between Yeats and Giraldus (*Vision*, 1962, p. 54). Yeats seems to be seeking to dissolve the partiality for the antithetical that Owen Aherne complained of in the 1925 edition (*Vision*, 1925, p. xxiii) and to absorb and express both tinctures in himself in 1937. Giraldus is still needed for the Robartes story, which embodies the primary-antithetical contrast of Aherne and Robartes; but the ben Luka story is no longer strictly necessary and is slighted in 1937.

The 1925 Robartes story is well known. After thirty-years' separation, Aherne encounters Robartes by chance in the National Gallery contemplating a Pre-Raphaelite picture, the story of Griselda. Robartes asks for Yeats, and Aherne reminds him that both he and Robartes had quarreled with Yeats in the past:

> Mr Yeats had given the name of Michael Robartes and that of Owen Aherne to fictitious characters, and made those characters live through events that were a travesty of real events. (*Vision*, 1925, p. xvi)

Aherne points out that Yeats described Robartes's death in connection with certain associations that must seem "highly disagreeable to an honourable man," but Robartes replies that, while he minded once, he subsequently found that Yeats had done him a service (*Vision*, 1925, p. xvi). Robartes was certainly still angry in "The Phases of the Moon," where he refuses to help Yeats in his pursuit of wisdom. The cause of the quarrel, as John Aherne notes, seems largely directed against Yeats's style:

> *Robartes.* He wrote of me in that extravagant style
> He had learnt from Pater, and to round his tale
> Said I was dead; and dead I choose to be.[63]

Now, however, he finds that rumors of his death have allowed him to pursue his studies in the East without interruption from his old fellow students.

As the two old friends walk toward Yeats's lodgings, Robartes relates his life to Aherne: his affair with the ballet dancer, his travels to Cracow and his affair there with a lower-class girl, which leads to his discovery of Giraldus's *Speculum Angelorum et Hominorum* (the title was corrected in 1937 to *Speculum Angelorum et Hominum*, "The mirror of angels and men").[64] Robartes's absorption in the book causes a final quarrel with the peasant girl; in despair, Robartes goes to pray at the Holy Sepulchre and, from there, on to Damascus to learn Arabic and continue his prayers at Mecca. Traveling in the desert, he notices strange markings in the sand that correspond to the diagrams in Giraldus. He abandons his pilgrimage and works among the local tribes as a doctor, hoping to make contact with this strange, nomadic tribe that, like Robartes himself, is noted for "the violent contrasts of character amongst them, for their licentiousness and their sanctity" (*Vision*, 1925, pp. xviii–xix).

He finally gets his chance when an old man of the Judwalis seeks out his medical skill. Noticing the Giraldus book on Robartes's table, the Arab explains that the diagrams are the same as those in "The Way of the Soul between the Sun and the Moon," a lost book written by the tribe's founder, Kusta ben Luka, a Christian philosopher at the court of Harun Al-Raschid (*Vision*, 1925, p. xix). (Yeats later changed the spelling to Rashid.) Robartes is allowed to travel with the tribe and learns that the doctrine of ben Luka, which he thinks may also be Syriac in origin, is preserved in the tribe by a tradition of instructing the young Judwalis to trace the philosophical diagrams in the sand during a dance.

By this time, Aherne and Robartes have reached Yeats's Bloomsbury lodgings. There is a light in the window, but suddenly, Robartes changes his mind. He will not see Yeats now; they must make an appointment. He is sure to be out. To this point, the tale has been little more than adventure; Robartes, himself, has seemed sure of himself and deliberate. Now, for the first time, he is flustered and uncertain. He has not forgiven Yeats, and his call is not a social one. Robartes has a mission; and having lived so long as a solitary desert wanderer, he is uncertain how to make his story public:

> I have great gifts in my hands and I stand between two enemies; Yeats that I quarrelled with and have not forgiven; you that quarrelled with me and have not forgiven me. (*Vision*, 1925, p. xx)

The quarrel between Robartes and Aherne has not been recorded, unless it is the difference of temperament discussed in "The Tables of the Law." There is no "incident" of a quarrel, only brief references to the fact that, since youth, the two men have been prone to violent arguments (*Vision*, 1925, p. xxi). Although it is known, by hearsay, that there was a quarrel with Yeats, it has not been recorded as an incident. What the passage seems to mean is that Aherne and Yeats are primary and antithetical symbols, and their opposition is representative of the partisanism of modern times that is also evident in the brief reference Robartes makes to the war (*Vision*, 1925, p. xv). Aherne has a strong personal antipathy toward Yeats that emerges later in a quarrel as to how Robartes's manuscripts should be edited.[65] Robartes, who, it is important to note, has no "gift of expression" himself (*Vision*, 1925, p. xx), accuses Aherne of being too Christian (that is, too primary) in his editing, while Aherne remarks that Yeats does no better in being too antithetical (*Vision*, 1925, p. xxiii).

Robartes, although he is antithetical in the early stories and in the final *Vision*, seems here to be neutral, holding in his hands the means of reconciliation, or at least, understanding, between the two tinctures and the two men. Since a living man can represent only half of the system (*Vision*, 1925, p. 251), Robartes knows that whichever writer he chooses will distort the truth. Robartes's uncertainty disrupts the narrative flow and suggests an implied analogy with Yeats's difficulty in finding the proper style for *A Vision*. The same patterning of men's personalities is evident in 1937; but there, significantly, it is Aherne and Robartes who are in opposition and Yeats who is neutral.

If Robartes's uncertainty is a veiled allusion to the stylistic difficulties with the material, Yeats opts, finally, for his own modified lyricism. At first, Robartes assigns Aherne the editorship of the papers, and the two men travel through France and Ireland. They stay at Aherne's Dominick Street house, the scene of "The Tables of the Law," and on a walking tour in Connaught, pass Thoor Ballylee, where they hold a conversation something like that in "The Phases of the Moon." As though to point up the polarity of Aherne and Yeats, Yeats has Aherne remark of Robartes that "as his friendship with me grew closer, his animosity against Mr Yeats revived" (*Vision*, 1925, p. xxi).

Suddenly, a violent quarrel erupts. Robartes accuses Aherne of neglecting the antithetical side of the system, of interpreting it as a form of Christianity, and decides to give all the material to Yeats. Aherne, angry in his turn, asks if Robartes would give his papers to a man "who has thought more of the love of woman than of the love of God," and Robartes answers yes, "I want a lyric poet, and if he cares for nothing but expression, so much the better, my desert geometry will take care of the truth" (*Vision*, 1925, p. xxi). Aherne's angry retort reveals the full animosity he feels for Yeats:

Mr Yeats has intellectual belief but he is entirely without moral faith, without that sense, which should come to a man with terror and joy, of a Divine Presence, and though he may seek, and may have always sought it, I am certain that he will not find it in this life. (*Vision*, 1925, pp. xxi–xxii)

Robartes repeats this idea in 1937: "We desire belief and lack it" (*Vision*, 1962, p. 53). Apparently, it is an echo of a remark he has made before, possibly around 1917 or 1918 when he and Aherne passed Thoor Ballylee. Now Robartes, angrier than ever, "revives" an old quarrel of thirty years ago, saying that Aherne is "but a free man for a moment," and even asking him if he has consulted his confessor on the matter.

The fighting becomes so intense that Yeats is forced to break in with a footnote: "I think Mr Aherne has remembered his own part in this conversation more accurately than that of his opponent" (*Vision*, 1925, p. xxii). The note is puzzling. Strictly speaking, Yeats was not present when the words were exchanged and cannot know whether Aherne is embroidering. Is this concern for accuracy regarding the remark about the confessor an acknowledgment on Yeats's part that he is distorting the Aherne of thirty years ago who, as has been shown, was not the prim, conservative Christian of 1925, but at least in the beginning of "The Tables of the Law," a man every bit as daring as Robartes himself?

The quarrel blows over, and Aherne considers himself well out of the writing of *A Vision*. Yeats assumes the editorship with the stipulation that Aherne write the introduction and any notes he cares to, and Robartes returns to Mesopotamia (*Vision*, 1925, p. xxii).

The interesting point about Robartes's story, so far as this study is concerned, is the way it changes in tone over the years. In "Rosa Alchemica," as we have seen, the village riot that ended the Order of the Alchemical Rose was considered as tragic; Robartes was dead or thought to be, and the news spread even to the remote villages in the western islands of Ireland, where the three old men in "The Adoration of the Magi" heard of it. In "The Phases of the Moon," published in 1919, Robartes is alive but angry with Yeats over the story of his death, or more to the point, the style in which it was reported. By the time of the 1925 *Vision*, Robartes's anger has cooled, but the incident of the riot is still serious; two old friends died at the temple, and this had turned Robartes, temporarily, from his occult studies (*Vision*, 1925, p. xvii). In 1937, Yeats makes a point of deflating the originally tragic end of Robartes and the Order; John Aherne writes to Yeats:

A foolish rumour got out among the herring or mackerel sorters, and some girls (from Glasgow, my brother says, for they come from all parts) broke the window. (*Vision*, 1962, p. 55)

Robartes, too, has changed. His adventures are much the same as in 1925, but now highly condensed and colored with a tragic love absent in the original. Robartes is more emotional in 1937, much more involved in the movement of the gyres. He is no longer the neutral balancer between the antithetical Yeats and the primary Aherne as in 1925, but now more himself the antithetical man, even the prophet of the coming antithetical age.

Yeats was fascinated by the prophetic aspects of the system, but as the omission of the conclusion of "Dove or Swan" indicates, he was uncertain as to how to incorporate his predictions into *A Vision*. Another omitted section, "Michael Robartes Foretells," written sometime after 1932, appears in *Yeats and the Occult*. Walter Kelly Hood, who edited the piece, believes it would have been placed at the end of the book, thus enclosing the system in a fictional frame. Seven years would have seemed to have intervened between the first meeting of the pupils in London and their second meeting at Thoor Ballylee. The piece concerns the political manifestations that signal the new era,[66] and it is significant that Yeats omitted it; for although he was deeply concerned with politics late in his life, *A Vision* is, remarkably, an apolitical book. This controlled exclusion of topical material indicates that he intended the work to be an artistic image, not an actual history. *On the Boiler* provided a much better format for topical ideas and may have been devised to accommodate ideas Yeats rejected for *A Vision*.

Michael Robartes, despite his prophetic power, must have proved an inadequate spokesman for Yeats's political ideas. In the 1937 version, he is seen caught in the movement of the gyres. He knows the sorrow of love, and at one point describes life as "an irrational bitterness" (*Vision*, 1962, p. 40), a distinctly different type of remark in tone from one made in 1925: "But why should we complain, things move by mathematical necessity" (*Vision*, 1925, p. xvi). Robartes's discovery is less an adventure tale and more a philosophical parable in 1937. For example, Robartes does not pursue the Judwali tribe after accidently coming across their tracks in the desert; here, the old Arab is "sent" to him to explain the doctrinal diagrams (*Vision*, 1962, p. 41)—significantly, just after he, like Yeats, had ."ceased all active search, yet had not ceased from desire" (*Vision*, 1925, p. xi). In general, this motif of "spiritual intervention" is more evident in the 1937 stories than in those of 1925, where events happen largely by human effort. In 1937, Robartes is a seer, and the lives of all the characters are more strongly predestined. The emphasis is more upon instinctual knowledge than upon hard-won scholarly learning; and this new emphasis forces significant changes in the style and structure of the later work.

Robartes's Friends: Biography Changed into Myth

One of the most significant changes in the 1937 version is, of course, the addition of the stories of Robartes's friends: Peter Huddon, John Duddon, Daniel O'Leary, Denise de L'Isle Adam, John Bond, and Mary Bell. All of these are new characters in Yeats, assembled, theoretically, as Robartes's pupils, those selected by him or perhaps merely sent to him in his morning visions to contemplate "the terror that is to come" (*Vision*, 1962, p. 50), the coming antithetical age. The idea of a small group of initiates who watch for the coming age is not a new idea in Yeats; it appears in "The Tables of the Law." To some extent, his early fellow students of the occult formed such a group, and the idea finds its way into *The Speckled Bird*. Yeats's 1925 dedication, "To Vestigia" (Moina Mathers), is written both to her and to others who believed that, if one had faith, revelation would "find him at the fitting moment," or that "some messenger would make himself known" (*Vision*, 1925, pp. x–xi). The idea of that early, secret group of believers is, after thirty years, still very attractive to Yeats, for he predicts in 1925 that such a group will welcome in the new era:

> A decadence will descend ... When the new era comes bringing its stream of irrational force it will, as did Christianity, find its philosophy already impressed upon the minority who have, true to phase, turned away at the last gyre from the *Physical Primary*. (*Vision*, 1925, p. 213)

Yeats speaks of this minority in terms of "organic groups" or "*covens* of physical or intellectual kin ... the brood of Leda, War and Love; history grown symbolic, the biography changed into a myth" (*Vision*, 1925, p. 214).

Are Robartes's pupils the "brood of Leda"? Have they turned away from the physical primary? Northrop Frye has written that according to Yeats's system, the antithetial age will be contrasted to the present primary as individuality is to unity, tragedy is to comedy, freedom is to necessity, evil to good, art to science, Robartes to Aherne.[67] Robartes thunders to his pupils, "After an age of necessity, truth, goodness, mechanism, science, democracy, abstraction, peace, comes an age of freedom, fiction, evil, kindred, art, aristocracy, particularity, war" (*Vision*, 1962, p. 52). Yet, Robartes's friends seem to have few of these antithetical traits. They certainly are not evil; they do not seem to represent freedom. Far from being tragic, they are decidedly comic.

In fact, the stories as a whole seem to lampoon not only the system itself, but many of Yeats's cherished ideas. Mary's timid, ridiculous act of adultery with John Bond could be a reductive parody of Leda and the Swan; Denise and her impotent or cowardly lover, Duddon, a comment on the falling away from the passion and idealism represented by Sara and Axel, two iconoclasts who more nearly represent the antithetical.[68]

Yeats could be a capable social satirist, and to some extent "Stories of Michael Robartes and His Friends" does draw a satiric picture of modern society, set up in opposition to, perhaps in mockery of, the coming antithetical age, a portrait of a decadent, ridiculous culture, incapable of receiving a mythology. In short, the stories seem to represent not the waiting coven, but a sham secret group that is in fact no different than the decadent majority that must be swept away before the new era can be born. On a personal level, they represent a reexamination of many of Yeats's earlier selves, for example, the theater-reforming Daniel O'Leary and the armchair philosopher, Mr. Bell. The satiric is certainly present in the 1937 *Vision* as it was in *The Speckled Bird*; but as in the earlier work, it is not the main purpose. Internal evidence suggests that Yeats was setting many old arguments straight in 1937; in a manner almost too subtle and personal to be fully traced, he was saluting old friends and creating a unique form of autobiography. Finally, he was forging a wild, new style, drawn from the incredible energy of his last years and based, in part, on the style of his brother, Jack, and on the contemporary authors he had rejected in 1925 at the conclusion of "Dove or Swan."

In order to understand this highly personal late style, it is necessary to identify the stories' various autobiographical strains. The first character one encounters in "Stories of Michael Robartes and His Friends" is Daniel O'Leary, and it is difficult not to see a great deal of Yeats, the theater reformer, in O'Leary's hatred of the modern "kitchen gabble" and his interest in the establishment of "a small theatre for plays in verse" (*Vision*, 1962, p. 33). He begins his story by recalling how, in the years before the Great War, "the realists drove the last remnants of rhythmical speech out of the theatre" (*Vision*, 1962, p. 33), and goes on to tell the assembled group at Robartes's how, during a recent performance of *Romeo and Juliet*, he yielded to an impulse and flung his boots at the performers. Yeats would have approved of this gesture. In 1936, he pleaded with his readers to take action along similar lines:

> If anybody reads or recites poetry as if it were prose from some public platform, I ask you, speaking for poets, living, dead, or unborn, to protest in whatever way occurs to your perhaps youthful minds; if they recite or read by wireless, I ask you to express your indignation by letter.[69]

Unfortunately, O'Leary missed the actors and instead struck a member of the orchestra, and having, like Yeats, a hatred and dread of musicians,[70] ran, bootless, out of the theater and into the waiting arms of Aherne, who subsequently brought him, on Robartes's instructions, to the house. O'Leary's action, like Duddon's later, is meant to announce the theme of the stories: free will versus determinism. O'Leary thinks he has "decided" to fling his boots at just that instant, but Robartes sees beforehand that the action is determined by the system. In effect, the plot of the stories is that the characters are educated away from this illusion of free will, but such wisdom, it is implied, may bring suffering.[71]

If O'Leary is an autobiographical character, what about the others? Most of the assembled group seem to have specific or generalized allegorical significance. Huddon is War, Duddon is Art, and Denise, Love (*Vision*, 1962, p. 37). War and Love, Huddon and Denise, are the brood of Leda Yeats wrote of in 1925; in terms of the stories and the system in general, they are both of the past and of the future—symbols, perhaps, of the incarnation of the classical antithetical as Aherne may be thought of as the symbol of the present primary. Since the coming antithetical age will resemble the past classical era, Huddon and Denise belong in the grouping, but since the new era will also differ significantly from the old classical age, Mary, rather than Denise, is its proper representative. Both Huddon and Denise, therefore, seem to have negligible roles in the annunciation. Duddon, on the other hand, the artist and the most dedicated of Robartes's pupils (he alone keeps records and notes on the teachings), seems different from his friends, more significant in the plot. Art, which he represents, may be that which breaks the third shell when Robartes and Mary Bell have buried the lost egg of Leda to hatch in the warm desert sand (*Vision*, 1962, p. 51), for art is the central trait of the coming antithetical era.

Huddon, it should be noted, has no story of his own to tell and no real autobiographical significance for Yeats except that, as War, he may represent the lifetime of love-hate struggle with the affairs of the world that Duddon-Yeats, the artist, must accept as his Body of Fate. War, the public, the press, the holder of the purse, is the patron of Art; but Art is liberated only in striking down its patron as Duddon does, a symbol of the coming interchange of the tinctures when art will replace science. On a thematic level, it is clear that a figure of war as well as one of art must be present in the stories, for the coming antithetical age is also characterized by war. Explaining in *On the Boiler* why Robartes urges his pupils to prepare for war, Yeats writes that during the writing of *A Vision*, he had the word *terror* impressed upon him. The motif of war, on a personal level, seems to be a reaction to the mechanistic decay of the modern world, for Yeats writes, "The danger is that there will be no war, that the skilled will attempt nothing, that the European civilisation, like those older civilisations that saw the triumph of their gangrel stocks, will accept decay."[72]

Significantly, Duddon furnishes the point of attack for the stories as a whole. He is the narrator, and the plot begins not with O'Leary's, but with Duddon's arrival at Robartes's. If Yeats is masking behind ben Luka, Giraldus, and O'Leary, it seems reasonable to suspect that there is an autobiographical element in Duddon as well. The text of the stories gives little concrete evidence that Huddon represents Yeats's Body of Fate, but the idea that Duddon is Yeats becomes more plausible in light of the close biographical links between Yeats's life and the romantic triangle of Huddon, Duddon, and Denise.

Denise de L'Isle Adam, whose name implies that she is, in a sense, rewriting the work of Villiers, is reading *Axel* in bed late one night. In the section entitled "Ordeal by Gold and Love" (a title that sums up Duddon's trials as well as Axel's, for he is tormented by his love for Denise and his financial dependency on his patron, Huddon), she encounters Axel's remark that Sara's hair is full of the odor of dead roses and dreams that some man may one day say that of her. Whether Yeats has forgotten the line or whether he is deliberately misquoting in order to emphasize Denise's self-centered attitude, it is actually Sara herself who describes her hair as full of the odor of dead roses. Axel has threatened to kill her; but reversing roles, Sara claims him as a prisoner of her beauty and, urging him to let himself be seduced, promises to veil him with her hair. "All the favours of all other women," she cries, "are as nothing, set in the scale against my cruelties!"[73] To judge by Yeats's biography, this sentiment might well have applied to Maud Gonne, and there are other hints that suggest an identity between Denise and Maud.

Denise reads on, into the section called "The Supreme Choice" where she encounters the famous line, "Live? Our servants will do that for us!"[74] The choice in *Axel* is primarily Sara's, and it is a choice between life and death. For Denise, who in her preoccupation with the power of her own beauty misreads the play, missing the conflict of poetic dream and reality, the choice is one between the sensitive Axel (Duddon and Yeats) and the worldly Commander (Huddon, Major MacBride, and possibly Lucien Millevoye, the French political journalist and father of Iseult Gonne).[75]

Suddenly the candle goes out. Duddon has crawled through the window and presented himself, unsuccessfully, as a lover. The problem, as it turns out, is that Duddon is used to Huddon's cast-off romances; Duddon himself cannot initiate the physical side of a romance, Huddon must take the lead. Denise, misunderstanding Duddon's artistic sensitivity for mere shyness, has a simple solution: "Fetch the Commander" (*Vision*, 1962, p. 43).

It seems clear that Huddon and Duddon represent the split between body and soul, that they are male counterparts to the chambermaid and the lady in "The Three Bushes." Their situation reflects the limitation, the lack of unity, in incarnate life that Robartes says brings life's bitterness.[76] The material and the spiritual, the primary and the antithetical, when combined, represented unity; but such a combination is impossible. The coda to the tale, which takes place in Florence, restates the contrast between Huddon and Duddon in terms that suggest the system. Denise sends Huddon a cigarette case containing one cigarette in memory of their first sexual encounter. She makes clear that it is Duddon she loves even though she is Huddon's mistress, and then adds, enigmatically, "When a man gives me a cigarette, and I like the brand, I want a hundred, but the box is almost empty" (*Vision*, 1962, p. 44). Denise, unable to understand the poetic implications of *Axel*, can be won only by the commanding Huddon who represents the physical primary; but being primary herself, she is attracted to the poetic Duddon who represents the coming antithetical, not only because he is her opposite—her Daimon—but because, as she realizes, "the box is almost empty": the physical primary is nearly exhausted.

If Denise's story is a veiled autobiographical account of Yeats's romance with Maud Gonne,[77] it represents a significant change in attitude toward her late in Yeats's life. It is certainly a different picture of her than one gets in the earlier poems; but by the time of the second version of *A Vision*, Yeats and Maud Gonne were somewhat estranged. They quarreled openly in 1918 when Yeats, newly married, refused to shelter her from the authorities while she was visiting Ireland illegally. The disturbance, he judged, might upset his new wife, who was ill at the time.[78] He berates her in "A Prayer for My Daughter"; and in 1923, when she was arrested and jailed, Yeats, although he wanted to help, sensed the immense gulf of politics that had always lay between them:

> The day before her arrest she wrote to say that if I did not denounce the Government she renounced my society for ever. I am afraid my help in the matter of blankets, instead of her release (where I could do nothing), will not make her less resentful. She had to choose (perhaps all women must) between broomstick and distaff and she has chosen the broomstick—I mean the witches' hats.[79]

By 1929, they had apparently ceased to communicate on any deep level. Yeats writes to Mrs. Shakespear:

> When Lady Gregory goes, and she is now very frail, I too shall have but one old friend left. (M[aud] G[onne] has been estranged by politics this long while.)[80]

The "one old friend" is Mrs. Shakespear herself, to whom Yeats wrote often and intimately in his later years. Mrs. Shakespear was a cousin to Lionel Johnson and the sister of a Mr. Tucker, whose wife, formerly Mrs. Hyde-Lees, was George Hyde-Lees's mother.[81] It was through her that Yeats met his future wife; but Yeats and Mrs. Shakespear, who was married to a man much older than she, were also at one time lovers, even sharing Yeats's lodgings at Woburn Buildings for a time. She is the Diana Vernon of his memoirs,[82] on which he worked at the same time he worked on *A Vision*. Remembering the past, he wrote to her during that period:

> I came upon two early photographs of you yesterday, while going through my file—one that from *Literary Year Book*. Who ever had a like profile?—a profile from a Sicilian coin. One looks back to one's youth as to [a] cup that a mad man dying of thirst left half tasted. I wonder if you feel like that.[83]

The mellow, mature affection he felt for Olivia Shakespear and for Mrs. Yeats seemed, toward the end, to replace the more dramatic passion he had felt for Maud Gonne. Perhaps he believed though, looking back, that he had wronged Mrs. Shakespear; and if he could not write openly of their early illicit love, he reminds her of it often, as in a letter of 1934 that discusses the memoirs:

> I am just beginning on Woburn Buildings, building up the scene there—alas the most significant image of those years must be left out.[84]

But if he could not write of her in the memoirs, he could pay homage to her in *A Vision* where she merges with the qualities of another important woman in his life, Lady Gregory.[85]

Mary Bell has a special place in the stories. She is chosen to place the lost egg of Leda in the warm desert sand to hatch. As her name suggests, she is the Madonna figure of the new age, but she is also an adulteress, for the new antithetical age—the "rough beast" to be born—must have a different annunciation from the birth of Christ that initiated the primary Christian age. Yeats writes in *A Vision* that this new age will be "neither from beyond mankind nor born of a virgin, but begotten from our spirit and history" (*Vision*, 1962, p. 262). In *On the Boiler*, much the same idea is expressed: "Yet we must hold to what we have that the next civilisation may be born, not from a virgin's womb, nor a tomb without a body, not from a void, but of our own rich experience."[86] It would seem that Yeats now sees the coming antithetical age as much more a product of man himself than he did in the early stories, but the Madonna is still an outsider, like the lawless harlot in "The Adoration of the Magi":

> When the Immortals would overthrow the things that are to-day and bring the things that were yesterday, they have no one to help them, but one whom the things that are to-day have cast out. Bow down and very low, for they have chosen this woman in whose heart all follies have gathered, and in whose body all desires have awakened; this woman who has been driven out of Time and has lain upon the bosom of Eternity. (*M.*, p. 312)

The style of portraiture has changed drastically; the high seriousness is replaced by farce in 1937, but the core idea is similar. The Madonnas, like Yeats's muse, are women of nature and the night who give themselves to sailors and afterward return to talk of Chinese porcelain. Neither art nor the antithetical are abstract; both need contact with nature (*Vision*, 1962, p. 24).

John Bond, Mary's lover, whose name, as Hazard Adams has pointed out, derives from Blake, may suggest, in the idea of bonding, the organic group or coven that will welcome the new age. He is the spiritual figure, parallel to the natural Mary. He is also an expert on migratory birds, and birds are symbolic in myth of the spirit and soul.[87] In a note to *Four Plays for Dancers* (1921), Yeats explains that he uses birds as "symbols of subjective life" and that this symbolism is intimately connected to the Robartes material.[88] Is John, then, the parallel to the Holy Ghost who, like a cuckoo, leaves his offspring to hatch in the nest of the Joseph figure, the primary Christian Mr. Bell? Is their son, the product of an antithetical impulse, who is to be raised, as Yeats would have him raised, in a find old aristocratic house, the symbol of the new age?

Mary Bell's story is the most complex and the most ridiculous in the series. She and John meet at Cannes and fall in love; but when she learns that she is pregnant, she returns to her husband's house where her son is born. Five years later she comes to John at the Dublin Museum to consult with him about certain birds' nests that she wishes to construct with her own hands; and a month later, John is summoned by telegram to her country house. Her husband is dying, and ignorant of John and Mary's relationship, he wishes to consult with him on some scientific work he is doing. John arrives and is taken to Mr. Bell, who explains his philanthropic work, the teaching of caged cuckoos to nest. He has chosen this form of serving God because he does not wish to leave the luxury of his estate. His work has come to nothing, however, and now, old and dying, he has called upon John's expertise to help the work go on. As they are talking, however, Mary enters the room, holding a finished nest that she herself has made in secret, and Mr. Bell dies, happy in the thought that his work has not been in vain.

The details of this story are especially pertinent. As Mary and John walk through the "deplorable semi-gothic gateway" to the eighteenth-century house, she points out the "great sycamores and lucombe oaks and the clump of cedars," and the "great plantations behind the house" (*Vision*, 1962, p. 46), which represent the confidence of generations in their descendants. It is difficult not to compare the Bell estate to Coole, another great eighteenth-century house noted for its woods. Joseph Hone describes it in this way:

> The unpretentious gates of Coole open on an avenue of great trees, their leafy embracing branches a tunnel of twilight on the sunniest day. . . . More woods spread out behind the house.[89]

On their walk, Mary remarks on the "noble and generous confidence" of those who planted the trees for their descendants (*Vision*, 1962, p. 46), and in his memoirs, Yeats writes much the same thought:

> Lady Gregory is planting trees; for a year they have taken up much of her time. Her grandson will be fifty years old before they can be cut. We artists, do not we also plant trees and it is only after some fifty years that we are of much value?[90]

A Vision is, in many ways, the summing up of fifty years.

There are other parallels. Mr Bell had been in the Foreign Office (*Vision*, 1962, p. 47); Sir William Gregory was a former governor of Ceylon.[91] The walls of the Bell house are covered with portraits of famous writers, artists, and politicians of the 1860s and 1870s, dueling swords and pistols, placed there by "generations who did not care how incongruous the mixture that called up their own past history" (*Vision*, 1962, p. 47). The same was true of Coole:

> Many generations, and no uncultured generation, had left images of their service in the outlines of wood and fields at Coole, in sculpture and pictures, in furniture, in a fine library with editions of the classics and books on plants and agriculture.[92]

There seems no doubt that the Bell estate was modeled on Coole Park; and in her nobility and generous, gentle nature, Mary is somewhat like Lady Gregory. The necessity for a generous aristocracy that fosters the artist is, of course, a central concept in Yeats's ideal society. Harun Al-Raschid, ben Luka's patron, is another such figure: "He is the greatest of all traditional images of generosity and magnanimity."[93] John is like Yeats; both are interested in things of the spirit, symbolized by birds; both are taken into and nurtured by a great house. But it is, of course, the Olivia Shakespear elements in Mary that point up the parallel between John and Yeats as the lover figure.

The story is not an easy puzzle; the parallels are not exact, and often two or three persons merge in one character (Olivia, Lady Gregory, and George Yeats in Mary). Throughout the various stories, Yeats himself divides into many characters, each representing a certain period in his life (John Bond, John Duddon, Mr. Bell, Daniel O'Leary), and each revealing a great deal about his final attitude both toward himself and toward the creation of *A Vision*. The style is opaque, but the purpose is to pay homage to those who helped create not only the book, but the final, contented Yeats himself, those who helped him to nest and to build a nest, a system, for the wandering spirits, the migratory birds.

Maud Gonne was a bird fancier, often taking several with her on her travels, including a large Donegal hawk. Before important political rallies, she had a private ritual of releasing caged birds to symbolize the release of Ireland from bondage to England.[94] The Yeatses, too, kept caged canaries in the window, but, as the letters reveal, it was Olivia Shakespear whom Yeats probably identified with the nest builder, Mary Bell. Yeats writes her often about the birth of young canaries and the personalities of their parents:

> How much do I owe you for the nest? I forgot to ask you. The hen-bird is now sitting on two eggs and there is peace. The cock-bird brings her food and only chirps reproaches when she leaves the nest for a moment. He never pecks her and indeed I am inclined to think that he was never a sadist but that they had quarrelled because she insisted on "marriage lines." "Marriage lines" are plainly in the canary language a nest. They used to roost at opposite ends of their perch but now the cock-bird goes to sleep as close to the nest as he can. He sings more than ever.[95]

One can, I think, cautiously suggest that Yeats is reading a bit of his own married life into that of the birds, and the passage implies that Mrs. Shakespear was also a bird lover and sent various nesting materials to Yeats for his pets. In fact, he writes her again on this same topic later:

> Will you help my canaries who are nest making but with sheep's wool and green moss which they dislike? Can you get me at the bird-shop a bundle of nesting material? The shops all sell it.[96]

The nest-building process fascinated Yeats and apparently Mrs. Yeats as well. In his next letter to Mrs. Shakespear, he thanks her for the nesting materials and goes on to write:

> I have no doubt that in a few weeks' time we shall be the embarrassed owners of 20 new born canaries. I have suggested a pie but George won't hear of it. There is also a nest of stares in a hole over my bed-room window, no end of jackdaws in the chimneys, so George must be satisfied. I have just reminded her that when we came here first [Ballylee] she asked me if I thought anybody would give us a couple of crows, and if I thought the crows, if they did, could be got to build in the big tree.[97]

Nest building became a metaphor for instinct in Yeats's quarrel with abstract knowledge, and this running quarrel, prevalent in most of his late prose, forms an underlying intellectual structure for "Michael Robartes and His Friends."

Given the nest-building motif from the letters, it seems plausible to suggest that Mary is a portrait of Olivia Shakespear, with touches of George Yeats, who of course made a nest (home) for Yeats as well as the system, another kind of nest. Yeats is present in John Bond, both as the student of migratory birds (things of the spirit) and as Mary's illicit lover, and less obviously present in Mr. Bell, the foolish philosopher. At first, the parallel can easily go unnoticed. Because Mr. Bell is lord of the Bell estate (identified with Coole) and is Mary's husband, logic would demand that he be seen as Sir William Gregory and/or Mr. Shakespear; but "Stories of Michael Robartes and His

Friends" is not a work that progresses logically. Mr. Bell's behavior fits neither of these men; it does, however, fit Yeats as the struggling philosopher.

Mr. Bell's story introduces a second theme: instinct versus reason. The misguided Mr. Bell is essentially of the Christian primary era. Although he understands, dimly, that the birds are "the passions of Adam, torn out of his breast" (*Vision*, 1962, p. 48)—that is, things of the spirit, moods Yeats would call them—he misunderstands, like the old voteen in "The Old Men of the Twilight," the duality of history. The birds are antithetical, representing the other half of existence that he cannot see, let alone appreciate. Instead, he cages the things of the spirit and, like a good Christian, attempts to "save" the sinful birds from robbing and killing each other, that is, from war, their antithetical occupation. Naturally, they languish. He wants to teach them to nest, that is, to "weave" materials "into a structure" (*Vision*, 1962, p. 49); he wants, in other words, to replace antithetical instinct with primary knowledge.

In *A Vision* Yeats was also attempting to weave fragments into a structure, and there is ample evidence throughout the 1937 version to suggest that he remained unsatisfied with the "artificial unity" he had created: "Only dry or drying sticks can be tied into a bundle" (*Vision*, 1962, p. 302). It is instinct alone, not knowledge, that can understand the coming antithetical era, hence the influx of antithetical freedom and the celebration of the mysterious Thirteenth Cone that close the book. Mr. Bell's mistake is Yeats's own. All his scholarly toil and knowledge did not produce *A Vision*; the system, the nest for the free antithetical spirit, came through a woman, as did Mr. Bell's triumph, the nest made by Mary. It is the intuitive power, which Yeats perceived in Mrs. Shakespear and his wife, the stillness of waiting—which he describes in "The Symbolism of Poetry" and in "Earth, Fire and Water" in *The Celtic Twilight*—that alone can call down the spirits, not the aggressive search for knowledge. The fact that the nest is a fraud indicates Yeats's realization that a mere system is not a living mythology; a system is, like a nest or a work of art, a form for the spirits to inhabit, a breeding ground for the egg.

The lost egg of Leda, the symbol of the coming antithetical era, had other associations for Yeats as well. The legendary Merlin used crystal "serpents' eggs" for the purpose of scrying,[98] and the egg was an ancient Egyptian symbol that Yeats probably first encountered in conversation with Madame Blavatsky.[99] The work of Henry More and Ochorowicz suggested to Yeats that the root of personality, the soul perhaps, was oval or egg-shaped,[100] and Yeats wrote of the "ethereal body," the root of "natural warmth," as "a round or oval figure."[101] Yeats probably saw in the egg the symbol of unity composed of two opposites, white and yolk; it may have reminded him of the Chinese "symbol of *yen* and *yin*, those two forms that whirl perpetually, creating and recreating all things."[102] Certainly, it fit his concept of history with its alternation of antithetical and primary eras, the gyres changing direction every 2,000 years, for Robartes calls the universe "'a great egg that turns inside-out perpetually without breaking its shell'" (*Vision*, 1962, p. 33). It could also represent the disembodied spiritual universe, the system's sphere, the true reality that is mirrored by material life (*Vision*, 1962, p. 73, p. 193).

Yeats was fascinated by "those marble eggs, or objects of burnished steel too drawn up or tapered out to be called eggs, of M. Brancussi [sic]" (*Vision*, 1925, p. 211) and put them in evidence of the new art in which "it is as though the forms in the stone or in their reverie began to move with an energy which is not that of the human mind" (*Vision*, 1925, p. 211). The egg represents something about to be born, a blood revolution, and this "thing" emanates from the spiritual world. By 1931, Yeats had sufficiently defined his ideas about this symbol of the coming era to write:

> Let images of basalt, black, immovable,
> Chiselled in Egypt, or ovoids of bright steel
> Hammered and polished by Brancusi's hand,
> Represent spirits. If spirits seem to stand
> Before the bodily eyes, speak into the bodily ears,
> They are not present but their messengers.
> Of double nature these, one nature is
> Compounded of accidental phantasies.
> We question; it but answers what we would
> Or as phantasy directs—because they have drunk the blood.[103]

This discussion of "Stories of Michael Robartes and His Friends" is neither exhaustive nor definitive, for the symbolism, perhaps intentionally, is too elusive to be traced with absolute accuracy. Yeats leaves much, like the significance of John's and Mary's son, unexamined. Biographical figures merge with one another in a single fictional character, or as with Yeats himself, split into several characters, making it difficult to explicate the one meaning of the tales. The stories as a whole seem to cut both ways. In one sense they are definitely satiric, aimed at deflating not only modern society, but the poet himself. Duddon, Bond, and Bell are all highly humorous and remarkably honest self-portraits. On the other hand, Mary Bell seems to be a sincere compliment to Olivia Shakespear, Lady Gregory, and George Yeats;[104] and the ideas of Robartes are, of course, Yeats's own, meant to be taken seriously. The stories are autobiographical and represent both Yeats's intention to acknowledge, under the veil of fiction, his emotional debts and to assert his convictions regarding determinism and instinct. Another story—that of Huddon and Duddon—reinforces Yeats's argument for a form of poetic epistemology that relies on aristocratic breeding and instinct rather than factual knowledge.

Hudden, Dudden, and Donald O'Nery

If, as Richard Ellmann has said, *A Vision* was for Yeats "a huge projection of his own life, filled with autobiography and rationalization of his personal crises and temperament,"[105] one would expect to find in it all the various preoccupations that thread through his long career. Virginia Moore, among others, has traced the influences of the various occult traditions on the work, and an earlier portion of this study discussed how autobiographical elements enter into "Stories of Michael Robartes and His Friends." A third enduring influence on Yeats was folklore, in which he saw living proof of the workings of the Great Mind and Great Memory he had postulated in the 1901 essay, "Magic." This interest, too, finds its way into the 1937 *Vision* and furnishes there, in the little poem of Huddon, Duddon, and Daniel O'Leary, the symbolic foundation for Yeats's defense of instinct as the true basis of knowledge.

Huddon, Duddon, and Daniel O'Leary (or Hudden, Dudden, and Donald O'Neary, as they are called in *Celtic Fairy Tales*, edited by Joseph Jacobs in 1891) are universal figures in traditional folklore. Yeats used them in his 1888 *Fairy and Folk Tales of the Irish Peasantry* under the title "Donald and His Neighbours," where the spelling was Hudden, Dudden, and Donald O'Nery.[106] In these stories, two greedy farmers, Hudden and Dudden, attempt to gain possession of the land of their neighbor, Donald. Donald, however, a quick-thinking, humorous character with luck on his side, can always turn the tables on his enemies and profit by their villainy. For example, when Hudden and Dudden kill Donald's cow in an attempt to drive him off the land, Donald, by trickery, is able to sell the hide to the innkeeper in town for a fabulous price. He then convinces Hudden and Dudden that the hide market is booming, and they promptly slaughter their own herds, only to find that Donald has tricked them and the hides are worthless. Finally, enraged, Hudden and Dudden capture Donald and tie him in a sack, intending to drown him in a nearby lake. Again, Donald outsmarts them. By pretending that he is being taken to a wonderful destiny, he persuades a passing herdsman to take his place in the sack, asking for the herdsman's cattle in return. The herdsman is drowned in Donald's place and Donald, now a prosperous cattleman, convinces Hudden and Dudden that he found the cattle at the bottom of the lake. Greedy to the end, Hudden and Dudden run to the lake and jump to their own deaths.

Edward Callan, one of the few critics who has given close attention to this poem, argues that Yeats included the story because of its universality. His argument runs as follows: Yeats's *Autobiographies* and other prose reveal his conviction that the speech of imagined characters is the closest one can come to truth because it comes from the poet's instinct and has the sanction of the ancient Great Mind and Memory. To cite an example, Yeats writes in the "Introduction to 'The Words upon the Window-pane'" of 1931:

Thought seems more true, emotion more deep, spoken by someone who touches my pride, who seems to claim me of his kindred, who seems to make me a part of some national mythology, nor is mythology mere ostentation, mere vanity if it draws me onward to the unknown; another turn of the gyre and myth is wisdom, pride, discipline.[107]

Callan's example is from *Autobiographies*:

> I know now that revelation is from the self, but from that age-long memoried self, that shapes the elaborate shell of the molusc and the child in the womb, that teaches the birds to make their nest; and that genius is a crisis that joins that buried self for certain moments to our trivial daily mind.[108]

In 1937, Yeats wished to elaborate this theory since, as Callan implies, *A Vision* itself was a product of the workings of the Great Mind and Memory. (Were not Spengler's discoveries unaccountably close to Yeats's own, both in time of publication and in the dating of historical periods?) Yeats was familiar with Jacobs's work and admired its scholarship, Callan argues, a quality he himself did not possess. Consequently, he includes the Hudden and Dudden tale, a story Jacobs found remarkable in its universality (it is known in Ireland, Sicily, Afganistan, and Jamaica), as proof of the existence of the Great Mind and Memory. Yet, far from being, as Jacobs argued, an example of cross-cultural borrowing, the tale's history was like the simultaneous discoveries of Yeats and Spengler; the spirit world was expressing a truth, metaphorically, through men's imaginations. This is why Yeats mocks "men of thought," Jacobs among them, who believe, like Locke and Russell, in the "corked bottle" theory of mind—that is, that the mind at birth is a blank sheet and that all knowledge comes through learning. To Yeats, mind is instinctual; it discovers the truths locked in the Great Memory through imagination, a power that has affinities with the nesting instinct of birds. *A Vision*, then, in Callan's view, not only sets forth a system, but argues for the validity of that system and its methods by appealing to an epistemology of the imagination and instinct:

> The strategy of the 2nd edition of *A Vision* is designed to reveal how wisdom is propagated among men, not through the medium of libraries only, but through the psychic channels of a common mind, or a deep, archetypal memory—analogous, for example, to the instinct of birds. The wisdom stored in this memory was accessible only through the imagination and its works: through one's own fictional characters like Hanrahan, Robartes, and Aherne, through fictions of the folk-imagination like Huddon, Duddon and Daniel O'Leary.[109]

Callan's work helps to explain further why birds and nesting play such an important part in the "Stories of Michael Robartes and His Friends": *A*

Vision was achieved through imagination, not logic, and is to be read in the same way. It is not an abstract philosophy, but a living myth, as Yeats makes clear in 1937:

> My imagination was for a time haunted by figures that, muttering "The great systems," held out to me the sun-dried skeletons of birds, and it seemed to me that this image was meant to turn my thoughts to the living bird. That bird signifies truth when it eats, evacuates, builds its nest, engenders, feeds its young; do not all intelligible truths lie in its passage from egg to dust? (*Vision*, 1962, p. 214)

During the last few years of his life especially, Yeats's eye was constantly focused on the living bird. As will be shown later, the difference in style between the two versions reflects Yeats's struggle to conquer the abstractions he found in conventional philosophy and to invest his own system with the energy and life of myth.

What is missing in this discussion is the deeper significance that the symbol of the nesting bird implies. Yeats did, as Callan suggests, take his argument from Locke's remark that the nesting instinct of birds was insignificant to his work because he had called his book *A Philosophical Essay upon Human Understanding*. To Locke, Yeats opposed Henry More who considered that this instinct proved the existence of the Anima Mundi.[110] Yeats's own pet birds set before him the problem Locke had ignored, and he concludes with More that their actions, like those of his daughter, reveal a knowledge from beyond their own training in life. The same connection to the Anima Mundi holds for the artist, especially when his work is like that of *A Vision*: "When a man writes any work of genius, or invents some creative action, is it not because some knowledge or power has come into his mind from beyond his mind?"[111]

What is this power from beyond the mind? It is, first, the knowledge of the dead: "The bees and birds learn to make comb and nest from that *Anima Mundi* which contains the knowledge of all dead bees and birds."[112] But, more than that, it is the dead themselves who still live. Yeats's Anima Mundi has a more ghostly aspect than any psychological theory of the unconscious would imply:

> The dead living in their memories are, I am persuaded, the source of all that we call instinct, and it is their love and their desire, all unknowing, that make us drive beyond our reason, or in defiance of our interest it may be; and it is the dream martens that, all unknowing, are master-masons to the living martens building about church windows their elaborate nests; and in their turn, the phantoms are stung to a keener delight from a concord between their luminous pure vehicle and our strong senses. (*M.*, p. 359)

One is taken back, thematically, to the early kidnapping fairy stories Yeats collected at the beginning of his career and, more importantly, to the theme of the active Daimon Yeats discussed in the 1925 *Vision*. In both cases, Yeats's purpose was to reveal how much control the dead have over the events of life, and to a great extent *A Vision* is a book of the dead. The relationship between the living and the dead pierces to the center of Yeats's theory of artistic creation and implies the very theme and source of *A Vision* in the world of the Spirits.

With this core of meaning in mind, two further remarks about Callan's study should be made. First, it does not go far enough; it abstracts a quality from the history of the tale, universality, and assumes that this quality is Yeats's sole reason for including it. Callan never really looks at the story itself. While Yeats is certainly arguing for an epistemology of the imagination—and the tale is included as evidence of that theory—the Hudden and Dudden material has as much to say about the theme of *A Vision* as it does about the methods of discovering that theme. Second, Callan assumes a partisanism in Yeats that is not supported by the poem, the style of *A Vision*, or the artistic stance of Yeats's later life. In a book of *A Vision*'s scope, any choosing of sides, whether it be the antithetical over the primary as in 1925, or the instinctual over the rational as Callan argues, could not help but spoil the effect of a total vision, a timeless sacred book in which all points of view balance. The work represents the equanimity of Yeats's old age.

This discussion may seem belabored, but the Hudden and Dudden material has much to say about the themes and methods of *A Vision*. Why did Yeats choose this particular story? He must have known dozens that were equally universal, and there are factors to argue against it. First, as Joseph Jacobs points out, the story was not Celtic but European and was only Celtic by "adoption and by colouring."[113] The whole of *Celtic Fairy Tales* was, in fact, written to attract English schoolchildren. Thus, the collection is not really scholarly, and Jacobs confesses as much. Discussing his rewriting and blending of the Celtic and European elements in the tales, he says: "I trust I shall be forgiven by Celtic scholars for the changes I have had to make to effect this end."[114] On the other hand, Yeats's supposed lack of scholarship is exaggerated. In his early career as a journalist, Yeats faulted Lady Wilde for lack of documentation in her *Ancient Cures, Charms, and Usages of Ireland*, a folklore collection;[115] and he was keenly aware of the problem of mixing scientific and poetic approaches to folk material. Thus, on two counts, the argument that Yeats chose the story because he admired Jacobs's scholarship seems weak.

Finally, the story is not, on the surface, typically Yeatsian, dealing as it does with mere trickery and greed. In *The Celtic Twilight*, there are few stories, "The Three O'Byrnes and the Evil Faeries" being the notable example, in which greed and worldly success figure as motives for action. In this story, fairy gold is promised to the O'Byrne family, but only after three of them have dug for it and died. It is not typical of the volume; most of the stories concern visions of the beautiful otherworld, kidnapping fairies, or famous ballad singers and storytellers. Even the O'Byrne's greed is forgiven because of the world's present state of decay:

> In the dim kingdom there is a great abundance of all excellent things. There is more love there than upon the earth; there is more dancing there than upon the earth; and there is more treasure there than upon the earth. In the beginning the earth was perhaps made to fulfill the desire of man, but now it has got old and fallen into decay. What wonder if we try and pilfer the treasures of that other kingdom! (*M.*, p. 86)

The digging for gold here is clearly symbolic of a longing for the beauties of the otherworld; and thus, on a symbolic level if not on the level of plot, the story expresses the theme of the two kingdoms, the day-to-day real world and that otherworld of eternal beauty which the fairies and the instructors of *A Vision* inhabit. It seems needless to document here that Yeats believed in the existence of this otherworld; the theme runs throughout his work—whether the other kingdom is the fairy world, the alchemical realm of the moods, or the sphere of reality in *A Vision*.[116] This is the world that imagination discovers; it contains the truth that can only be discovered by instinct, but it is important to note that such a discovery can often mean death.

Like many of his characters, Yeats longed for this other kingdom, the land he had seen and heard in vision. Once, when he was visiting the Belfast Naturalists' Field Club, he told the following story, which was faithfully recorded by the club secretary:

> When he was a child he was told that there was a submerged city at the bottom of Sligo Lake, and that from its tower came up sometimes at evening a far-off murmur of fairy bells. Once when eight years old he gazed upon that lake, and he imagined, so much did the story possess his mind, that he could hear the murmur of the bells creep up through its waters.[117]

Sometimes fairy music leads men to their death, but it also can mark a man as a poet:

> Many a mortal have they enticed down into their dim world. Many more have listened to their fairy music, till all human cares and joys drifted from their hearts, and they became great fairy doctors, or great musicians, or poets like Carolan, who gathered his tunes while sleeping on a fairy rath; or else they died in a year and a day, to live ever after among the fairies.[118]

Yeats's childhood belief has much in common with the Hudden and Dudden tale that he, too, records in *Fairy and Folk Tales of the Irish Peasantry* in 1888. In Yeats's version, the villains, Hudden and Dudden, attempt to drown Donald O'Nery in a river that Donald, having tricked them, says is filled with "all the sight of cattle and gold that ever was seen."[119] In Jacobs's version, the place is the "Brown Lake of the Bog" that leads to the "Land of Promise,"[120] and Donald embroiders much more on the beauties of this other world. In Jacobs, Donald escapes the sack by hinting that he is being taken off to marry a princess, but in Yeats, Donald is going to heaven, where he will be "free from trouble."[121] In Jacobs, the clouds overhead are reflected in the lake and appear to be cattle beneath the water, while in Yeats, Donald simply throws a stone in the river to indicate where the others are to jump. Although Jacobs's version may seem better to suggest the otherworld Yeats experienced as a child and later wrote of in *The Celtic Twilight*, Yeats's note to the *Vision* poem states that as a child he pronounced O'Leary to rhyme with "dairy," which suggests that he was thinking of his own version with Donald O'Nery, not Jacobs's O'Neary (*Vision*, 1962, p. 32), when he worked on the material late in life. Whatever version he was using, the important element is not the universality of the tale, but the element of another world that exists beneath some body of water; for water represents the "image-making power" (*Vision*, 1962, p. 93). It is through the symbol of elemental water that one can call up spirits, that is, in more prosaic terms, imagine that other world:

> Did not the wise Porphyry think that all souls come to be born because of water, and that "even the generation of images in the mind is from water"? (*M.*, p. 80)

In choosing the Hudden and Dudden story, Yeats's interest was in the theme of the two kingdoms, *A Vision* being the product and promise of that unseen other kingdom. Here water plays a highly significant role. Once when A.E. was painting a deep, stagnant pool on Lady Gregory's estate, he grew inexplicably melancholy and morose. Yeats writes of it:

> I divined that something was wrong, for with men of his kind all is an evocation, and not daring to give him a symbol, persuaded him to paint the garden in hot sunlight. At once he became cheerful again and told me that he had seen in the stagnant pool figures that promised him all wisdom if he would but drown himself.[122]

To Yeats, his friend's danger was very real, just as was the narrator's in the 1897 stories, for he writes elsewhere in his 1909 journal:

> All civilization is held together by a series of suggestions made by an invisible hypnotist, artificially created illusions. The knowledge of reality is always by some means or other a secret knowledge. It is a kind of death.[123]

Donald's promise of riches compels his enemies to jump foolishly to their deaths; in *A Vision*, this amusing bit of trickery becomes a grim joke. No living man can know more than half of the system (*Vision*, 1925, p. 251). To attempt to see both sides—all of reality—is to risk a kind of death. This is true of the average man as well as the visionary; it was Aherne's fate in 1897.

Yet, on the other hand, to know only one side of the system is to be but another kind of fool. The Hudden and Dudden of the folktale are a "roaring, ranting crew," probably primary, physical in nature, interested in material wealth. Those Yeats substitutes for them "despair" and "love wench Wisdom's cruel face" (*Vision*, 1962, p. 32). They are probably antithetical. Or the distinction might be between the mass the mankind—Hudden, Dudden, and Donald O'Nery—and the coven—the minority awaiting the new era, represented by Robartes's satirically drawn friends. It is all one; Yeats mocks both "hard-living men and men of thought" (*Vision*, 1962, p. 32). They both spend their lives for nothing, for there is nothing to achieve, neither wealth nor wisdom, in a predestined pattern. All is as it must be. Yeats is, in the poem and the fictional section of *A Vision*, the neutral figure Robartes was in 1925, above the struggles for either material wealth or intellectual knowledge, in tune, instinctively, with the vast historical processes. He can watch the world with a "cold eye," with the same sort of disinterested delight with which a child hears a folktale, "for the world only exists to be a tale in the ears of coming generations" (*M.*, p. 300). Because he is, in a sense, all men present, the teachers and the pupils of the system, he alone can see the paradox and mock the world, mock even his own system. Being an old man, a fact he insists on in the 1937 version, he can even mock death.

4
Style: The Playing of Strength

Sources of the Change in Style

"STORIES of Michael Robartes and His Friends" is, as much as *The Herne's Egg* or the Crazy Jane poems, central in the examination and assessment of Yeats's late style; yet strangely, it is his most neglected and misunderstood work. Helen Vendler misses the work's modernity entirely when she dismisses the stories as "stage scenery," tales that "now have a faded antiquarian savor in their remoteness, their rather perverse and precious humor, and their artificial tone."[1] Richard J. Finneran, in his study, *The Prose Fiction of W. B. Yeats: The Search for 'Those Simple Forms,'* deliberately omits them as "so limited in purpose and so intimately connected with the philosophical system as to be distinct from the prose fiction proper."[2]

Of course, the stories would lack focus without the system, but this hardly renders them negligible. They represent, after all, the only prose fiction of Yeats's late period, and more importantly, they mark a radical departure in style from his earlier stories. In them, the familiar occult themes, the suggestion of folklore in the Hudden and Dudden material and a significant contemporary artistic setting come together, woven into a wild new style that Yeats had derived in part from his contemporaries.

Robartes had complained bitterly of the old "extravagant" style Yeats had learned from Pater.[3] He was still angry in 1937, as John Aherne's letter testifies:

> He is, however (and this I confirm from my own knowledge), bitter about your style in those stories and says that you substituted sound for sense and ornament for thought.[4]

John tries to argue that Yeats's style was merely the style of the period, the equivalent of "absolute" or "pure" poetry and that, while it lacked speed and variety, it would have acquired them in time, as did Elizabethan prose. He pleads that "romance driven to its last ditch had a right to swagger" (*Vision*, 1962, p. 55). But, Robartes is adamant:

> He answered that when the candle was burnt out an honest man did not pretend that grease was flame. (*Vision*, 1962, p. 55)

The image of the burnt-out candle, soon to be extinguished in the violent, dark winds of modernity, appears as a frontispiece in the 1929 *Packet for Ezra Pound*, as it does in many Cuala volumes, and reflects a contemporary concern with finding an adequate style to meet the demands of a coldly scientific civilization. One remembers the young Yeats from *Autobiographies* who was "in all things Pre-Raphaelite,"[5] arming himself with "a fardel of stories, and of personages, and of emotions, inseparable from their first expression."[6] In 1937, the old man has a new, hard-edged weapon.

Robartes complained specifically of the speed and variety of the early style, and that seems a good place to begin comparing Yeats's early and late prose. A passage chosen at random from "Rosa Alchemica" or, for that matter, any of the stories from the 1890s, typically shows a long, convoluted sentence. The speed is deliberately slowed by an abundance of modifying phrases, often placed so as to interrupt the natural word order of the sentence. Abstract, multisyllabic diction further slows the lines. The tone is formal; the pace one of meditation. In 1937, the stories still show an abundance of modifying phrases, for this is in fact a hallmark of Yeats's prose, but the phrases are shorter and the trick is used less often. In the late style, Yeats also uses an abundance of coordinating conjunctions to keep the sentences, in effect, compound rather than compound-complex, and thus to propel the narrative forward more rapidly. The diction has been greatly simplified.

Yeats realized that his old style would not do and took pains to change it. And what he was attempting to change in himself, he criticized in others. In 1932, he reviewed A.E.'s *Song and Its Fountains* somewhat severely because of its language:

> My friend, whose English at the close of the civil war was so vigorous and modern—I remember an article which found its way into the prisons and stopped a hunger strike—writes as though he were living in the 'nineties, seems convinced that spiritual truth requires a dead language. He writes "dream" where other men write "dreams," a trick he and I once shared, picked up from William Sharp perhaps when the romantic movement was in its last contortions. Renaissance Platonism had ebbed out in poetic diction, isolating certain words and phrases as if they were metaphors that seem to me like those wax flowers of a still older time I saw in childhood melted on the side towards the window.[7]

Yeats's characteristic prose had always a delicacy like poetry; the subtle, wavering rhythms, elaborate allusions, and the frequent rhetorical questions that double the meaning back upon itself evoke a mood of speculation, of belief or a longing for belief, rather than of certainty. In his style, he invites the reader to speculate upon the difficult concepts of *A Vision*.

It would seem, however, that the more certain Yeats became in his opinions, and the more pressure the rational twentieth century put upon him as one of the last romantics, the more this style faded. In *On the Boiler*, the prose is tougher, the rhythms more insistent, and in the late stories, evocation is replaced by a method of stark, flatly stated correspondences. If one looks at the 1937 stories, one notices not only the absence of the gorgeous description of "Rosa Alchemica" and the absence of any attempt to make the dialogue realistic, but a certain bluntness of statement. The symbols are not vague and evocative like the rose, but now almost allegorical: Denise is Love; Huddon, War; and Duddon, Art.

It is perhaps a mistake, however, to claim that this style is really new, for it has deep roots in Yeats's occult studies. The persistence and power of the symbol had been his lifelong study; and as early as 1901, he had set forth his credo in "Magic":

(1) That the borders of our mind are ever shifting, and that many minds can flow into one another, as it were, and create or reveal a single mind, a single energy.
(2) That the borders of our memories are as shifting, and that our memories are a part of one great memory, the memory of Nature herself.
(3) That this great mind and great memory can be evoked by symbols.[8]

The evocation of the power of the Great Mind and Memory was not a form of aimless or chance reverie, but a precise methodology. Often in Yeats's writing about his occult experiments, he will confess to imagining the wrong symbol, thus calling up in his partner a distorted or partial vision. The same thing could happen in poetry because every symbol, invested in life with a material aspect (color, form, sound), had an exact equivalent in the nonmaterial realm of the Great Mind and Memory. As Yeats writes in "The Symbolism of Poetry," in 1900:

All sounds, all colours, all forms, either because of their preordained energies or because of long association, evoke indefinable and yet precise emotions, or, as I prefer to think, call down among us certain disembodied powers, whose footsteps over our hearts we call emotions; and when sound, and colour, and form are in a musical relation a beautiful relation to one another, they become, as it were, one sound, one colour, one form, and evoke an emotion that is made out of their distinct evocations and yet is one emotion.[9]

Yeats is careful to point out that no two of these "modulations or arrangements" of symbols evoke the same emotion,[10] and one gets a hint from this passage of how inherently schematic Yeats's mind was. The young man who collected and classified butterflies and moths would later classify the Irish fairies in the same way in "Irish Fairies, Ghosts, Witches, Etc.," an article that appeared in the theosophical magazine, *Lucifer*, in 1889, and in *Irish Fairy Tales*. So eager was he to study Blake's complicated system that one should not be surprised that he later devised an equally complex system of his own, although some critics still see him as a dreamy nonintellectual. His ritual for the Castle of Heroes was highly schematic and allegorical; even his friends were classified as symbols.

This natural predilection for classification that, in a literary context, can become allegory, found a tradition already prepared for it in occultism. Kathleen Raine and Virginia Moore, among others, have documented Yeats's intense study of ancient symbols and myths and the way in which symbols were literally dramatized in occult rituals. When Yeats was initiated as a neophyte (0-0) in the Golden Dawn on 7 March 1890, for example, he wore a symbolic green robe, red shoes, and a rope belt. He was blindfolded. After certain oaths were made, he was led around the hall to symbolic spots corresponding to the four points of the compass. At one point, his path was barred by a wand. He passed between two pillars, one black and one white, representing Severity and Mercy. He learned secret steps and salutes.[11] In another ritual, he symbolically enacted the discovery of the tomb of Christian Rosencreutz[12] with Mathers taking the part of Christian. In his 5-6 initiation ritual, Yeats was suspended on a cross by means of ropes while the Second Chief of the Order held out the Rose Crucifix and said, "The Symbol of Suffering is the symbol of strength." Yeats replied; "I, Demon Est Deus Inversus, a member of the Body of Christ, do this day spiritually bind myself, even as I am now bound physically upon the Cross of Suffering, that I will to the utmost lead a pure and unselfish life."[13]

These ritualized performances of a symbol's meaning must have made the patterns of myth not just an objective intellectual system, but a total way of life.[14] It would be natural, after such initiations, for Yeats to ritualize his own life and see his friends as symbols. Micheál MacLiammóir, in fact, has noted the humorous extremes to which this ritualism could be carried in Yeats's personal life: "There was a gravity, an almost ecclesiastical ritualism, about the way in which he signed a cheque or put on his overcoat, and he would order a waiter to bring him a mutton chop in the tones of one who seeks the Holy Grail."[15] Yet, in Yeats's work—"All Souls' Night" or "Stories of Michael Robartes and His Friends," for example—this deliberate mythmaking served a highly serious purpose, that of shaping personal experience into usable aesthetic content.

The rituals also offered a stylistic model that appealed to Yeats's naturally schematic mind. Not only his themes, but to a great extent, his method and style were derived from occult tradition. To take a further example, *The Chymical Marriage of Christian Rosencreutz*, the central document in the Rosicrucian tradition, is an extended allegory. In Virginia Moore's summary of the story, Christian travels to a far country to attend the wedding of a king and queen, symbolic of the male and female principles. On his way and at the castle, he encounters many strange persons and events, obviously symbolic of alchemical doctrines. The full plot of *The Chymical Marriage* need not be set forth here, for the important thing one notes is that there is no attempt to make the story credible or to maintain continuity in the plot; the symbolic skeleton alone seems important.[16]

Of course, the style of "Stories of Michael Robartes and His Friends" is not modeled directly on Yeats's 5-6 initiation or on *The Chymical Marriage*, but the style of the documents that were his daily study throughout most of his life did influence his fiction. Many of these documents, those in the hermetic tradition, were based on the doctrine of correspondence that states, "What is below is like that which is above, and what is above is similar to that which is below, to accomplish the wonders of one thing."[17] Yeats, in all probability, first learned this doctrine from Madame Blavatsky's discussion of the Emerald Tablet.[18] The doctrine's affinity with the two-kingdoms motif in Irish folkore would have attracted him, and doubtless it played a part in shaping the aesthetic theories of "The Symbolism of Poetry." More importantly for the purpose here, the doctrine of correspondence dictated the language of the Order's rituals as a bare, simple, one-to-one allegorical pattern. In this, perhaps, Yeats saw that the simple act of naming, of setting down symbol and significance in bold, allegorical strokes, could give his work a power that the delicacy of elaborate imagery could not attain. In the later poems, this boldness of statement becomes more apparent, as for example in the conclusion of "A Prayer for My Daughter":

> Ceremony's a name for the rich horn,
> And custom for the spreading laurel tree.[19]

or in "Lapis Lazuli":

> Over them flies a long-legged bird,
> A symbol of longevity.[20]

As Richard Ellmann writes of Yeats's work after *A Vision*, "The power to classify is the power to control, and a new sense of strength comes into his writing."[21]

Of course, as critics have noted, Yeats fought a lifelong battle against abstraction. Perhaps one of his best-known pronouncements on this subject appears in the introduction to *The Cat and The Moon*, a play written under the spell of the initial excitement *A Vision* brought to his work:

> I had to bear in mind that I was among dreams and proverbs, that though I might discover what had been and might be again an abstract idea, no abstract idea must be present.[22]

In his journal of 1909, he explains how abstract philosophy enters the work of art and is eventually absorbed by the plot and characters, a process that might also describe the writing of "Stories of Michael Robartes and His Friends":

> In Christianity what was philosophy in Eastern Asia became life—biography, drama. A play passes through the same process in being written. At first, if it has psychological depth, there is a bundle of ideas, something that can be stated in philosophical terms; my *Countess Cathleen*, for instance, was once the moral question, may a soul sacrifice itself for a good end?—but gradually philosophy is eliminated more and more until at last the only philosophy audible, if there is even that, is the mere expression of one charcter or another. When it is completely life it seems to the hasty reader a mere story.[23]

The demands and beauties of life must, for Yeats, the poet, always triumph over rational thought and abstraction; but the battle with abstraction *was* a battle for Yeats precisely because, unlike Pound perhaps, he saw something of merit in it. As Warwick Gould has pointed out, classification and one-to-one correspondences, allegory and the act of naming called down the disembodied moods; these things formed the ancient language that gave the magician his power.[24] As he grew older, Yeats may have seen that in his Pateresque prose, he was fighting the evils of modernity with an outmoded and ineffectual weapon and that he had had all along in occultism the rudiments for the forging of a new style.

In the 1930s, the various threads of Yeats's life seemed to be coming together: Irish folklore could still contribute to the themes of his late work; occultism could provide not only disguised content, but a new style. Had he persisted in his early Pateresque style, he might have isolated himself from younger writers; in fact, he saw himself as apart from them in the conclusion of "Dove or Swan" in 1925. With a new contemporary style, evident in 1937, he could integrate his work successfully with theirs.

There seems little question that Yeats was experimenting with a new style, and John Aherne's remarks about *his* brother's diaries can be taken as a hint from Yeats:

> Should I live, and my brother consent, I may publish some part of these, for they found themselves, as always, where life is at tension, and met, amidst Free State soldiers, irregulars, country gentlemen, tramps and robbers, events that suggest, set down as they are without context or explanation, recent paintings by Mr. Jack Yeats where one guesses at the forms from a few exciting blotches of colour. (*Vision*, 1962, p. 53)

Yeats, too, was learning from his brother.

In 1938, Jack Yeats published *The Charmed Life*, a unique novel-length record of the ramblings of two Irish tramps, Mr. Nomatter and his friend, Bowsie. They remind one, sometimes strikingly, of the later Beckett tramps, Estragon and Vladimir, in *Waiting for Godot:* comfort loving, sentimental, alternately wise and foolish philosophers, one constantly looking out for the other's welfare. To take one particularly Beckett-like sample: At one point, having nothing better to do, Bowsie and Nomatter decide to walk in opposite directions on two low headlands, stand with the bay of the sea between them, and commune with their "nonsensical souls."[25] The incident is trivial and insignificant, but perhaps because of the positioning of the characters, it seems to mean much more. There is a touch of sorrow in these two comic figures something like that in Robartes and in Yeats's other late fictional characters, but it is objectified by the humor of the setting and narrative style.

In another passage, Bowsie falls off a bridge and is nearly swept out to sea; a chance whim of the waves saves him and, as in *La La Noo*, there is something significant about the event, in terms of myth and symbol, which Jack Yeats keeps tauntingly out of reach. Symbols recur, notably the sea, the star, and the rose, but their meaning is never pinpointed. There is no plot, only miniature portraits and vivid, humorous description and sketches. One must "guess at the form from a few exciting blotches of colour." For example, how are we to think of Bowsie from this little incident, described by Mr. Nomatter:

> Bowsie is looking neat, and imposing, still. He has the artificial rose in his coat. But, passing by a furze bush, an idea comes to him. He takes the rose from his coat, and fastens it securely, with its wire stem well twisted, to the topmost spray of the bush. Bowsie, with that poetic droop in his eyelids, says, "Wave there, noble flower, and long may you wave over the little young things of the wild—under the rose."[26]

Yeats, who may be the model for the Bowsie of this particular passage, liked the book and remarks on it in *On the Boiler*, discussing the falsehood of all knowledge:

> And now comes my brother's extreme book, *The Charmed Life*. He does not care that few will read it, still fewer recognise its genius; it is his book, his *Faust*, his pursuit of all that through its unpredictable, unarrangeable reality least resembles knowedge. His style fits his purpose, for every sentence has its own taste, tint, and smell.[27]

Although *The Charmed Life* was published after the second *Vision*, Jack Yeats's evolving style in painting and prose had been influencing Yeats for some time; and it was this same extreme style, grasped by the reader's intuition rather than by reference to the conventional frameworks of "knowledge," that Yeats was attempting in the second version of *A Vision*. "Stories of Michael Robartes and His Friends" lacks the rich, visual description of Jack Yeats's work, and the characters do not share the same warmth of affection as Bowsie and Nomatter. The prose is much less adorned, starker and simpler syntactically; but the same elusiveness surrounds the seemingly symbolic incidents. Why does O'Leary accidentally strike a musician? Why are the time designations of the incidents so carefully recorded? (The group first meets at eleven o'clock; Denise is reading *Axel* between twelve and one on 2 June; Mary visits John at the museum at four o'clock.) Why does Duddon blow out the candle?

Jack Yeats's painting style, as Micheál MacLiammóir has noted, changes in old age much as his brother's writing does. The landscapes become wild, and the work reflects a savage energy. New images appear (city streets, theater scenes, urban faces)—all depicted in glittering light.[28] Yeats, visiting him in 1929, wrote to Lady Gregory:

> I went out to Jack's this afternoon and saw there much of his new work—very strange and beautiful in a wild way. Joyce says that he and Jack have the same method.[29]

It is interesting that Yeats should recall Joyce's remark, for Joyce was one of those writers of Phase 23 whom Yeats discussed in the 1925 conclusion of "Dove or Swan":

> I find at this 23rd Phase which is it is said the first where there is hatred of the abstract, where the intellect turns upon itself, Mr Ezra Pound, Mr Eliot, Mr Joyce, Signor Pirandello, who either eliminate from metaphor the poet's phantasy and substitute a strangeness discovered by historical or contemporary research or who break up the logical processes of thought by flooding them with associated ideas or words that seem to drift into the mind by chance; or who set side by side as in "Henry IV," "The Waste Land," "Ulysses," the *physical primary*—a lunatic among his keepers, a man fishing behind a gas works, the vulgarity of a single Dublin day prolonged through 700 pages—and the *spiritual primary*, delirium, the Fisher King, Ulysses' wandering. It is as though myth and fact, united until the exhaustion of the Renaissance, have now fallen so far apart that man understands for the first time the rigidity of fact, and calls up, by that very recognition, myth—the *Mask*—which now but gropes its way out of the mind's dark but will shortly pursue and terrify.[30]

Joyce worked by paralleling myth and reality, by intertwining them, yet keeping the correspondences inexact and open-ended. His purpose was not like Yeats's to "restore mythology" to the modern world, but to dramatize the gap between myth and reality while at the same time asserting the identity between them. Significantly, too, Joyce added the satiric humor, the hatred, and aloofness Yeats had rarely displayed in his early work. Still essentially a romantic in 1925 and not recognizing some of his own goals and principles in Joyce's work, Yeats stood apart from his contemporaries in "Dove or Swan." He objects in his notes that the new art makes physical and mental objects alike material and that "man in himself is nothing."[31] Obviously, such an art is incompatible with the occult ideas reflected in the Blake book. Further, it breaks the correspondence of object and meaning necessary to the symbolist and undermines the persona of the lyrical poet. In a later essay, he rejects the "new naturalism" of Joyce and Pound because in it the "consciousness" of the artist has "shrunk back," become passive rather than active, and man is "helpless before the contents of his own mind."[32]

Yeats was never entirely sure of his assessment of these younger artists, however, and by 1937, he was using many of the same techniques himself, especially the inexact, mismatched humorous parallels between the bare traditional symbol and the real-life equivalent. This mismatching created a gap in which the force of the artistic personality could play. Although the styles had similarities, there was an essential difference: Joyce's approach was intellectual; the observing eye was purely analytical, with the personality of the artist "refined out of existence." Yeats's approach was personal; the observer took a more subjective stance, dramatizing himself as the link between myth and reality. In "Stories of Michael Robartes and His Friends," autobiography, with its real-life personages, becomes personal, not intellectual, myth. There is the same gap; and one intuits identities, many of them comic, which one cannot "prove" by the intellect. Echoes of meaning remain elusive, like the sketchy figures in Jack Yeats's later paintings.

This is a far different, and far less serious, method of using myth than Yeats employed in, say, "No Second Troy" or even in the late poem, "Beautiful Lofty Things," where there is almost no distinction between myth and reality:

> Maud Gonne at Howth station
> waiting a train,
> Pallas Athene in that straight back
> and arrogant head.[33]

Although the description here is vivid, it has no tension in itself. Maud and Athene are the same; one does not comment upon the other. Both are mythological figures with little reality to balance them. In the late plays and some of the later poems, like the Crazy Jane series, the reality that balances the myth can become coarse and grotesque as it does in Joyce, but it does so in order to express the personal view of the author, not an objective intellectual pattern.

Although the symbolic skeleton and the autobiographical approach were the same elements Yeats had used all his life, he now saw that the slight mismatch of identities and the gap it created made the stories more universal, more mysterious, reckless, like the incidents in Joyce. This style seemed to have more energy and life, and to leave more room for the poetic personality, the hidden yet constantly present sensibility representing the imagination, which bound the two identities together by the simple act of perceiving them together. It was the style Yeats would later admire in his brother's book, and its discovery may be the reason that he omitted the conclusion of the 1925 "Dove or Swan" in 1937. There was by then less distance between his own work and that of other "modern" authors. The revised *Vision*, in fact, now even illustrated some of these new artistic principles.

Another artist Yeats criticized in 1925 was Wyndham Lewis, whose work he used as an example of the distinction between personal dream and mechanical form. Having moved away from recognizable subject matter, Lewis, like Brancuşi, had, he thought, moved away from personality, which had long been central to Yeats's stance as a lyric poet. Their forms were mathematical; their rhythms, geometrical patterns imposed on, not issuing from, the mind: "They are all absorbed in some technical research to the entire exclusion of the personal dream" (*Vision* 1925, p. 211).

Yeats discussed this new art with his father in their letters. He saw in Lewis's pictures a confusion of the rhythmical, which is a living thing, with abstraction, the equivalent of rhetoric in writing, which was "incompatable with life."[34] It was a fine distinction and one with which Yeats struggled in his own work, for he saw that the world and he himself were changing; the old style would not do. In 1925, he had characterized himself as a lyric love poet (*Vision*, 1925, p. xxi). Now *energy*, not *world-weariness*, became his key word. Style was a surplus of energy, "the playing of strength when the day's work is done."[35] By 1927, he was praising the "abounding natural life" in a countryman's novels, "that tragic farce we have invented."[36] His response was the same to Lewis's *Time and Western Man*:

> I am reading *Time and the Western Man* [sic] with ever growing admiration and envy—what energy!—and I am driven back to my reed-pipe. I want you to ask Lewis to meet me—we are in *fundamental* agreement.[37]

Significantly, Lewis had "found an expression for my hatred—a hatred that being half dumb has half poisoned me."[38] Again in 1927, Yeats wrote:

> Tell Wyndham Lewis ... that I am in all essentials his most humble and admiring disciple. I like some people he dislikes but I accept all the dogma of the faith.[39]

Energy rather than thought is the mark of the coming antithetical age; it manifests itself in what Yeats calls plasticity, a quality he finds in *The Apes of God* and in Pirandello's work.[40] His admiration for *Time and Western Man*, a vehement attack on romanticism, illustrates how far Yeats had diverged from his early poetic preferences.

By 1929, when the first Cuala edition of *A Packet for Ezra Pound* was published, Yeats felt he had misjudged his contemporaries. One passage in particular reflects Yeats's concern that he remain contemporary, able to judge the younger artists of his age, and shows that he was consciously working toward a radically new style:

> It is almost impossible to understand the art of a generation younger than one's own. I was wrong about "Ulysses" when I had read but some first fragments, and I do not want to be wrong again—above all in judging verse. Perhaps when the sudden Italian spring has come I may have discovered what will seem all the more, because the opposite of all I have attempted, unique and unforgetable.[41]

In this volume, as in the 1937 version of *A Vision*, Yeats devotes considerable space to Pound's plan for the structure of the cantos, a structure "like that of a Bach Fugue" (*Vision*, 1962, p. 4). As in John Aherne's letter, the style is compared to painting,

> where everything rounds or thrusts itself without edges, without contours—conventions of the intellect—from a splash of tints and shades; to achieve a work as characteristic of the art of our time as the paintings of Cézanne, avowedly suggested by Porteous, as *Ulysses* and its dream association of words and images, a poem in which there is nothing that can be taken out and reasoned over, nothing that is not a part of the poem itself. (*Vision*, 1962, p. 4)

In other words, the work appears to be fragmented; but in fact it is unified to the point of defying analysis by the overriding, unifying presence of the artist. The same preference for intuition over analysis that motivated the nest analogy in the stories is obvious here in the opening sections of *A Vision*, where Yeats instructs one to read with imagination, for personal imagination is ultimately the true means of unification:

> I may, now that I have recovered leisure, find that the mathematical structure, when taken up into imagination, is more than mathematical, that seemingly irrelevant details fit together into a single theme. (*Vision*, 1962, p. 5)

Yeats now sees that the mechanics of reason or pure thought, which he criticized in his contemporaries in 1925, drive civilization to its final phase.[42] Nonrepresentational art is a symptom of the return to the primary tincture of the final phases (*Vision*, 1962, p. 258). It represents the necessity of the predetermined pattern; and in 1937, Yeats is more willing to accept this necessity and incorporate it into his own work than he was in 1925. He can now accept the work of Lewis or Joyce; he can even, to show his own modernity, his place in literary history, write like them, as he does in "Stories of Michael Robartes and His Friends." Yet, he is still not one of them. The old romantic power of the personal imagination, not the intellect, still governs and transforms mechanical abstractions and places them in a larger context. His own work, including the early folktales like "Donald and His Neighbours," seen not merely in chronological order but with this power of imagination, now seems to form a larger circle that both anticipated and can include the coming age. He was, Yeats seems to be saying, ahead of his time, and this has given him a certain equanimity, a perspective:

> Perhaps now that the abstract intellect has split the mind into categories, the body into cubes, we may be about to turn back towards the unconscious, the whole, the miraculous; according to a Chinese sage darkness begins at midday. Perhaps in my search, as in that first search with Lady Gregory among the cottages, I but showed a first effect of that slight darkening.[43]

Farce and Absurdism

The term *allegory* has been used to denote the one-to-one correspondences found in Yeats's late work and to distinguish this style from the vague and more evocative style of his earlier symbolism. Yet, to call Yeats an allegorist, a writer of extended metaphor with a moral purpose, is obviously to place him in the wrong literary category. Two other genres suggest themselves: absurdism and farce.

While an absurdistlike tension informs the total structure of *A Vision*, farce, by which is meant a kind of broad, satiric humor, perhaps best describes "Stories of Michael Robartes and His Friends" taken in isolation. Northrop Frye calls farce a "nonmimetic form of comedy,"[44] and identifies it with ritual.[45] It is the genre of such popular spectacles as puppet plays, pageants, masques, folk plays, and pantomimes, but its roots lie in mythology. Thus it expresses, often in a grotesque or at least burlesque, manner the most ancient and central beliefs of a race. It is not a form for the middle class, and this would have suited well Yeats's developing concept of the ideal society.

The artist alone, he was coming to feel, makes a permanent contribution to society by ordering and unifying it in archetypal patterns. Two classes could assist him: the nobles, who served as patrons, and the beggar men, who furnished a vast "reservoir of energy and imagery" that grounded the artist's conceptions in an earthy tradition.[46] The startling language and the savage gaiety of the lower class, as Yeats undoubtedly learned from Lady Gregory and Synge, could infuse an archetypal structure with new vitality:

> John Synge, I and Augusta Gregory, thought
> All that we did, all that we said or sang
> Must come from contact with the soil, from that
> Contact everything Antaeus-like grew strong.
> We three alone in modern times had brought
> Everything down to that sole test again,
> Dream of the noble and the beggar-man.[47]

Farce, like the clean, straight-line syntax of the rituals of the Order, allowed the symbols to stand out in clear relief. Farce fit Yeats's concept of the artist's unifying role in society; farce also, and perhaps most importantly, was the genre of energy. Writing in his journal of 1909, he distinguishes it from tragedy, which is passion, and pure comedy, which is largely characterization:

> Tragedy is passion alone and, instead of character, it gets form from motives, the wandering of passion; while comedy is the clash of character. Eliminate character from comedy and you get farce. Farce is bound together by incident alone.... Comedy is joyous because all assumption of a part, of a personal mask, whether the individualized face of comedy or the grotesque face of farce, is a display of energy, and all energy is joyous.[48]

In his next entry, he associates the various genres with the classes of society:

> The tragic mask expresses a passion or mood, a state of the soul; that only. (The mask of musician or of the dying slave.) The mask of comedy an individual. (Any modern picture.) The mask of farce an energy; in this the joyous life by its own excess has become superficial, it has driven out thought. (Any grotesque head.) Then these are connected in some way with the dominant moods of the three classes which have given the cradles, as it were, to tragedy, comedy, and farce: aristocracy, the middle class, and the people—exaltation, moral force, labour.[49]

It is needless to examine in any great detail the instances of farce in Yeats's later work: the fight with the table legs and the ritual rape of Attracta in *The Herne's Egg*, the Crazy Jane poems, the fool who echoes Cuchulain, and finally, "Stories of Michael Robartes and His Friends," with its loose, episodic structure and wooden characters. All represent Yeats's attempts to come to terms with the concerns of his late period: the remodeling of society and the role of the modern artist, the search for an appropriate new style, and his scorn of abstract thought in favor of joyous energy. Farce was often the style of Yeats's later work. His themes, seen in retrospect, seem to foreshadow modern absurdist drama.

Balachandra Rajan, in his *Tri-Quarterly* article, "Yeats and the Absurd," and in his book, *W. B. Yeats: A Critical Introduction*, has done most to advance the case for absurdism in Yeats's plays. Yeats was no nihilist, as Rajan points out; he was writing tragedy, from which the absurd is derived,[50] or in some cases, farce. He read none of the founders of existentialism except Nietzsche,[51] certainly had no "philosophy" of absurdism, and in his constant belief that man could refute the indifference of the universe with his creative acceptance, his "tragic joy" in defeat, he avoided the pessimistic tone of some of the later absurdists. Still, reading his late plays today, one senses the seeds of absurdism in his work.

If Yeats was not consciously or even precisely an absurdist, his work still tended increasingly toward the stark absurdist contrast between the hero and his desire, between the human will and an indifferent universe. As Rajan says in "Yeats, Synge and the Tragic Understanding," Yeats's later work is "concerned with the hero's struggle to maintain his nature in the face of circumstances designed to ensnare or to assault that nature."[52]

Of course, the fact that a "system" does exist serves to protect the dignity of Yeats's heroes. It provides a rational framework, absent in true absurdism, by which the characters can make sense of their own actions and the workings of the universe. Only in *The Herne's Egg* is reason as a guiding principle for human action ever seriously questioned. Further, Yeats's heroes are protected by a social context, by history, and a kind of artistic salvation. The severed head can still sing, and Cuchulain is remembered in popular legend. As in "Lapis Lazuli," a creative temperament or the created work itself transcends and transfigures the indifference of the universe. The heroic dimensions of this transcendence, however, take on a darker cast as the pressures of modernity force upon the romantic poet an understanding of the widening distance between aspiration and actuality.

This "tragic understanding" of the distance between the hero's ideal self and the hostile or irrational circumstances in which he must now realize this self provides the tension of many of Yeats's later plays; as Rajan has noted, this tension increases from play to play:

> As Yeats's possession of this understanding deepens, as he grows in poetic confidence and in the clarity of his quarrel with himself, he is able to maximize the resistance against which the statement of dignity must be made. The resources for that statement are steadily diminished; it is threatened increasingly by humiliation and mockery. The trap tightens, restricting the room for manoeuvre.[53]

The extreme tension is reached when Cuchulain is killed by the blind man in *The Death of Cuchulain*, but the theme of man and his desire goes as far back as "The Wanderings of Oisin." Between these two works, the tension slowly tightens.

If this distancing were only a poetic device, it would soon ring false; the fact that it does not indicates that the culture verifies the sense of increased distance between man and his desire, the material and the spiritual. So long as the possibility for fulfillment of this desire continues, as it does in Yeats's work, the drama is not precisely absurd. Increased loss of faith, mythological disorientation, automation, separation from nature, and scientism eventually produced the modern absurd play; but these factors were influencing Yeats's thinking toward the absurd perspective in the 1930s if not before.

Although, as Peter Ure points out, Yeats was carefully not to let the system intrude too obviously in his plays, *A Vision*, quite naturally, influenced his other work, and a loose parallel can be observed between Yeats's development as a dramatist and his evolving philosophy. In the introduction to *The Cat and the Moon*, Yeats speaks extensively of Vico and the cycles of the sun and moon, for example, but he also stresses that the theory and the stagecraft must be kept separate:

> The blind man was the body, the lame man was the soul.... But as the populace might well alter out of all recognition, deprive of all apparent meaning, some philosophical thought or verse, I wrote a little poem where a cat is disturbed by the moon, and in the changing pupils of its eyes seems to repeat the movement of the moon's changes, and allowed myself as I wrote to think of the cat as the normal man and of the moon as the opposite he seeks perpetually, or as having any meaning I have conferred upon the moon elsewhere. Doubtless, too, when the lame man takes the saint upon his back, the normal man has become one with that opposite, but I had to bear in mind that I was among dreams and proverbs, that though I might discover what had been and might be again an abstract idea, no abstract idea must be present.[54]

For Yeats's essays, this seems an unusually lucid and straightforward passage and is evidence for Ellmann's interpretation of how Yeats used his system to avoid abstraction.

It may have been the system, with its insistence on the violence of the coming antithetical age, which led Yeats to incorporate a wilder, more violent imagery into his later plays. The image of the severed head comes immediately to mind. In *A Full Moon in March* a new age is born, symbolized by the conception of the child. It is significant to note that the symbol of the achievement of the anti-self here is blood, not the rather mild image of the lame man taking the saint upon his back that appears in *The Cat and the Moon*. The blood is deliberate and is evidence of Yeats's attempts at a new style. In 1934, he writes to Edmund Dulac, who had apparently criticized this violent image:

> You may be right about *The Full Moon in March* [sic] but I am not sure. I thought you would say what you have said, for I have been working at something opposed to the clear, bright dry air of your genius. I do not understand why this blood symbolism laid hold upon me but I must work it out. If I had a volume of my poems I could show you when it began about

six years ago. Such things come from beyond the will, they exhaust themselves and the mind turns to some opposite.[55]

A. Norman Jeffares, among others, has noted Yeats's identification of sex, blood, and water.[56] The water imagery of his early poems, identified there with romantic love, becomes blood, which is identified with sex, in the later work. In 1934, Yeats wrote to Olivia Shakespear about the "four ages of civilization" that correspond to four ages in individual man:

> First age, *earth*, vegetative functions. Second age, *water*, blood, sex. Third age, *air*, breath, intellect. Fourth age, *fire*, soul etc. In the first two the moon comes to the full—resurrection of Christ and Dionysus. Man becomes rational, no longer driven from below or above.[57]

Jeffares, following Yeats's letters, identifies the second age as the "armed sexual age, chivalry" and the age of fire, a purging away of civilization through hatred, with our own era;[58] but Yeats's correspondences are tricky. In *A Vision*, 1937, Yeats identifies the second quarter of the wheel of the Faculties, that is, the wheel of the individual man, as the quarter of elemental water with its "image-making power" (*Vision*, 1962, p. 93). Thus, in the context of his own work, the blood-water symbol seems to suggest an additional meaning: Yeats's powerful late poetic drive:

> Never had I more
> Excited, passionate, fantastical
> Imagination, nor an ear and eye
> That more expected the impossible.[59]

The blood symbol has both a personal significance and a significance within the historical scheme of *A Vision*. Yeats's concern that his poetic powers might dwindle with old age may have driven him to insist upon them with violent, bloody imagery; or finding he was stronger than ever, he may have found an appropriate celebration in the wild, even grotesque, incidents and characters of his late work.

In his letter to Edmund Dulac in 1934, Yeats traces his preoccupation with blood symbolism from around 1928, but this more violent imagery is evident even earlier. In *Calvary*, probably written in 1920, Christ stands with his arms outstretched upon the Cross, a highly ritualistic and dancelike gesture, while in *The Resurrection* of 1925, a virgin cuts the living heart from a god, and later the Greek discovers that "the heart of a phantom is beating!"[60] He reacts in terror, as Yeats says he himself did when he encountered the story in Crookes's *Studies in Psychical Research*: "The sense of spiritual reality comes whether to the individual or to crowds from some violent shock."[61] As early as *The Resurrection*, the symbol of revolution is blood:

Odour of blood when Christ was slain
Made all Platonic tolerance vain
And vain all Doric discipline.[62]

The contact with the supernatural is much more realistically presented here than in *The Dreaming of the Bones* (1917), just as the severed head, only a possibility in *The Green Helmet* (1910), becomes real in *A Full Moon in March*. This increased violence echoes the new, violent Robartes calling for war in the 1937 *Vision*.

Perhaps the best evidence for Yeats's "absurdism" is *The Herne's Egg*. The play is, of course, a farce; but Congal's eventual isolation, his ignoble rebirth as a donkey, and the doubt cast upon reason as a guide to human action move the theme somewhat out of the genre of comedy and toward the truly absurd. Congal's heroic stance is left in question at the end of the play: Has he been killed by a fool, or is he the fool in driving himself to his own destruction because of a strange bird-god he himself does not believe in?

Yeats knew the story of Congal from his early studies of Irish myth and Irish poets, particularly Samuel Ferguson, whose poem, "Congal," Yeats discusses in an early article, "The Poetry of Sir Samuel Ferguson, I." Not only the historical moment of Ireland's transition to Christianity, the focus of Ferguson's poem, but the sheer audacity of Congal himself seems to have attracted Yeats:

> It is the story of the death in the seventh century, at the battle of Moyra (or Moira) of Congal Claen. Congal was a heathen; his enemy, the archking Ardrigh, was a Christian. This was the sunset of Irish heathendom. Across Ireland, eager for the battle, march Congal and his warriors.[63]

Congal's forces meet the "Washer of the Ford," an old spirit woman who washes the bodies of those slain in battle; she turns over the body of one of the victims, and Congal sees his own dead face, but he marches on:

> Still on they go, these indomitable pagans. Surely nothing will resist their onset. Will they not even shake the throne of God in their sublime audacity? No; Congal when he has accomplished deeds of marvellous valour is slain by the hand of an idiot boy who carries a sickle for sword, and the lid of a cauldron for shield. Ah, strange irony of the Celt.[64]

The play Yeats made from this material represents a definite progression toward the absurd in that it not only displays an absurd theme, more clearly here than in *The Death of Cuchulain* where Cuchulain's heroic nature, whatever his fate, is never in doubt, but it also dramatizes that theme in an absurd manner. In *The Theatre of the Absurd*, Martin Esslin makes a distinction between the theater of Camus and Sartre, who present absurd themes from within the theatrical convention of rational plot and character; and the later, true absurdists, who discard this convention of rational discourse in order to express truly their theme in its own terms.[65] Yeats here, on a smaller scale, seems to be taking a similar step in his drama. The style itself is chaotic, with abrupt changes of tone; there is no overview, no aesthetic distance. The spectator is plunged into confusion. Further, as Rajan notes, the disparity between matter and spirit is greatly widened:

> What is also represented is a further evolution in Yeats' always sharp sense of the absurd. Man is not only defeated but defeated without dignity; the holy mountain lies under the "moon of comic tradition." In these circumstances it is hardly answer enough to reply that man's arrogance brings on his defeat. His humiliations, moreover, are now such that he can no longer respond to absurdity by nobility. All he can do is to refuse to surrender and even in fighting for himself he can no longer be sure that he is not really doing the Herne's will. Taken in the context of Yeats' work, *The Herne's Egg* seems to represent a further and even an impetuous step forward in the segregation of the supernatural from the natural. The terms of the opposition can no longer co-exist, let alone involve each other creativity.[66]

This is the only Yeats play in which the hero (if Congal is a hero) suffers humilitation—that is, total defeat of human dignity in terms of the world. Cuchulain still stands in the post office; the Swineherd is an eternal image of art; but Congal has, like Camus's Sisyphus, only his subjective "posture of scorn" to defend his dignity from his fate, and even that is in doubt.

Having detected the seeds of absurdism in Yeats's late plays, it would be reasonable to look for it in "Stories of Michael Robartes and His Friends" as well; and to a certain extent, the stories are illuminated by a reading of them in this light. Yet, if one takes as the core of absurdism the idea of the dignity of man under attack from a reductive or irrational universe, not much of this tension is found in the characters themselves. A truly absurd character consciously perceives the unbridgeable gap between man, with his often noble, or at least human, aspirations to understand and improve his condition, and the seemingly indifferent, perhaps irrational, universe that is silent on questions of meaning, success, or failure. Further, fully cognizant of this gap, the absurd character persists in attempting to bridge it. He or she seeks an impossible reconciliation, risks total defeat, and lives, like the old men of the twilight, in constant uncertainty.

According to this definition, Aherne and Robartes cannot be called absurd characters. They represent the system, and though Robartes finds life bitter, they both accept the unalterable necessity of life as it is. They recognize that they are predestined, while the other characters in the stories still operate under the illusion, or delusion, of free will. It is, in fact, partly to lure them away from this illusion that Robartes has called his friends together. Could they recognize and accept the deterministic nature of existence, Robartes must feel, they would in effect be saved from the painful absurd perspective, for acceptance nullifies the absurdist tension. (Perhaps Yeats shared this same motive in writing *A Vision*.) Yet, ironically, none of Robartes's pupils really stands in need of this salvation, for none of them has a keen sense that anything is seriously amiss in the universe. They do not suffer as Robartes does because they do not sense the painful disjunction between desire and necessity.

Mr. Bell, on the other hand, could be an absurd character, for he does sense the gap between the actual and the ideal, and he does risk defeat. The terms of this defeat, however, lie not in the world (he has never seen the world, as Robartes has, but has chosen to remain on his estate); he is defeated by his own muddleheaded misunderstanding of the nature of the universe. Truly absurd characters do not make such mistakes. Their heroism, like Cuchulain's, lies in recognizing their situation and confronting it. The absurd character cannot be deluded; Mr. Bell is no absurdist.

Yet, if the characters of the stories are not trapped in an absurd situation, the stories as a whole still lend an absurd tone to *A Vision*.[67] It is Yeats, perhaps, who risks defeat and stands in uncertainty. Yeats is, in a sense, the main character of the stories and of *A Vision* as a whole; he masks behind many of the characters, and his sensibility informs the system and directs the reader's response to it. Yet, if he took the system seriously, believed it, or, at the least felt it to be of major importance—and one cannot doubt that he did—why does he undermine it with these lightweight, puzzling stories? Their tone does not match that of *A Packet for Ezra Pound* or the personal tone of the poet elsewhere in the book. Certainly, they are at odds with the somber material of the system itself and, in effect, undercut it severely.

While one cannot adequately document Yeats's frame of mind during the period between 1925 and 1937, and thus "prove" that he adopted a different attitude toward *A Vision* during those years, the structure and tone of the two versions, when compared, seem to show that Yeats's perspective on the system had changed radically by 1937. In 1925, he wrote that he "would restore to the philosopher his mythology" (*Vision*, 1925, p. 252). He contemplated the world "without terror, in exultation almost" (*Vision*, 1925, p. xiii), and predicted that if his fellow students would only master the system and act upon it, "the curtain may ring up on a new drama" (*Vision*, 1925, p. xii). Although he realized that myth and fact, formerly united, had now fallen far apart, he felt that the very recognition of the rigidity of fact in the modern world might, in reaction, call up myth, the Mask (*Vision*, 1925, p. 212). In other words, he was still seeking, in 1925, to apply the theory of the individual adopting the Mask, the artistic pose, the gesture, the thing most difficult, to the culture. Technical study and mechanization were the false Mask; myth was the true Mask that would "save" modern civilization.

The view was a romantic one, perhaps based on an imperfect understanding of the system; the work was an attempt at a true "explanation of life," an attempt to create mythological truth in the same way that the plays for dancers would create a true ritual. The problem was, as critics have pointed out, that Yeats's audience had no common ground in which a mythology might live; Yeats was attempting to manufacture a tradition, not following one that already existed.[68] In 1937, as the telling grease-and-flame remark indicates, Yeats realized that such an approach was unworkable.

Modernity was exerting a distorting pressure on the artist, for an artist must, in part, draw his mythology and style from the world, and the world was changing. As early as 1904, Yeats compared the inspiration of the modern writer to that of Cervantes and Boccaccio:

> I have felt that these men, divided from one another by so many hundreds of years, had the same mind. It is we who are different; and then the thought would come to me, that has come to me so often before, that they lived in times when the imagination turned to life itself for excitement. The world was not changing quickly about them. There was nothing to draw their imagination from the ripening of the fields, from the birth and death of their children, from the destiny of their souls, from all that is the unchanging substance of literature. They had not to deal with the world in such great masses that it could only be represented to their minds by figures and abstract generalisations.... It is the change that followed the Renaissance, and was completed by newspaper government and the scientific movement, that has brought upon us all these phrases and generalisations, made by minds that would grasp what they have never seen.[69]

Boccaccio and Cervantes had the "same mind"; in ancient Byzantium, "religious, aesthetic and practical life were one" (*Vision*, 1962, p. 279). Unity of culture was a central ideal in Yeats's thinking, but the modern world was fragmented and disintegrating. By 1937, Yeats saw that he could not create a myth in defiance of fact, could not impose a Mask of unified myth on a disordered culture; the Mask, to be contemporary and true to phase, must include fact. It must appear fragmented. The "unnatural" story of 1925, a seamless but archaic unity, gave way to the farcical, disjointed tales of 1937 and the straightforward account of the system's source in automatic writing. Modern civilization, the reality of fact and fragmentation, had to be included in the myth, and Yeats himself, as mythmaker, had to take a more active part. Thus the 1937 version presents not only the myth—the system—but also a dramatization of the absurdity of attempting to create a myth in the face of modern civilization. It is in this sense that one can say that "Stories of Michael Robartes and His Friends" adds the "absurd" tension to *A Vision* as a whole.

When the first edition came out, there was little critical response; Yeats wrote to Olivia Shakespear in March 1926:

A Vision reminds me of the stones I used to drop as a child into a certain very deep well. The splash is very far off and very faint. Not a review except one by AE—either the publisher has sold the review copies or the editors have—and no response of any kind except from a very learned doctor in the North of England who sends me profound and curious extracts from ancient philosophies on the subject of gyres. A few men here are reading me, so I may found an Irish heresy.[70]

The 1937 version got little better response. Cecil Salkeld reviewed it intelligently, but only to point out that it was a personal system, inaccessible to analysis.[71] This time, however, Yeats anticipated the response. He advised Ethel Mannin to read only the first fifty pages: "The rest is not for you or for anybody but a doctor in the North of England with whom I have corresponded for years."[72] A favorable review in the *Irish Church Gazette* partially made up for the "stupidities of men who attribute to me some thought of their own and reply to that thought,"[73] but by now Yeats seemed content to remain isolated in his thought. A new concern with artistic expression replaced the fretful concern for accuracy and clarity in the first edition; Yeats wrote of his reviewers:

> They all think I was bound to explain myself to them. It is just that explaining which makes many English books empty. A Frenchman thinks of his friend and his friend's mistress, with whom he dines at some café, an Englishman of the chance woman he brings down to dinner. I have always deliberately left out this explaining. Intensity is all. I want to be some queer man's companion.[74]

Yeats's movement here, like his movement toward a small, aristocratic theater, is toward a philosophy for a few friends, not for the general populace. It is "absurd" to expect Denise or Huddon or Mr. Bell to accept the mythology they so much need; the true coven consists of Yeats himself, George Yeats, the English doctor, and Pound. The distance between what Yeats is attempting and the ludicrous society in which he must attempt it gives a tension to the 1937 *Vision* as a whole that one misses in the uniform deception of 1925. The system is not now easily given to the world; instead one sees the poet struggling with its expression, trying first one mode then another. The 1937 version is, in short, a lyric dramatization of mythmaking; Yeats sees himself now "set in a drama where I struggle to exalt and overcome concrete realities perceived not with the mind only but as with the roots of my hair."[75]

Yeats keeps this struggle alive in two ways in *A Vision*: by devising the vivid, farcical stories that, by their humorous and puzzling nature, nag at the reader's consciousness, asking to be explained; and by including himself in the prefatory sections and in the narration of the system as a dramatization of the modern poetic sensibility. This drama takes the form of a struggle between the intellect and faith of man and the nature of a universe that can be known, if at all, only partially. In this sense, Yeats's self-drama is analogous in the nature of its conflict to modern absurdist drama—but of course, it is never precisely absurd. Yeats is not defeated in his struggle. The world, even the modern world, is not an irrational void, nor is the isolation that his vision imposes, described in "All Souls' Night," more than a dramatizing pose. Like Cuchulain's at his death, Yeats's creative acceptance of the terms of the struggle, supported by the influx of man's mysterious freedom at the end of the book, saves the conflict from meaninglessness. Nevertheless, the comparison of *A Vision* and absurdism remains a valid means of exploring the tone of Yeats's late work, for he seems to have foreseen in this complex, often frustrating work the problems that the absurdists would later confront. He may have sensed, too, the time coming when the vast poetic statement would seem little more than an eccentricity.

Self-Dramatization

As has been shown, Yeats had difficulty in deciding upon the best manner in which to present his system. His initial approach was to present the material as a dialogue between Robartes and Aherne, a format that was abandoned when the material grew in detail and subtlety.[76] Constrained in dealing directly with the origins of the material and aware of its probable effect on his readers, he invented the tale of Robartes's discovery, hoping its romanticism would soften the unpleasant rigidity of the system, establish its antiquity, and invite the imagination to play upon the central symbol. Although he himself was to act as editor, in fact the mask of Aherne handles most of the editorializing. Yeats contributes only the brief dedication, the poems, and the final two sections (15 and 16) of "The Gates of Pluto." In 1937, however, as Ellmann notes, Yeats was "more confident and willing to speak in his own person,"[77] and the role of the fictional characters in the presentation of the system is cut drastically.

One might well wonder why Yeats retained and even elaborated upon the Robartes fiction in the 1930s; but perhaps paradoxically, attributing the material to fictional characters maintained the truth of the system and indicated Yeats's belief that it was not his alone, but had been given him from the Anima Mundi. Yeats did not invent the system, although he subscribes to it. Rather, it is like a timeworn shell cast up from the waters of the Great Mind and Memory. He has *discovered* the eternal image of art and life.

The found-book motif, which runs through the history of *A Vision* and occultism in general, is an obvious symbolic representation of the tendency of spiritual truth to submerge and then reappear in a culture, always manifesting itself to just the right person at just the right time. It is in this sense that Yeats can be said to be "writing out of" *A Vision*; the symbols are not his personal symbols, although of course he shares them, but the universal symbols of the culture. *A Vision* is not Yeats's notebook, but just that—a vision, the history of man seen through the imagination. By implication, anyone can and should use its symbols, for they constitute, to borrow Northrop Frye's term, a "grammar," albeit a previously submerged one. In this connection, one might make a case for Yeats's mythology as a more genuine and universal body of symbols than Blake's, which, although it uses conventional symbolism, seems more clearly personal and "invented." For Yeats, the poet in modern society is not the romantic rebel but the cultural unifier, the modern shaman, the one to whom the vision comes.

Yeats then, is not inventing but recording the history of the soul of man, and this is not merely a chronology of facts; it is mythology. This history has divine or spiritual authority by virtue of the fact that a pattern may be discerned in it, a pattern within which each individual acts out his or her part. Yeats's part is self-dramatization, the enactment of the bringing forth of the unifying mythology. The pattern illustrates recurrence; and since man is a part of the pattern, reincarnation and a kind of immortality are established. The pattern also shows images of perfection or symbols that are eternal and by which man perceives the system; thus man, being part of the pattern, must also be capable of perfection and a type of immortality in the Thirteenth Cone. Mythology, as opposed to mere historical chronology, is meaningful by virtue of the patterns it exhibits; it has a spiritual authority. This spiritual authority in Yeats's mythology comes through the Record, which is a repository of the eternal recurrent patterns accessible to man through imagination, communion with the Great Memory:

> Certainly when sleep is interrupted by vision the seer goes back to remote times, and the seer amidst brilliant light discovers myths and symbols that can only be verified by prolonged research. He has escaped from the individual *Record* to that of the race. (*Vision*, 1925, p. 250)

Yeats's pride in the powers of his imagination and the immense significance he attributed to the system that had found expression through him should not, however, give the reader the impression that Yeats is speaking ex cathedra in *A Vision*. In fact, the genius of the book is that Yeats consistently sees himself as caught within the system, as having only partial vision and struggling to understand and express his perceptions. He writes in 1925 that "much of this book is abstract, because it has not yet been lived, for no man can dip into life more than a moiety of any system" (*Vision*, 1925, p. 251). He struggles not only with ideas, but with their expression: "I find a statement that for the supreme magical work no word or symbol can be used that is still a part of living tradition" (*Vision*, 1925, p. 250). Perhaps the best evidence that Yeats did not take a godlike perspective toward this vision appears at the conclusion of the 1925 dedication. It shows, not that *A Vision* enabled him to live more and more in a world of his own creation, as Ellmann has suggested,[78] but that it enabled him to live with joy in the natural world:

> I know that the new intensity that seems to have come into all visible and tangible things is not a reaction from that wisdom but its very self. Yesterday when I saw the dry and leafless vineyards at the very edge of the motionless sea, or lifting their brown stems from almost inaccessible patches of earth high up on the cliff-side ... I murmured, as I have countless times, "I have been part of it always and there is maybe no escape, forgetting and returning life after life like an insect in the roots of the grass." But murmured it without terror, in exultation almost. (*Vision*, 1925, p. xiii)

This is the function of myth—to integrate man and his universe; and surely this passage answers, emotionally if not logically, Bloom's insistence that the book should restore man to his unfallen state.

Bachchan remarks that Yeats's philosophy was a "secular mysticism." Although Yeats studied the Hindu belief that rebirth was a punishment for some failure to perfect the human life, escape from rebirth was not salvation: "For Yeats the salvation of life was the reliving of this actual life."[79] Robert O'Driscoll makes the same point when he elucidates Yeats's distinction between the transcendentalist, who sees matter as evil, and the symbolist, who loves material life because only through it can the spiritual be expressed: "The symbolist recognizes the uniqueness and sacredness of all living forms: he can see infinity in a grain of sand and eternity in an hour. He loves a thing for what it is in itself, not for what it represents, nor for the ulterior purpose to which it can be put. Symbolism, therefore, which is built on the concept of the individual holiness of all living things, concludes in mutual respect and love."[80] This is, perhaps, what Yeats meant when he said that "belief is love."[81] *A Vision* does not offer a means of escape from life, nor an apology for its shortcomings; it is a celebration of life in all its diversity, a living mythology.

Yeats's entrapment in the system seems to have bothered him in 1925. He faults his "ignorance of philosophy" and "doubts" if he can convey the system adequately (*Vision*, 1925, p. xii). He attempts to gloss the book's shortcomings by resorting to metaphor: a "net for a herring fisher" in 1925 (*Vision*, 1925, p. 251), and referring to the 1925 edition, a "rule of thumb" in 1937 (*Vision*, 1962, p. 81). He confesses frankly in 1925 that the book is incomplete and criticizes the early edition severely in 1937 (*Vision*, 1925, p. xiii; 1962, pp. 19, 80, 187). He was also, as has been shown, somewhat at war with modernity in 1925.

By 1937, he seems to have realized that these very shortcomings and his struggle with them could give the work a dramatic vitality. The best evidence that a drama is being deliberately constructed in 1937 is the short coda, "The

End of the Cycle." *A Packet for Ezra Pound*, which serves as an introduction to the system, explains the source of the material in automatic writing and the associations Yeats makes with the material; it records the genesis of the work. When the system has been fully explicated, Yeats adds a brief concluding section in which he records his feelings upon completion of the book. His work done, he writes, he sits and meditates on the system, turning its central symbol over in his mind, attempting to substitute the particulars of his life for the abstractions of the system, seeking to test current political situations, indeed, the convictions of his life, by its logic. Memories intrude, but he seeks to "find everything in the symbol" (*Vision*, 1962, p. 301). He expects to be rewarded with a vision of total unity, but "nothing comes" (*Vision*, 1962, p. 301). He wonders if he is too old and falls into despair regarding the system: "Only dry or drying sticks can be tied into a bundle" (*Vision*, 1962, p. 302). Has he created an "artificial unity," or as he asks in another place, "will some mathematician some day question and understand, as I cannot, and confirm all, or have I also dealt in myth?" (*Vision*, 1962, p. 213). Then suddenly, he understands: "The particulars are the work of the *Thirteenth Cone* or cycle which is in every man and called by every man his freedom" (*Vision*, 1962, p. 302).

As Richard Ellmann has noted, the Thirteenth Cone functions like divinity in the system; it is the whole, total unity. Yeats makes the identification clearly in his 1930 diary, basing his concept of God on Berkeley's: "He creates what we perceive. I substitute for God the Thirteenth Cone, the Thirteenth Cone therefore creates our perceptions—all the visible world—as held in common by our wheel."[82] As such, the Thirteenth Cone cannot be grasped by the intellect of the man caught in antinomies but must be intuited or taken on faith. It is, in Yeats's term, "secret" (*Vision*, 1962, p. 302). Yeats noted the same problem in conceptualization when he studied Blake:

> Sometimes the mystical student, bewildered by the different systems, forgets for a moment that the history of moods is the history of the universe, and asks where is the final statement—the complete doctrine. The universe is itself that doctrine and statement. All others are partial, for it alone is the symbol of the infinite thought which is in turn symbolic of the universal mood we name God.[83]

The sphere is reality (*Vision*, 1962, p. 73); the cone is the "empty coil" left behind as the whirling sphere moves on (*Vision*, 1925, p. 133). Yeats explores this same perceptual problem in 1937:

> The ultimate reality, because neither one nor many, concord nor discord, is symbolised as a phaseless sphere, but as all things fall into a series of antinomies in human experience it becomes, the moment it is thought of, what I shall presently describe as the thirteenth cone. (*Vision*, 1962, p. 193)

The Heracles whom men thought they saw, bow in hand, like Lear in "Rosa Alchemica," inhabits this coil; he was an image in time. The *real* Heracles—the man—is seated "mid the gods that never die" (*Vision*, 1962, p. 226); that is, he inhabits the timeless Thirteenth Cone. Life, as we know it, is illusion.

Ellmann maintains that the inclusion of this final section establishes the system's "anti-self," a kind of surprise ending, a sudden reversal:

> All the determinism or quasi-determinism of *A Vision* is abruptly confronted with the Thirteenth Cycle which is able to alter everything, and suddenly free will, liberty, and deity pour back into the universe.[84]

As such, the Thirteenth Cone is perhaps too little and too late to give the system a genuine balance of freedom and determined necessity. Yeats himself was dissatisfied with his rendering of the Thirteenth Cone and wrote in his 1930 diary that he conceived of reality as both a single being and a "congeries of beings" and that the two could not be intellectually reconciled, as they would be in God. Yeats perceived God but his poet's allegiance to the multiplicity of life seemed to prevent him from writing of it: "Again and again with remorse, a sense of defeat, I have failed when I would write of God, written coldly and conventionally. Could those two impulses, one as much a part of truth as the other, be reconciled, or if one or the other could prevail, all life would cease."[85] The book, then, is about life as it is experienced, living and dead, within the "coil," not about the sphere, "which can be symbolised but cannot be known" (*Vision*, 1962, p. 193).

What should be pointed out particularly about this concluding passage, "The End of the Cycle," is the deliberate artfulness of it, the orchestration of moods within a classically dramatic pattern: meditation and search, doubt, despair, revelation, spiritual triumph. The passage is not mere autobiographical reporting, as when Yeats records the phenomena that accompanied the automatic writing, nor is it even the heightened, artistic autobiography of which he was an acknowledged master. When Yeats describes Pound feeding the cats, the scene is vividly rendered. Typically, Yeats fastens on one incident or observation and heightens it until this one gesture becomes the symbol not only of the whole man, but of some significant facet of the age. It is then an easy step to the "moral" of the observation: "Was this pity a characteristic of his generation that has survived the Romantic Movement, and of mine and hers that saw it die—I too a revolutionist—some drop of hysteria still at the bottom of the cup?" (*Vision*, 1962, p. 6).

In "The End of the Cycle," one has the sense that Yeats has invented an incident in order to make the statement; in other words, the passage is pure poetic construct, not a realistically based one. Its purpose is self-dramatization. It enforces the sense that what matters, ultimately, is the impact of the system on Yeats's life—Yeats, of course, standing for the modern poetic sensibility. In this way, despite its vast scope, *A Vision* is seen finally as personal and individual.

In Pound's style, as in that of Jack Yeats, what Yeats chiefly appreciated was the sense of the unique individual, the personality that infused the poem or painting. Writing in the 1929 *Packet for Ezra Pound*, Yeats notes especially the abandonment of traditional or even modern form for a kind of persona:

> He is not trying to create forms because he believes, like so many of this contemporaries, that old forms are dead, so much as a new style, a new man. Again and again he breaks the metrical form which the work seemed to require, or which, where he is translating, it once had, or interjects some anachronism, as when he makes Propertius talk of an old Wordsworthian, that he may pull it back not into himself but into this hard, shining, fastidious modern man, who has no existence, who can never have existence, except to the readers of his poetry.[86]

The power of this persona, its spontaneous, joyous energy, comes largely from the abandonment of traditional forms of knowledge and expression, forms replaced by a new self-possession that can play with the world; Pound's work exhibits "the grown man, in 'Cathay' his passion and self-possession, in 'Homage to Sextus Propertius' his self-abandonment that recovers itself in mockery, everywhere his masterful curiosity."[87]

A Vision, too, is a work of personality; the stories are a veiled autobiography, the concluding section a self-dramatization of the poet, and the introductory explanation of the source of the material a clear indication that Yeats intended the work to be seen as channeled through and focused upon one man's sensibility. The Anima Mundi had chosen Yeats; the instructors had come to give him (and through him, the world) a special gift, "metaphors for poetry" (*Vision*, 1962, p. 8). To express such a gift, Yeats explores almost every form of written expression: poetry, fiction, epistle, autobiography, philosophical speculation, and straight rhetorical reporting. He cross-references various intellectual disciplines: history, literature, archaeology, philosophy, art, and psychology. No single source and no single approach seem large enough to encompass the material.

Still the overall tone is uniquely Yeats's own; it has the force of personality. As in *Autobiographies*, one has the sense of mellow, deeply felt considerations, of a sensibility both objective and intimately involved in the concerns of the age. "Having the concrete mind of the poet," Yeats wrote in 1925, "I am unhappy when I find myself among abstract things, and yet I need them to set my experience in order" (*Vision*, 1925, p. 129). Unable or unwilling to write closely reasoned, abstract philosophy, he instead chose the model of Berkeley, who hated abstract ideas and used common words as a matter of principle. The effect, as Yeats notes about Berkeley's style, was that of conversation with a well-bred gentleman:

> Though he could not describe mystery—his age had no fitting language—his suave glittering sentences suggest it; we feel perhaps for the first time that eternity is always at our heels or hidden from our eyes by the thickness of a door. Something of this depends upon his use of common words, his sparing use of exact definitions, his conviction that he must as far as possible accept our point of view, upon his remaining, no matter what the theme, a conversationalist, an easy travelled man whose attention flatters us.[88]

This is Yeats's style when he discusses the twenty-eight incarnations—a light, gossiping urbanity—or when, in "Dove or Swan," he casually wrings a striking significance from an historical figure or a detail of sculpture. "The Soul in Judgment" is more condensed and urgent; "The Great Year of the Ancients," after initially inviting the reader to speculate on the theme of Christ and Caesar (the two poles of the system), is a fairly straightforward history of the concept of the Great Year. These are the sections of the work that Yeats revised and polished; they reflect a sense of control and mastery.

Elsewhere, Yeats insists on keeping the struggle with the material alive, and much of this struggle centers on his age. Yeats feared that he might not live to finish *A Vision*; but once, tried from overwork, he was cheered when Dolly Travers Smith, a medium, attempted automatic writing in his presence, revealing a message to him from the spirits: "Have no fear. You have time."[89] There are frequent references to his age in "Rapallo" also (*Vision*, 1962, p. 3), in the letter to Pound (*Vision*, 1962, p. 27), and in the conclusion. The dead romanticism implicit in the story of Pound and the cats, in the remembered concerns of his earlier life (the Cabala and the theater for plays in verse), and in John Aherne's letter reinforce Yeats's suspicion that he may be poorly equipped to forecast the future. He is out of place in the senate (*Vision*, 1962, p. 27). "Perhaps," he writes, "I am too old" (*Vision*, 1962, p. 301).

Then there is the struggle with the Frustrators, and Yeats's ignorance of philosophy, and the insistence of the instructors that he write the first book, however unprepared he felt to do so, and his consequent "shame" over the resulting first edition. Finally, there is Yeats's anxiety over the book's public reception:

> Some, perhaps all, of those readers I most value, those who have read me many years, will be repelled by what must seem an arbitrary, harsh, difficult symbolism. Yet such has almost always accompanied expression that unites the sleeping and waking mind. (*Vision*, 1962, p. 23)

The struggle evolves into a highly personal drama. The inclusion of the account of the source of the material in automatic writing puts Yeats in the foreground of the work, and that story has, in itself, an abundance of dramatic incidents. First of all, the instructors appear suddenly, just after Yeats has married, when after a lifetime of search and struggle for vision and his unhappy, confused courtship of Maud Gonne and her daughter, he is in despair. They come to "answer" a question raised in *Per Amica* "—whether some prophet could not prick upon the calendar the birth of a Napoleon or a Christ" (*Vision*, 1962, p. 9). It is as though, inadvertently, he has triggered the release of the great power he has always sought. Ironically, though Yeats can think and talk of nothing else, his wife, the crucial medium on which all depends, is "bored and fatigued by her almost daily task" (*Vision*, 1962, p. 9). There is the danger and mystery involved in the teaching process, the accompanying phenomena of scents and sounds, some of which were blessings, like the smell of roses at the birth of Michael Yeats or the signs of approval the Spirits sent while Yeats was writing the first edition (*Vision*, 1962, p. 18), and some of which were like the claptrap of fireside ghost stories, the "whistling ghost" that so disturbed the servants that Yeats asked to have the signal changed (*Vision*, 1962, p. 15). Then, there is the struggle with the Frustrators who, though Yeats could never quite define them, worked to confuse the manuscript or waste time (*Vision*, 1962, pp. 12–14). When the instructors' work was done, the Frustrators attacked Yeats's health and that of his children in order to prevent the completion of the work.

The instructors themselves provide considerable dramatic tension within the work, though critics generally have refused to take them as anything more than Yeats's own, and perhaps his wife's, unconscious mind. Some interpreters of the system make a slight bow to the work by calling the instructors Yeats's Daimon, but again, it is usually assumed that the term is only a poet's name for the unconscious. Virginia Moore summarizes the possibilities of interpreting the phenomenon of automatic writing extensively, but forms no ultimate judgment on precisely what the instructors were.[90] Richard Ellmann maintains that Yeats "never wholly gave up" the idea that the instructors were indeed Spirits; but he is open-minded about automatic writing, considering it as a sort of psychological phenomenon, and adds that the skeptic may assign it simply to the unconscious mind.[91] Helen Vendler believes that Mrs. Yeats's admission that she undertook the experiment to distract "her moody husband" offers sufficient explanation of the instructors;[92] and Moore quotes Mrs. Yeats as saying that she attempted to "fake" the writing.[93]

Vendler's and Moore's positions, which many critics share to a greater or lesser degree, seem to dodge the issue. It makes no difference why Mrs. Yeats attempted the automatic writing or whether she knew what she was doing. The question here is, Did Yeats believe the instructors were a mutual dream of his and his wife's, or did he believe the material came from beyond his or her psyche? He seems to assert both positions. Certainly, as "Desert Geometry" shows, he valued his wife's contribution very highly, and a discarded dedication reads:

> To MY WIFE who created this system which bores her, who made possible these pages which she will never read, and who has accepted this dedication on the condition that I write nothing but verse for a year.[94]

Yeats's comment that Mrs. Yeats's "created" the system, incidentlly, throws an interesting light on the arguments of critics who would discount totally the idea of spiritual instructors as the source of *A Vision*. It seems unlikely that Mrs. Yeats could or would have deceived her husband for so long a time; Yeats was a conscientious skeptic. Further, if the whole business of automatic writing was a fake, as some critics feel it was, should one not be looking, not at what Yeats knew and believed, but at what George Yeats thought? No critic has seriously considered *A Vision* as a work *by* Mrs. Yeats, nor has much research been done to determine what portion of the mateial, if any, came from her conscious or unconscious mind.

The idea that Mrs. Yeats was, in fact, the creator of the work is one considered and discarded by Yeats himself. He claims that the instructors took nothing from his wife's store of reading (*Vision*, 1962, pp. 19–20) or apparently from his own, for he remarks that, "there was nothing in Blake, Swedenborg, Boehme or the Cabala to help me now" (*Vision*, 1962, p. 12). Vendler assumes that this remark means that Yeats "disclaimed any mystical orientation in *A Vision*";[95] actually it means just the opposite. When at last Yeats was permitted to read philosophy, and he read avidly for four years, he found almost no sources for the material in the history of ideas:

> Although the more I read the better did I understand what I had been taught, I found neither the geometrical symbolism nor anything that could have inspired it except the vortex of Empedocles. (*Vision*,1962, p. 20)

Yeats was a skeptic, and the idea of mutual dream as a source in the unconscious did occur to him, but he must have felt himself "overwhelmed by miracle" (*Vision*, 1962, p. 25) when he could find no easy rational explanation for the instructors or the strange phenomena that accompanied their visits, no parallels to the knowledge they brought.

On the other hand, the Spirits themselves said that they were "often but created forms," and Yeats writes in 1937, "Again and again they have insisted that the whole system is the creation of my wife's Daimon and of mine, and that it is as startling to them as to us" (*Vision*, 1962, p. 22). The question intrigued Yeats, as the poem, "Towards Break of Day," illustrates:

> Was it the double of my dream
> The woman that by me lay
> Dreamed, or did we halve a dream
> Under the first cold gleam of day?[96]

Even if the material is not supernatural in origin, however, *A Vision* is still in

Style: The Playing of Strength 165

a sense miraculous. If Yeats did pierce through to such an intimate contact with his Daimon, his accomplishment is as great as that of Oedipus:

> He knew nothing but his mind, and yet because he spoke that mind fate possessed it and kingdoms changed according to his blessing and his cursing. (*Vision*, 1962, p. 28)

The origins of *A Vision* posed questions that Yeats never really resolved, as his statement regarding belief, the passage on "stylistic arrangements," indicates. As late as 1929, in *A Packet for Ezra Pound*, he flatly rejects the idea of mutual dream;[97] but by 1937 he must admit that he half rejects, half accepts such an explanation:

> Much that has happened, much that has been said, suggests that the communicators are the personalities of a dream shared by my wife, by myself, occasionally by others—they have, as I must some day prove, spoken through others without change of knowledge or loss of power—a dream that can take objective form in sounds, in hallucinations, in scents, in flashes of light, in movements of external objects. (*Vision*, 1962, pp. 22–23)

What must be borne in mind, however, is that the Daimon is not precisely the equivalent of the unconscious, however much more comfortable that identification may be for the modern mind. In 1925, Yeats spoke at length of "covens." These are more than just persistent ideas in history; they are beings made up of the Daimons of individuals, and they in turn have a Daimon of their own:

> That which we must deduce from the doctrine is that there can be no philosophy, nation, or movement that is not a being or congeries of beings, and that which we call proof of some philosophy is but that which enables it to be born. (*Vision*, 1925, p. 171)

He conceives of the world, in this passage, as a "drama" that has neither cause nor effect because all is "coeternal"; thus a coven is "unique, life in itself" (*Vision*, 1925, pp. 171–72). Yeats made much the same claim about the Golden Dawn in 1901, when during the crisis of the Order he wrote "Is the Order of R. R. & A. C. to Remain a Magical Order?" The Order was a coven:

> Because a Magical Order differs from a society for experiment and research in that it is an Actual Being, an organic life holding within itself the highest life of its members now and in past times, to weaken its Degrees is to loosen the structure, to dislimn, to disembody, to dematerialize an Actual Being.[98]

Thus, claiming that *A Vision* comes from Yeats's Daimon does not solve the problem. The Daimon itself may be a Spirit, or the instructors may be a coven, made up of the Daimons of all those predecessors who shared Yeats's thought regarding the system (*Vision*, 1962, p. 209). James Olney, who has traced the evolution of the concept of the Daimon from Hesiod through Heraclitus and Empedocles, through the medieval Christian scholars and finally to Jung, has clearly established that the Daimon is no mere eccentricity of Yeats's thinking, but what may be termed the classic "archetype of the self," a figure with a rich and ancient cultural history. Furthermore, the *unconscious* is no innocuous psychological term, but according to Jung (and probably Yeats), a reference to the "mythic land of the dead."[99]

Perhaps the wisest remark made about the issue of automatic writing was Northrop Frye's:

> The well-known introduction to *A Vision* explains how it was dictated to Yeats by invisible spiritual instructors who worked through his wife's gift for automatic writing. Not having any explanation of my own to offer of this account, I propose to accept his at its face value.[100]

Taken in the light of modern psychical and parapsychological research, Yeats's supernatural experiences are not all that fantastic. What is surprising is not that such a dignified poet should have had such an inexplicable lapse of reason, but that given the recent upsurge in interest in the supernatural, Yeats's writings in this genre are not better known to psychic researchers than they apparently are. As Kathleen Raine has noted:

> W. H. Auden was typical of his generation in blaming Yeats for not being sufficiently aware of the leading ideas of his time (he presumably meant left-wing political ideologies). But is it not already becoming clear that Yeats's thought *was* the leading thought of his time?[101]

It should be remembered also that Yeats was still unraveling the puzzles that *A Vision* posed after the 1937 version was published, for that book, he declared, was only his "public philosophy," dealing with history. His "private philosophy" dealt with the individual mind, but as he wrote to Ethel Mannin in 1938, he only half understood it.[102]

The ultimate source of *A Vision* remained something of a mystery even for Yeats, but two factors remain constant throughout the long history of the problem: the affirmation of a "Communion of the Living and the Dead" (*Vision*, 1962, p. 23), and the conception of the world as a drama. Once, thinking of his unknown instructors, Yeats asks:

> Was he constrained by a drama which was part of conditions that made communication possible, was that drama itself part of the communication, had my question to be asked before his mind cleared? (*Vision*, 1962, p. 13)

If the instructors were under such a constraint, Yeats was equally checked and governed by the drama. While Yeats seems to feel freer in 1937 to speak in his own voice, to reveal his problems and plans in correcting the work,[103] and to allow his imagination more play, he is still decidedly under the rule of the Spirits. For example, "I have been told to make these numbers correspond to the phases of the moon," he says in once place (*Vision*, 1962, p. 78), and in another, "I am told to give Phases 1, 8, 15, 22 a month apiece" (*Vision*, 1962, p. 196). He shows more confidence in the system and in his own scholarship in 1937 than he did in 1925. Compare, for example, his interpretations of Swedenborg (*Vision*, 1925, p. 128; 1962, p. 69). Nevertheless, the Spirits resist his interpretations, often to the point of violent quarrel, in order not to accept false reasoning from their pupil. After one such quarrel, which came nearly four years after the publication of the first edition when the instructors returned to correct the book, Yeats remembered:

> I had half forgotten—there had been no communication longer than a sentence or two for four years—how completely master they could be down to its least detail of what I could but know in outline, how confident and dominating. (*Vision*, 1962, p. 21)

This tension between the aspiring imagination of man and the rigid logic of the absolute informs all of the 1937 version and makes it a much more human and dramatic book than the 1925 version. In one place, the contrast is identified as that between "reality and justice," with the system serving as a means of holding both in the mind (*Vision*, 1962, p. 25). In another, the tension is set up as a division between concrete expression and abstract thought: Yeats's instructors have forbidden him to read philosophy, but they encourage him to read history and biography in order that he might give "concrete expression to their abstract thought" (*Vision*, 1962, p. 12). When his reading slackens, they send him word that they are "starved" for concrete particulars by means of a signal, the scent of an extinguished candle (*Vision*, 1962, p. 16). Perhaps this is why Yeats chose that symbol to express the abstract modern age, still littered with the outworn romanticism of his own youth.

In 1925, Yeats had also tried to balance the rigid abstract philosophy of the system with the concrete romantic tale of Robartes's discovery; but Yeats was never at his best in prose fiction, and the story, with its 1890s setting and formal dialogue, is not successful. By 1937, he realized that romanticism was as abstract as the philosophy itself; a fresher, more irreverent style is used in "Stories of Michael Robartes and His Friends." Further, his immersion in philosophy may have made him realize once again that he was primarily a lyric poet, and that his strongest artistic resources were self-dramatization and personal emotion.

As mentioned in chapter 2, the 1925 edition shows more concern with the individual than does the later version, as though Yeats were using the system then to solve his own personal problems. The 1937 version concentrates on the social and historical implications of the system, and the personal stance is much more secure. In 1925, Yeats the Poet was a kind of self-caricature, a diminutive, eccentric Yeats. In 1937, there is the self-possession Yeats admired in Pound and exhibited in his strongest late poems. He feels this strength himself in the later version:

> The other day Lady Gregory said to me: "You are a much better educated man than you were ten years ago and much more powerful in argument." And I put *The Tower* and *The Winding Stair* into evidence to show that my poetry has gained in self-possession and power. I owe this change to an incredible experience. (*Vision*, 1962, p. 8)

Yeats had also acquired Pound's mockery, as a significant change in the poem about Huddon and Duddon illustrates. In the 1931 Cuala edition of *Stories of Michael Robartes and His Friends*, the final line of the poem reads: "But how they mock us burning out."[104] In 1937, it is Yeats who mocks.

Daniel Albright, in his study of Yeats's imagination in old age, writes extensively of the poet's late efforts to unify all his previous thought.[105] His life itself was seen, then more strongly than ever, as a metaphor of his own time and race.[106] Albright writes in regard to "The Tower":

> We can see that the poet has attained in old age the perfect objectification of himself: he has become impersonal, stiffened into a pose, a mask, and his genius is "no flower of himself but all himself"—he has become one with his achievement.[107]

Yeats would have objected to the word *impersonal*, for the sense of personality informed all of his work. As he notes in three lectures given in 1910, the personal was the keystone of the Rhymers; it is the new generation of poets that is impersonal.[108] Still Yeats's concept of personality was a sophisticated one, certainly nothing like "confessional"; Albright is right to call *A Vision* "Yeats's real autobiography."[109] One recognizes in it, as in the memoirs, the heightening of biographical fact to symbolic gesture and the narrative voice as metaphor for the very type of the artist.

Toward the end of the work, Yeats describes civilization as a struggle to maintain self-control (*Vision*, 1962, p. 268). It is that sense of self-control, tragic dignity, and joy kept ceremoniously, even under the most humiliating or hysterical circumstances, which is, as Rajan points out, the essence of creativity. Yeats celebrates this tragic dignity in Cuchulain and embodies it himself in many of his most powerful poems. This power unites the antinomies of reality and justice, or concrete expression and abstract theory. In *A Vision*, it is also the power that gives the imagination the license to play with solemn abstractions and to see the one symbol reflected in many mirrors (*Vision*, 1962, pp. 213-14, 240).

In balance with this sense of control is the play of the imagination. "When I relate this symbol to reality," Yeats writes in 1937, "various fancies pass before the mind" (*Vision*, 1962, p. 205). In another place, he writes that the work of Josef Strzygowski "haunts" his imagination (*Vision*, 1962, p. 257). In the later work on the system, the imagination has a much more expansive role. Yeats sees Rapallo as a mystical place, for example (*Vision*, 1962, p. 16); he can even visualize the muse as licentious women of the night (*Vision*, 1962, p. 24). With "those hard symbolic bones under the skin," his mind turns back to art (*Vision*, 1962, p. 24). "What if," he writes, clearly inviting by that construction an imaginative approach to the system (*Vision*, 1962, pp. 28-29). Most obviously at the beginning of "The Soul in Judgment," with its speculative contrast of Valéry and the singing girl (*Vision*, 1962, pp. 219-20), or in the beginning of "The Great Year of the Ancients," where Christ and Caesar are set in contrast (*Vision*, 1962, pp. 243-45), Yeats is allowing his speculative powers full rein to play upon the system and encouraging the same approach in his readers.

The mirrors of the imagination reflect many moods. Some parts of the book, like the conclusion of "The Soul in Judgment," are difficult and quite serious; other sections are urbane, as when Yeats discusses the personality types of the various phases. Some sections are objective reporting; some show despair. Some, like the Valéry passage, are dreamy and meditative. But, the tone that critics most often miss in *A Vision* is the humor.

Yeats saw not only the pity, but also the humor of Pound's feeding the cats and savored T. S. Eliot's[110] remark, "some of them so ungrateful" (*Vision*, 1962, p. 6). The tone in *A Packet for Ezra Pound* is definitely light and often self-mocking, especially in the letter to Pound, advising him not to be elected to the senate, and in the section on churches, where Yeats decides he is "too anaemic for so British a faith" (*Vision*, 1962, p. 7). The quotation from Swift, criticizing the practice of "publishing introductions to books, that are God knows when to come out" (*Vision*, 1962, p. 8), points up that both *A Packet* and *Stories of Michael Robartes*, used as introductory material in 1937, had been published before and provides a humorous comment on the ragged, piecemeal manner in which *A Vision* evolved. The humor in "Stories of Michael Robartes and His Friends" is broader and more coarse, depending often on the juxtaposition of raw sexuality and male timidity. "I am afraid of unfamiliar women in pyjamas," Duddon confesses to Denise (*Vision*, 1962, p. 42). Some of the humor is satiric, aimed at Yeats himself, and some is social satire, like John's and Mary's reaction to love: "Brought up in the strictest principles of the Church of Ireland, we were horrorstruck" (*Vision*, 1962, p. 44).

In allowing his natural good humor to emerge in the prefatory material, however, Yeats is not signaling, as many critics have supposed, that *A Vision* is no more than some elaborate literary joke. Too many years and too much effort went into the making of Yeats's system for him not to have taken it seriously. Unquestionably, the surrounding stories and poems are sometimes ironic and satiric, but that does not seem to "prove" that all of *A Vision* is satire, or more precisely, after Northrop Frye's definition in *Anatomy of Criticism*, Menippean satire or anatomy.[111] This label, though convenient, seems forced, aimed more at covering what is not understood than at carefully explicating what is, in fact, a complex and singular book. However much parts of *A Vision* may be bent to fit the definition of anatomy in the abstract, the work as a whole certainly does not read like a Menippean satire, and a reader is surely tone-deaf who classifies *A Vision* with *Gulliver's Travels* and *Tristram Shandy* rather than *Paradise Lost* or the writings of Blake.

Although *A Packet for Ezra Pound* (1929) and *Stories of Michael Robartes and His Friends* (1931) originally appeared separately, they were seen to have obvious thematic ties to the 1925 *Vision*. By bringing all the material together in 1937, Yeats and later his editors seem to be indicating that he wished it to be read and considered as an artistic whole,[112] and further, that he wished the labor, the evolution, the process of mythmaking itself to be visible. This is typical of Yeats's tendency to make public his struggles with his art and with his belief that the poet's life, the raw material of the poetic personality that is the center of all great art, should be open to candid examination: "A poet is by the very nature of things a man who lives with entire sincerity, or rather the better his poetry the more sincere his life; his life is an experiment in living and those that come after have a right to know it."[113] By concentrating on the system alone, one misses the whimsey and self-mockery that are intricate parts of the work as a whole. It is to miss the style, the mark of this artistic personality. Speaking in a 1910 lecture on Synge, Yeats describes style as "a double attitude of the mind"[114] that involves both the visionary eye and the shaping joy or mastery of the hand:

> The vision looks out at all the great things that have been said to all the traditional images. It is so in all poetic arts, and in the hands there is shaping joy, *mastery*, exultation, a complete contradiction between the melancholy submissive dreaming soul—between what comes in at the visionary eye—and what is in the hand. When you find in a man's *hand* this fantastic *power*, this whimsical strength, you feel that man is a strong nature, a strong man.[115]

As Yeats wrote in his Blake book, "The most perfect truth is simply the dramatic expression of the most complete man."[116]

Helen Vendler and Northrop Frye rest their readings of *A Vision*, in part, on Valéry's definition of cosmogony from "On Poe's *Eureka*," and it is worth

Style: The Playing of Strength 171

duplicating the quotation in order to place the work in its true, if somewhat exclusive, genre:

> It [*Eureka*] belongs to a department of literature remarkable for its persistence and astonishing in its variety; cosmogony is one of the most ancient literary forms.... Just as tragedy touches on history and psychology, so does the cosmogonic form touch on religion, with which it is confused at many points, and on science, from which it is necessarily distinguished by the absence of experimental proof. It includes sacred books, splendid poems, outlandish narratives full of beauty and nonsense, and physico-mathematical researches often so profound as to be worthy of a less insignificant object than the universe. But it is the glory of man to waste his powers on the void, and it is something more than that. Often such crack-brained researches lead to unforeseen discoveries. The role of the nonexistent exists; the function of the imaginary is real; and we learn from strict logic that *the false implies the true*. One might say that the history of thought could be summarized in these words: *It is absurd by what it seeks, great by what it finds.*[117]

A Vision has a unique fascination and sparks a creative response in the reader who comes to it unintimidated, the reader who finds it as Robartes found Giraldus's book.

Cosmogony, which should not be confused with cosmology, implies the creation of a world—perhaps, in artistic terms, a new world—not the meticulous analysis of the scientifically verifiable universe. No one should miss the playful, energetic, ironic tone of Valéry's definition; to substitute cosmology, the study of the universe as an orderly system, for cosmogony is to change this tone to one too somber for *A Vision* in its entirety.

At bottom, Yeats believed that this work had been *given* to him, and thus he believed that it contained objective truth. But the question of belief is never simple for modern man, as Yeats not only realized but took pains to dramatize. Often, he doubts—perhaps feeling that this work, too, is only another clever invention. The double perspective of certainty and doubt gives the book its richness, particularly in 1937, when self-dramatization and humor reflect upon the abstract thought. The whimsey of the book, then, is half a self-mockery to cover this doubt, half the play of the self-possessed imagination upon the system.

If *A Vision* fits Valéry's category, Yeats has created his own universe, not copied either that of previous poets or that of contemporary science. A "stylistic arrangement" means, not an abstracted pattern of the given but a creative act, an arrangement of experience in the manner of one's own style; when one recalls Yeats's definition of style as a surplus of energy, the playing of strength when the day's work is done, the playful, energetic tone of *A Vision* begins to match Valéry's. Balanced against the individual creative act is the eternal pattern of all created things; *A Vision*, by its vacillation between faith and doubt, keeps both in communion, one mirroring the other, choice and chance at one.

Notes

Chapter 1. An Irish Heresy

1. W. B. Yeats, *A Vision* (London: Macmillan & Co., 1962), p. 9.
2. W. B. Yeats, *Essays and Introductions* (London: Macmillan & Co., 1961), p. xi.
3. Although *A Vision* was not actually published until 15 January 1926, I have preferred to use the date on the title page—1925 (see Walter Kelly Hood, "Michael Robartes: Two Occult Manuscripts," in *Yeats and the Occult*, ed. George Mills Harper [Toronto: Maclean-Hunter Press, 1975], p. 215). My spelling and capitalization, for the most part, follow the 1962 edition.
4. Ibid., p. 209.
5. W. B. Yeats, *The Letters of W. B. Yeats*, ed. Allan Wade (New York: Macmillan Co., 1955), p. 700.
6. W. B. Yeats, *A Critical Edition of Yeats's 'A Vision'* (1925), ed. George Mills Harper and Walter Kelly Hood (London: Macmillan & Co., 1978), p. xi. For a full account of the automatic writing, see George Mills Harper, "'Unbelievers in the House': Yeats's Automatic Script," *Studies in the Literary Imagination* 14 (Spring 1981): 1–16.
7. Ibid., pp. xiii–xv.
8. Ibid., p. xvii. Note that when Yeats develops more mastery over the system's symbols, and they become specifically lunar, the solar aspects of the system are represented by darkness, the lunar by light (see W. B. Yeats. *A Vision: An Explanation of Life Founded upon the Writings of Giraldus and upon Certain Doctrines Attributed to Kusta ben Luka* [London: T. Werner Laurie, 1925], p. 12).
9. Ibid., pp. xii, xvii.
10. W. B. Yeats, *Vision*, 1962, pp. 28–29.
11. Ibid., p. 78.
12. Northrop Frye, "The Rising of the Moon: A Study of 'A Vision,'" in *An Honoured Guest: New Essays on W. B. Yeats*, ed. Denis Donoghue and J. R. Mulryne (London: Edward Arnold, 1965), p. 9.
13. Ibid.
14. Northrop Frye, "Yeats and the Language of Symbolism," in *Fables of Identity* (New York: Harcourt, Brace & World, 1963), p. 218.
15. Ibid., p. 220.
16. Ibid., pp. 220–21, 227.
17. Hazard Adams, "Symbolism and Yeats's 'A Vision,'" *Journal of Aesthetics and Art Criticism* 22 (Summer 1964): 429.
18. Ibid., pp. 429–30.
19. Frye, "Yeats and the Language of Symbolism," p. 236.
20. Northrop Frye, "The Top of the Tower: A Study of the Imagery of Yeats," in *The Stubborn Structure: Essays on Criticism and Society* (Ithaca: Cornell University Press, 1970), p. 257.
21. Ibid., pp. 257–59.

22. Northrop Frye, *Spiritus Mundi: Essays on Literature, Myth and Society* (Bloomington: Indiana University Press, 1976), p. xii.
23. W. B. Yeats, *Critical Edition of "A Vision,"* p. xi.
24. Frye, "Rising of the Moon," p. 13.
25. Ibid., p. 14
26. Ibid.
27. Helen Hennessy Vendler, *Yeats's "Vision" and the Later Plays* (Cambridge: Harvard University Press, 1963), pp. 253–54.
28. W. G. Fay, "The Poet and the Actor," in *William Butler Yeats: Essays in Tribute,* ed. Stephen Gwynn (Port Washington, N. Y.: Kennikat Press, 1965), pp. 127–31.
29. Hazard Adams, *Blake and Yeats: The Contrary Vision,* Cornell Studies in English, vol. 40 (New York: Russell & Russell, 1968), pp. 48–49.
30. Ibid., pp. 49–50.
31. Vendler, *Yeats's "Vision,"* p. 3.
32. W. B. Yeats, *Letters,* ed. Wade, p. 211.
33. W. B. Yeats. *Essays and Introductions,* p. 49.
34. W. B. Yeats, *A Vision,* 1925, p. xxiii.
35. Vendler, *Yeats's "Vision,"* pp. 19–20.
36. Ibid., p. 5.
37. Ibid., p. 2.
38. Ibid., p. 255.
39. Ibid., p. 253.
40. W. B. Yeats, *Essays and Introductions,* p. 149.
41. W. B. Yeats, *A Vision,* 1925, p. xii.
42. W. B. Yeats, *Explorations* (London: Macmillan & Co., 1962), p. 392.
43. Richard Ellmann, *Yeats: The Man and the Masks* (New York: Macmillan Co., 1948), pp. 235–36.
44. W. B. Yeats, *A Vision,* 1962, p. 8.
45. W. B. Yeats, *Letters,* ed. Wade, p. 742.
46. Ellmann, *Man and Masks,* p. 262.
47. W. B. Yeats, *The Collected Poems of W. B. Yeats* (London: Macmillan & Co., 1969), p. 185.
48. Harold Bloom, *Yeats* (New York: Oxford University Press, 1970), p. 224.
49. Ibid., p. 219.
50. Frye, "Top of the Tower," pp. 272, 275.
51. Frye, "Rising of the Moon," pp. 28–29.
52. See Adams, "Symbolism and 'A Vision,'" pp. 427–29.
53. W. B. Yeats, *A Vision,* 1925, p. 212.
54. Ibid., p. 252.
55. Bloom, *Yeats,* p. 213.
56. Ibid., p. 215.
57. Ibid., p. 471.
58. Ibid., p. 211.
59. Ibid., p. 470.
60. Ibid., p. 471.
61. W. B. Yeats, *A Vision,* 1962, p. 206.
62. Ibid., p. 40.
63. Ibid., pp. 194–95.
64. Ibid., p. 29.
65. W. B. Yeats, *Critical Edition of "A Vision,"* p. 13 (note to original p. 27, ll. 14–15); pp. 22–23 (note to original p. 78, l. 18).
66. Erich Neumann, *Depth Psychology and a New Ethic,* trans. Eugene Rolfe (New York: G. P.

Putnam's Sons, 1969), pp. 16–17.

67. W. B. Yeats, *A Vision*, 1962, p. 8.

68. W. B. Yeats, *A Vision*, 1925, p. xi.

69. Erich Neumann, *Art and the Creative Unconscious*, trans. Ralph Manheim, Bollingen Series 61 (Princeton: Princeton University Press, 1969), pp. 8–10.

70. Ibid., pp. 16–19.

71. Ibid., pp. 43–45. Neumann does not discuss female patterns of artistic development.

72. Ibid., p. 24.

73. W. B. Yeats, *A Vision*, 1925, pp. xi–xii.

74. Ibid., pp. 251–52.

75. John F. Lynen, *The Pastoral Art of Robert Frost* (New Haven: Yale University Press, 1960), p. 168.

76. Ibid., p. 169.

77. Frye, "Rising of the Moon," pp. 9–10.

78. Ibid., pp. 17–18.

79. Ibid., p. 15.

80. W. B. Yeats, *A Vision*, 1925, p. 12. This solar darkness is true of the wheel of the Faculties only; in the realm of the Principles, the situation is reversed (see Yeats's note in *A Vision*, 1962, p. 220). This distinction causes some confusion in applying the system's symbols to the poetry, and I am grateful to Robert O'Driscoll for pointing it out to me.

81. W. B. Yeats, *A Vision*, 1962, p. 79.

82. Harbans Rai Bachchan, *W. B. Yeats and Occultism* (Delhi: Motilal Banarsidass, 1965), pp. 132–37,

83. W. B. Yeats, *A Vision*, 1962, pp. 78, 80.

84. W. B. Yeats, *Collected Poems*, p. 187.

85. W. B. Yeats, *A Vision*, 1962, p. 73.

86. Ibid., p. 81.

87. Louis MacNeice, *The Poetry of W. B. Yeats* (London: Oxford University Press, 1941), p. 234.

88. Ibid., p. 129.

89. John Unterecker, *A Reader's Guide to William Butler Yeats* (New York: Noonday Press, 1965), pp. 15–16.

90. W. B. Yeats, *A Vision*, 1962, p. 84.

91. W. B. Yeats, *Autobiographies* (London: Macmillan & Co., 1966), pp. 102–3

92. W. B. Yeats, *A Vision*, 1962, p. 40.

93. W. B. Yeats, *A Vision*, 1925, p. 225. Yeats tells this story often. In *A Vision* it relates to life after death, but since its core is the exorcism of the antinomies of life, it seems to fit Robartes's situation as well.

94. W. B. Yeats, *A Vision*, 1962, p. 40.

95. Unterecker, *Reader's Guide*, p. 16.

96. W. B. Yeats, *Collected Poems*, p. 188.

97. W. B. Yeats, *A Vision*, 1962, p. 302.

98. W. B. Yeats, *A Vision*, 1925, p. 25.

99. Ibid., p. 251.

100. Ibid., p. 149.

101. W. B. Yeats, *A Vision*, 1962, p. 33.

102. Edmund Wilson, *Axel's Castle: A Study in the Imaginative Literature of 1870–1930* (New York Charles Scribner's Sons, 1959), p. 54.

103. W. B. Yeats, *A Vision*, 1962, p. 8.

104. Ibid., p. 25.

105. W. B. Yeats, *Collected Poems*, p. 339.

106. W. B. Yeats, *Mythologies* (London: Macmillan & Co., 1959), p. 319. Subsequent references to this work will appear in the text as *M*.

107. Yeats, *Essays and Introductions*, pp. 50–51. Subsequent references to this work will appear in the text as *E. & I.*

108. Willam Blake, *The Works of William Blake*, ed. Edwin John Ellis and William Butler Yeats (London: Bernard Quaritch, 1893), 1: 95–96. Subsequent references to this work will appear in the text as *Works of Blake*.

109. W. B. Yeats, *A Vision*, 1925, p. 251.

110. Ibid., p. 134.

111. Mary Catherine Flannery, *Yeats and Magic: The Earlier Works*, Irish Literary Studies, vol. 2 (New York: Harper & Row, 1978), p. 39. For a further interpretation of Blake and Yeats based on occult tradition, see Kathleen Raine, *From Blake to "A Vision,"* New Yeats Papers 17 (Dublin: Dolmen Press, 1979).

112. W. B. Yeats, *A Vision*, 1962, p. 70.

113. It must be remembered that Yeats was working from documents, and the documents simply gave no attention to the origin of life or the question of good and evil (see W. B. Yeats, *A Vision*, 1925, p. 176). Yeats does allow his imagination to play upon these ideas, however (see ibid., p. 149).

114. William H. O'Donnell, "Yeats as Adept and Artist: *The Speckled Bird*, *The Secret Rose*, and *The Wind among the Reeds*," in *Yeats and the Occult*, pp. 55–79.

115. Frye, "Yeats and the Language of Symbolism," p. 232.

116. W. B. Yeats, *A Vision*, 1925, p. xi.

117. W. B. Yeats, *Critical Edition of "A Vision,"* p. 33 n. 133. Vendler also discusses the relation of "The Mental Traveller" and *A Vision* in *Yeats's "Vision,"* chap. 2, pp. 50–70.

118. W. B. Yeats, *A Vision*, 1925, p. 134.

119. W. B. Yeats, *A Vision*, 1962, p. 213.

120. W. B. Yeats, *A Vision*, 1925, pp. 133–34.

121. W. B. Yeats, *A Vision*, 1962, p. 12.

122. George Mills Harper and John S. Kelly, "Preliminary Examination of the Script of E[lizabeth] R[adcliffe]," *Yeats and the Occult*, pp. 130–71.

123. Ibid., p. 131.

124. Ibid., p. 138.

125. Ibid., p. 132.

126. Ibid., p. 138.

127. Ibid., p. 137.

128. Ibid., p. 148.

129. Ibid., pp. 136–37.

130. Ibid., p. 139.

131. W. B. Yeats, *Explorations*, p. 31.

132. Ibid., p. 31.

133. W. B. Yeats, *A Vision*, 1962, p. 9.

134. Kathleen Raine, *Yeats, the Tarot and the Golden Dawn*, New Yeats Papers, vol. 2 (Dublin: Dolmen Press, 1972), pp. 15–16. Morton Irving Seiden's *William Butler Yeats: The Poet as a Mythmaker, 1865–1939* (Michigan State University Press, 1962) is also a good source of basic occult information, especially chapter 1, "Sources and Analogues: 1885–1914."

135. W. B. Yeats, *A Vision*, 1962, p. 301.

136. W. B. Yeats, *Explorations*, pp. 52, 61–62.

Notes 177

Chapter 2. Circuits of Sun and Moon

1. W. B. Yeats, *A Vision*, 1925, p. xii. Subsequent references to this work will appear in the text as *Vision*, 1925.
2. W. B. Yeats, *A Vision*, 1962, p. 18. Subsequent references to this work will appear in the text as *Vision*, 1962. See also W. B. Yeats, *Letters*, ed. Wade, p. 695. There, Yeats refers to the book as "the first half" of his philosophy. See also pp. 699–700 in the same source.
3. W. B. Yeats, *Essays and Introductions*, pp. 156–57.
4. W. B. Yeats, *Mythologies*, p. 289.
5. Bloom, *Yeats*, p. 22.
6. Ibid., p. 215.
7. *Works of Blake*, 1: 287.
8. Ibid., p. 239.
9. Seiden, *Poet as a Mythmaker*, p. 103.
10. W. B. Yeats, *Critical Edition of "A Vision,"* p. 68 note 222. Harper and Hood note that the 1925 book 3 owes much to the experiments and publications of the Society for Psychical Research, particularly a book called *Human Personality and Its Survival of Bodily Death* by Frederic W. H. Myers.
11. E. Wilson, *Axel's Castle*, pp. 54–55.
12. W. B. Yeats, *Mythologies*, p. 80.

Chapter 3. Unnatural Stories

1. W. B. Yeats, *A Vision*, 1962, p. 19.
2. W. B. Yeats, *A Vision*, 1925, pp. xvi, xxi–xxii.
3. W. B. Yeats, *Explorations*, p. 259.
4. W. B. Yeats, *Collected Poems*, p. 532. This is the only reference to Robartes that survives in *Collected Poems*. There are, of course, numerous references in the original volumes of the poetry and plays.
5. Harper, "Unbelievers in the House," p. 6.
6. Adams, *Blake and Yeats, The Contrary Vision*, pp. 196, 199.
7. Bloom, *Yeats*, p. 210.
8. Vendler, *Yeats's "Vision,"* p. 7.
9. W. B. Yeats, [Ganconagh, pseud.], *"John Sherman" and "Dhoya,"* 2d ed. (London: T. Fisher Unwin, Pseudonym Library, 1891), p. 116.
10. Ibid., p. 170.
11. W. B. Yeats, *The Speckled Bird*, ed. William H. O'Donnell, Yeats Studies Series (Toronto: McClelland & Stewart, 1976), p. xxiv. Subsequent references to this book will appear in the text as *S. B.*
12. W. B. Yeats, *Autobiographies*, pp. 182–83.
13. W. B. Yeats, *Mythologies*, p. 271. Subsequent references to this work will appear in the text as *M*.
14. George Mills Harper, *Yeats's Golden Dawn* (London: Macmillan & Co., 1974), pp. 112–13.
15. Raine, *Yeats, Tarot and Golden Dawn*, p. 45.
16. Warwick Gould, "'Lionel Johnson Comes the First to Mind': Sources for Owen Aherne," *Yeats and the Occult*, p. 255.
17. Virginia Moore, *The Unicorn: William Butler Yeats's Search for Reality* (New York: Macmillan Co., 1954), pp. 172–76.

18. Ellmann, *Man and Masks*, p. 219.
19. V. Moore, *Unicorn*, pp. 225–26.
20. W. B. Yeats, "Clarence Mangan (1803–1849)," in *Uncollected Prose by W. B. Yeats*, ed. John P. Frayne and Colton Johnson (London: Macmillan & Co., 1970), 1: 116.
21. Raine, *Yeats, Tarot and Golden Dawn*, p. 9.
22. Harper, *Golden Dawn*, appendix A, p. 204.
23. Ibid., p. 176 n. 26.
24. Quoted by Raine, *Yeats, Tarot and Golden Dawn*, pp. 46–47.
25. Ibid., p. 45.
26. Ibid., p. 24.
27. Ibid., p. 15.
28. Ibid., p. 23.
29. Ibid., p. 18.
30. Ibid., pp. 18–20.
31. Ibid., p. 45.
32. Ibid., p. 5.
33. Ibid., pp. 6–7.
34. W. B. Yeats, *Collected Poems*, p. 184.
35. W. B. Yeats, *Memoirs: Autobiography—First Draft Journal*, ed. Denis Donoghue (London: Macmillan & Co., 1972), p. 138.
36. Flannery points out that the three "Rosa Alchemica" stories were originally intended to be published with the nine stories of *The Secret Rose*. Apparently, Yeats's publisher, Bullen, separated the stories into two books. Whatever Yeats's intentions regarding publication, however, it is obvious that the three stories share characters and themes and, therefore, are meant to reflect upon one another (Flannery, *Yeats and Magic*, p. 85).
37. Harper, *Golden Dawn*, pp. 9–10.
38. V. Moore, *Unicorn*, pp. 103–4.
39. W. B. Yeats, *Explorations*, p. 393.
40. W. B. Yeats, *Memoirs*, pp. 96–97. Warwick Gould gives further evidence for Johnson as the model for Aherne in *Yeats and the Occult*, as does Robert O'Driscoll in "*The Tables of the Law*: A Critical Text," *Yeats Studies: An International Journal*, no. 1 (1971): 96.
41. Philippe Auguste Mathias de Villiers de L'Isle-Adam, *Axel*, trans. H. P. R. Finberg, with a preface by W. B. Yeats (London: Jarrolds 1925), p. 7.
42. Ibid., p. 284.
43. Ibid., pp. 281–83.
44. W. B. Yeats, *The Collected Plays of W. B. Yeats* (London: Macmillan & Co., 1966), p. 449. Gould treats this same material regarding the name, Hearne, or Aherne, in *Yeats and the Occult*.
45. W. B. Yeats, *Explorations*, p. 259.
46. W. B. Yeats, *Letters*, ed. Wade, p. 644.
47. W. B. Yeats, *The Variorum Edition of the Poems of W. B. Yeats*, ed. Peter Allt and Russell K. Alspach (New York: Macmillan Co., 1973), p. 853.
48. W. B. Yeats, *Letters*, ed. Wade, p. 805.
49. W. B. Yeats, *Variorum Poems*, p. 852.
50. W. B. Yeats, *Collected Poems*, p. 532.
51. W. B. Yeats, *Letters*, ed. Wade, pp. 676–77.
52. W. B. Yeats, *Variorum Poems*, p. 852.
53. Ibid., p. 821. Michael J. Sidnell suggests that John Aherne is a fused recollection of Owen Aherne and John Hearne from *The Speckled Bird* in "Mr. Yeats, Michael Robartes, and Their Circle," in *Yeats and the Occult*, p. 229. Gould, in the same volume, finds a historical model for John Aherne (pp. 277–78).
54. W. B. Yeats, *Letters*, ed. Wade, p. 677. Sidnell discusses Yeats's notes and poems regard-

ing the *Vision* characters extensively in *Yeats and the Occult*.

55. W. B. Yeats, *Letters*, ed. Wade, p. 700.
56. V. Moore, *Unicorn*, pp. 63-65.
57. W. B. Yeats, *Letters*, ed. Wade, p. 675.
58. Ibid., p. 680.
59. Ibid., p. 691.
60. Ibid., pp. 666-67.
61. Sidnell, "Mr. Yeats," p. 248.
62. W. B. Yeats, *Collected Poems*, p. 281.
63. Ibid., p. 184.
64. In 1937, Robartes apparently discovers the book in Vienna, not Cracow (see *A Vision*, 1962, p. 38). There is no evidence in 1937 that Robartes visited Cracow as he did in 1925 (*A Vision*, 1925, p. xvii).
65. W. B. Yeats, *Critical Edition of "A Vision,"* pp. 6-7 n. 5, 19 n. 61. Harper and Hood find in the early drafts for *A Vision* the suggestion that Robartes turned away from Yeats's door because he feared he might encounter Ezra Pound inside. Pound, a man of Nietzsche's violent Phase 12, was Aherne's enemy in an early version of the story. Robartes has some sympathy for men of the hero's phase, and Yeats admired Pound's "intellectual hatred," but Pound was, nevertheless, eventually dropped from the 1925 version.
66. Walter Kelly Hood, "Michael Robartes: Two Occult Manuscripts," in *Yeats and the Occult*, pp. 204-24.
67. Frye, "Rising of the Moon," pp. 17-18.
68. Sidnell's interpretation focuses more upon the themes of history and ceremony than does mine, which lays more emphasis on the autobiographical elements of the stories. Sidnell sees the nest as history; I see it as a work of art, perhaps an Arcon, a primary image requiring antithetical expression (see *Yeats and the Occult*, pp. 252-54).
69. W. B. Yeats, *Essays and Introductions*, p. 508.
70. Ibid., p. 268.
71. Sidnell has pointed out the more immediate concern of the narrative—the search for the proper guardian of the lost egg of Leda (*Yeats and the Occult*, p. 253).
72. W. B. Yeats, *Explorations*, p. 425.
73. Villiers de L'Isle-Adam, *Axel*, p. 260.
74. Ibid., p. 284.
75. W. B. Yeats, *Memoirs*, pp. 132-33.
76. Sidnell discusses this point in *Yeats and the Occult*, p. 253, adding that the Huddon-Duddon arrangement is also a comment on the supposed autonomy of art that is ultimately dependent upon nature. His discussion of "The Dance of the Four Royal Persons" (p. 248) makes the same point about art.
77. Maud Gonne, somewhat like Sara, had wanted to enter a convent as a young woman (W. B. Yeats, *Memoirs*, p. 132). Like Denise, she was tall and had acting experience to match Denise's training as a model (idem, *A Vision*, 1962, p. 53).
78. Joseph Hone, *W. B. Yeats, 1865-1939* (London: Macmillan & Co., 1962), p. 314.
79. W. B. Yeats, *Letters*, ed. Wade, p. 697.
80. Ibid., p. 769.
81. Hone, *Yeats*, pp. 113, 258-59.
82. W. B. Yeats, *Memoirs*, p. 74.
83. W. B. Yeats, *Letters*, ed. Wade, p. 721.
84. Ibid., p. 820.
85. There is every reason to assume that Mary Bell's character was also shaped in homage to George Yeats; but probably, since Yeats gives her credit for her help in the making of *A Vision* openly in the prefatory parts of the book, he felt no need to draw her portrait in detail in the

stories. She must, I believe, figure directly in the making of the nest or system, but no identifying characteristics point up her identity with Mary Bell.

86. W. B. Yeats, *Explorations*, p. 437.
87. Neumann, *Art and the Creative Unconscious*, p. 8.
88. W. B. Yeats, *The Variorum Edition of the Plays of W. B. Yeats*, ed. Russell K. Alspach (London: Macmillan & Co., 1966), p. 789.
89. Hone, *Yeats*, p. 138.
90. W. B. Yeats, *Memoirs*, pp. 155–56.
91. Hone, *Yeats*, p. 139.
92. Ibid., p. 140.
93. W. B. Yeats, *Explorations*, p. 448.
94. Micheál MacLiammóir and Eavan Boland, *W. B. Yeats and His World* (London: Thames & Hudson, 1971), p. 38.
95. W. B. Yeats, *Letters*, ed. Wade, p. 669.
96. Ibid., pp. 680–81.
97. Ibid., p. 681.
98. V. Moore, *Unicorn*, p. 65.
99. Raine, *Yeats, Tarot and Golden Dawn*, p. 7.
100. W. B. Yeats, *Explorations*, p. 52. See also idem, *Essays and Introductions*, p. 441.
101. W. B. Yeats, *Explorations*, p. 64.
102. Ibid., p. 396.
103. Ibid., p. 367.
104. Harper and Hood also suggest that *A Vision* was "stimulated by and based on the mystery of Yeats's relations with three women: his wife and Iseult and Maud Gonne." The original automatic script was, in fact, largely concerned with Yeats, George, and their friends, but the Controls specially warned him against including any personal references in the book (W. B. Yeats, *Critical Edition of "A Vision,"* pp. xxiii–xxiv, xxxv).
105. Ellmann, *Man and Masks*, p. 235.
106. *Fairy and Folk Tales of the Irish Peasantry*, ed. W. B. Yeats (London: Walter Scott, 1888), p. 299.
107. W. B. Yeats, *Explorations*, p. 345.
108. W. B. Yeats, *Autobiographies*, p. 272.
109. Edward Callan, "Huddon and Doddon in Yeats's *A Vision*: The Folk Tale as Gateway to the Universal Mind," *Michigan Academician* (Summer 1973): 10.
110. W. B. Yeats, *Autobiographies*, p. 265.
111. Ibid., p. 272.
112. W. B. Yeats, *Essays and Introductions*, p. 414.
113. *Celtic Fairy Tales*, ed. Joseph Jacobs (New York: G. P. Putnam's Sons, n. d.), p. 270.
114. Ibid., p. vii.
115. W. B. Yeats, *Uncollected Prose*, pp. 173–75.
116. Although little attention is given in the final work to parallels between the fairy world and the world of the instructors, Yeats did question his Control on this matter. He replied: "The people of faery, the souls at one & fifteen and all other legendary states are but parts of one truth. The truth is in all but in some more concealed by fable & dreams than in others" (W. B. Yeats, *Critical Edition of "A Vision,"* p. 72 (note to original p. 229, l. 8).
117. Daniel Hoffman, *Barbarous Knowledge: Myth in the Poetry of Yeats, Graves, and Muir* (New York: Oxford University Press, 1967), p. 38.
118. W. B. Yeats, *Uncollected Prose*, p. 133.
119. *Fairy and Folk Tales*, p. 303.
120. *Celtic Fairy Tales*, p. 62.
121. *Fairy and Folk Tales*, p. 302.

122. W. B. Yeats, *Memoirs*, p. 131.
123. Ibid., p. 166. O'Donnell also notes that death is the price of spiritual wisdom in "Yeats as Adept and Artist," in *Yeats and the Occult*, p. 65.

Chapter 4. Style

1. Vendler, *Yeats's "Vision,"* p. 7.
2. Richard J. Finneran, *The Prose Fiction of W. B. Yeats: The Search for "Those Simple Forms,"* New Yeats Papers, vol. 4 (Dublin: Dolmen Press, 1973), p. 37.
3. W. B. Yeats, *Collected Poems*, p. 184.
4. W. B. Yeats, *A Vision*, 1962, p. 55.
5. W. B. Yeats, *Autobiographies*, p. 114.
6. Ibid., p. 116.
7. W. B. Yeats, *Essays and Introductions*, p. 415.
8. Ibid., p. 28.
9. Ibid., pp. 156–57.
10. Ibid., p. 157.
11. V. Moore, *Unicorn*, pp. 134–39.
12. Ibid., pp. 151–57.
13. Ibid., p. 149.
14. Ibid., p. 133.
15. MacLiammóir and Boland, *Yeats and His World*, p. 125.
16. V. Moore, *Unicorn*, pp. 115–22, 456.
17. Ibid., p. 104.
18. Ibid., pp. 103–4.
19. W. B. Yeats, *Collected Poems*, p. 214.
20. Ibid., p. 339.
21. Ellmann, *Man and Masks*, p. 236.
22. W. B. Yeats, *Explorations*, p. 403.
23. W. B. Yeats, *Memoirs*, p. 150.
24. Gould, "Lionel Johnson Comes the First to Mind," in *Yeats and the Occult*, pp. 270–71.
25. Jack B. Yeats, *The Charmed Life* (London: Georgy Routledge & Sons, 1938), p. 76.
26. Ibid., p. 106.
27. W. B. Yeats, *Explorations*, p. 450.
28. MacLiammóir and Boland, *Yeats and His World*, p. 113.
29. W. B. Yeats, *Letters*, ed. Wade, p. 764.
30. W. B. Yeats, *A Vision*, 1925, pp. 211–12.
31. W. B. Yeats, *Variorum Plays*, p. 569.
32. W. B. Yeats, *Essays and Introductions*, pp. 405–6.
33. W. B. Yeats, *Collected Poems*, p. 348.
34. W. B. Yeats, *Letters*, ed. Wade, p. 608.
35. W. B. Yeats, *Essays and Introductions*, p. 254.
36. W. B. Yeats, *Letters*, ed. Wade, p. 722.
37. Ibid., p. 733.
38. Ibid., p. 734.
39. Ibid., pp. 733–34.
40. W. B. Yeats, *Explorations*, p. 316.
41. W. B. Yeats, *A Packet for Ezra Pound* (Dublin: Cuala Press, 1929), p. 4.
42. W. B. Yeats, *Explorations*, p. 316.

43. Ibid., p. 404.
44. Northrop Frye, *Anatomy of Criticism: Four Essays* (Princeton: Princeton University Press, 1971), p. 290.
45. Ibid., p. 107.
46. Unterecker, *Reader's Guide*, pp. 121–22.
47. W. B. Yeats, *Collected Poems*, p. 369.
48. W. B. Yeats, *Memoirs*, p. 152.
49. Ibid., p. 153.
50. Balachandra Rajan, "Yeats and the Absurd," *Tri-Quarterly*, no. 4 (Winter 1965–66): 134.
51. Ibid., p. 131. For a full discussion of Nietzsche's influence on Yeats, see Otto Bohlmann, *Yeats and Nietzsche: An Exploration of Major Nietzschean Echoes in the Writings of William Butler Yeats* (Totowa, N. J.: Barnes & Noble, 1982).
52. Balachandra Rajan, "Yeats, Synge and the Tragic Understanding," *Yeats Studies: An International Journal*, no. 2 (1972): 67.
53. Ibid., p. 72.
54. W. B. Yeats, *Explorations*, pp. 402–3.
55. W. B. Yeats, *Letters*, ed. Wade, p. 803.
56. A. N. Jeffares, *W. B. Yeats*, Profiles in Literature Series (London: Routledge & Kegan Paul, 1971), pp. 64–65.
57. W. B. Yeats, *Letters*, ed. Wade, p. 826.
58. Ibid., p. 825.
59. W. B. Yeats, *Collected Poems*, p. 218.
60. W. B. Yeats, *Collected Plays*, p. 593.
61. W. B. Yeats, *Explorations*, p. 399.
62. W. B. Yeats, *Collected Plays*, p. 594.
63. W. B. Yeats, "The Poetry of Sir Samuel Ferguson, I," in *Uncollected Prose*, p. 84.
64. Ibid., p. 85.
65. Martin Esslin, *The Theatre of the Absurd* (London: Eyre Methuen, 1974), pp. 5–6.
66. Balachandra Rajan, *W. B. Yeats: A Critical Introduction* (London: Hutchinson University Library, 1965), pp. 163–64.
67. See also Sidnell, "Mr. Yeats," in *Yeats and the Occult*, pp. 252, 254.
68. John Rees Moore, *Masks of Love and Death: Yeats as Dramatist* (Ithaca: Cornell University Press, 1971), p. 197.
69. W. B. Yeats, *Explorations*, pp. 148–49.
70. W. B. Yeats, *Letters*, ed. Wade, p. 712.
71. Quoted by V. Moore, *Unicorn*, p. 419; and Hone, *Yeats*, pp. 462–63.
72. W. B. Yeats, *Letters*, ed. Wade, p. 899. Wade identifies the doctor as F. P. Sturm (p. 712).
73. Ibid., p. 905.
74. Ibid., pp. 905–6.
75. W. B. Yeats, *Explorations*, p. 302.
76. Ellmann, *Man and Masks*, p. 234.
77. Ibid., p. 235.
78. Ibid., p. 236.
79. Bachchan, *Yeats and Occultism*, p. 58.
80. Robert O'Driscoll, *Symbolism and Some Implications of the Symbolic Approach: W. B. Yeats during the Eighteen-Nineties*, New Yeats Papers, vol. 9 (Dublin: Dolmen Press, 1975), p. 13.
81. W. B. Yeats, *Explorations*, p. 400.
82. Ibid., p. 320.
83. *Works of Blake*, 1: 239.
84. Ellmann, *Man and Masks*, p. 282.
85. W. B. Yeats, *Explorations*, p. 305.

86. W. B. Yeats, *Packet for Pound*, p. 8.
87. Ibid., p. 8.
88. W. B. Yeats, *Essays and Introductions*, p. 403.
89. W. B. Yeats, *Letters*, ed. Wade, p. 744.
90. V. Moore, *Unicorn*, pp. 256-61.
91. Ellmann, *Man and Masks*, p. 222.
92. Vendler, *Yeats's "Vision,"* p. 3.
93. V. Moore, *Unicorn*, p. 253.
94. Quoted by Ellmann, *Man and Masks*, p. 262.
95. Vendler, *Yeats's "Vision,"* p. 3.
96. W. B. Yeats, *Collected Poems*, p. 208.
97. W. B. Yeats, *Packet for Pound*, p. 30.
98. W. B. Yeats, "Is the Order of R. R. & A. C. to Remain a Magical Order?" in Harper, *Golden Dawn*, p. 261.
99. James Olney, "Sex and the Dead: Daimones of Yeats and Jung," *Studies in the Literary Imagination* 14 (Spring 1981): 48-50. For a deeper exploration of the intellectual history behind Yeats and Jung's thinking, see idem, *The Rhizome and the Flower: The Perennial Philosophy—Yeats and Jung* (Berkeley and Los Angeles: University of California Press, 1980).
100. Frye, "The Rising of the Moon," p. 13.
101. Kathleen Raine, "Hades Wrapped in Cloud," in *Yeats and the Occult*, p. 81.
102. W. B. Yeats, *Letters*, ed. Wade, p. 916.
103. Yeats uses first-person narration much more freely in 1937 than in 1925 and makes a great many more methodological statements (see W. B. Yeats, *Vision*, 1962, pp. 71, 77, 187, 207).
104. W. B. Yeats, *Stories of Michael Robartes and His Friends: An Extract from a Record Made by His Pupils—And a Play in Prose* (Dublin: Cuala Press, 1931), p. ii.
105. Daniel Albright, *The Myth against Myth: A Study of Yeats's Imagination in Old Age* (London: Oxford University Press, 1972), p. 63.
106. Ibid., p. 4.
107. Ibid., p. 51.
108. W. B. Yeats, "Yeats's Lecture Notes for 'Friends of My Youth,'" ed. Joseph Ronsley, *Yeats and the Theatre*, Yeats Studies Series (Toronto: Maclean-Hunter Press, 1975), p. 78.
109. Albright, *Myth against Myth*, p. 2.
110. W. B. Yeats, *Letters*, ed. Wade, p. 748.
111. For other viewpoints on Yeats's humor, see Hazard Adams, "Some Yeatsian Versions of Comedy," *In Excited Reverie: A Centenary Tribute to William Butler Yeats*, ed. A. Norman Jeffares and K. G. W. Cross (New York: St. Martin's Press, 1965), pp. 152-70; Eugene Korkowski, "Yeats' Vision as Philosophic Satura," *Éire/Ireland* 12 (Fall 1977): 62-70; and Steven Helmling, "Yeats's Esoteric Comedy," *Hudson Review* 30 (Summer 1977): 230-46.
112. After Yeats's death, his publishers, in consultation with Mrs. Yeats, considered including the prefatory material and the stories in *Explorations* (1962). The fact that they did not do so seems to indicate that they felt that all the related material should be seen as a whole (see Richard J. Finneran, "A Preliminary Note on the Text of *A Vision* [1937]," *Yeats and the Occult*, p. 319). For a full account of *A Vision*'s publication history, see idem, "On Editing Yeats: The Text of *A Vision* (1937)," *Texas Studies in Language and Literature* 19 (Spring 1977): 19-34.
113. W. B. Yeats, "Friends of My Youth,". p. 74.
114. W. B. Yeats, "Yeats on Personality: Three Unpublished Lectures," ed. Robart O'Driscoll, *Yeats and the Theatre*, p. 48.
115. Ibid., p. 48.
116. *Works of Blake*, 1: 241.
117. Paul Valéry, "On Poe's *Eureka*," in *The Collected Works of Paul Valéry*, trans. Malcolm Cowley and James R. Lawler, Bollingen Series 45, vol. 8 (Princeton: Princeton University Press, 1972), p. 170.

Select Bibliography

Primary Sources

Blake, William. *The Works of William Blake*. Edited by Edwin John Ellis and William Butler Yeats. 3 vols. London: Bernard Quaritch, 1893.

Fairy and Folk Tales of the Irish Peasantry. Edited by W. B. Yeats. Camelot Series, edited by Ernest Rhys. London: Walter Scott, 1888.

Oxford Book of Modern Verse: 1892–1935. Edited by W. B. Yeats. Oxford: Clarendon Press, 1936.

W. B. Yeats and T. Sturge Moore: Their Correspondence. Edited by Ursula Bridge. London: Routledge & Kegan Paul, 1953.

Yeats, Jack B. *The Charmed Life*. London: George Routledge & Sons, 1938.

Yeats, William Butler. *Autobiographies*. London: Macmillan & Co. 1966.

———. *The Collected Plays of W. B. Yeats*. London: Macmillan & Co., 1966.

———. *The Collected Poems of W. B. Yeats*. London: Macmillan & Co., 1969.

———. *A Critical Edition of Yeats's "A Vision"* (1925). Edited by George Mills Harper and Walter Kelly Hood. London: Macmillan & Co., 1978.

———. *Essays and Introductions*. London: Macmillan & Co., 1961.

———. *Explorations*. London: Macmillan & Co., 1962.

———. [Ganconagh, pseud.]. *"John Sherman"* and *"Dhoya."* 2d ed. London: T. Fisher Unwin, Pseudonym Library, 1891.

———. *The Letters of W. B. Yeats*. Edited by Allan Wade. New York: Macmillan Co., 1955.

———. *Letters on Poetry from W. B. Yeats to Dorothy Wellesley*. London: Oxford University Press, 1940.

———. *Memoirs: Autobiography—First Draft Journal*. Edited by Denis Donoghue. London: Macmillan & Co., 1972.

———. *Mythologies*, London: Macmillan & Co., 1959.

———. *A Packet for Ezra Pound*. Dublin: Cuala Press, 1929.

———. *The Speckled Bird*. Edited by William H. O'Donnell. Yeats Studies Series, edited by Robert O'Driscoll and Lorna Reynolds. Toronto: McClellan & Stewart, 1976.

———. *Stories of Michael Robartes and His Friends: An Extract from a Record Made by His Pupils—And a Play in Prose*. Dublin: Cuala Press, 1931.

———. *Uncollected Prose by W. B. Yeats*. Edited by John P. Frayne and Colton Johnson.

2 vols. London: Macmillan & Co., 1970 and 1975.

——. *The Variorum Edition of the Plays of W. B. Yeats*. Edited by Russell K. Alspach. London: Macmillan & Co., 1966.

——. *The Variorum Edition of the Poems of W. B. Yeats*. Edited by Peter Allt and Russell K. Alspach. New York: Macmillan & Co., 1973.

——. *A Vision*. London: Macmillan & Co., 1962.

——. *A Vision: An Explanation of Life Founded upon the Writings of Giraldus and upon Certain Doctrines Attributed to Kusta ben Luka*. London: T. Werner Laurie, 1925.

Secondary Sources

Adams, Hazard. *Blake and Yeats: The Contrary Vision*. Cornell Studies in English, vol. 40. New York: Russell & Russell, 1968.

——. "Symbolism and Yeats's 'A Vision.'" *Journal of Aesthetics and Art Criticism* 22 (Summer 1964): 425–36.

——. "Yeatsian Art and Mathematic Form." *Centennial Review* 4 (Winter 1960):70–88.

Albright, Daniel. *The Myth against Myth: A Study of Yeats's Imagination in Old Age*. London: Oxford University Press, 1972.

Allen, James Lovic. "Yeats's Phase in the System of *A Vision*." *Éire/Ireland* 8 (1973): 91–117.

Bachchan, Harbans Rai. *W. B. Yeats and Occultism*. Delhi: Motilal Banarsidass, 1965.

Bloom, Harold. *Yeats*. New York: Oxford University Press, 1970.

Bohlmann, Otto. *Yeats and Nietzsche: An Exploration of Major Nietzschean Echoes in the Writings of William Butler Yeats*. Totowa, N. J.: Barnes & Noble, 1982.

Callan, Edward. "Huddon and Duddon in Yeats's *A Vision*: The Folk Tale as Gateway to the Universal Mind." *Michigan Academician* 6, (Summer 1973): 5–16.

Celtic Fairy Tales. Edited by Joseph Jacobs. New York: G. P. Putnam's Sons, n. d.

Ellmann, Richard. *The Identity of Yeats*. London: Macmillan & Co., 1954.

——. *Yeats: The Man and the Masks*. New York: Macmillan Co., 1948.

Engelberg, Edward. *The Vast Design: Patterns in W. B. Yeats's Aesthetic*. Toronto: University of Toronto Press, 1965.

Esslin, Martin. *The Theatre of the Absurd*. London: Eyre Methuen, 1974.

Finneran, Richard J. "On Editing Yeats: The Text of *A Vision* (1937)." *Texas Studies in Language and Literature* 19 (Spring 1977): 119–34.

——. *The Prose Fiction of W. B. Yeats: The Search for "Those Simple Forms."* New Yeats Papers, vol. 4 edited by Liam Miller. Dublin: Dolmen Press, 1973.

Flannery, Mary Catherine. *Yeats and Magic: The Earlier Works*. Irish Literary Studies, vol. 2. New York: Harper & Row, 1978.

Frye, Northrop. *Anatomy of Criticism: Four Essays*. Princeton: Princeton University Press, 1971.

——. *Spiritus Mundi: Essays on Literature, Myth and Society*. Bloomington: Indiana University Press, 1976.

———. "The Top of the Tower: A Study of the Imagery of Yeats." In *The Stubborn Structure: Essays on Criticism and Society*. Ithaca: Cornell University Press, 1970.

———. "Yeats and the Language of Symbolism." In *Fables of Identity*. New York: Harcourt, Brace & World, 1963.

Harper, George Mills. "'Unbelievers in the House': Yeats's Automatic Script." *Studies in the Literary Imagination* 14 (Spring 1981): 1–16.

———. *Yeats's Golden Dawn*. London: Macmillan & Co., 1974.

Helmling, Steven. "Yeats's Esoteric Comedy." *Hudson Review* 30 (Summer 1977): 230–46.

Henn, T. R. *The Lonely Tower: Studies in the Poetry of W. B. Yeats*. 2d ed. London: Methuen & Co., 1966.

Hoffman, Daniel. *Barbarous Knowledge: Myth in the Poetry of Yeats, Graves, and Muir*. New York: Oxford University Press, 1967.

Hone, Joseph. *W. B. Yeats, 1865–1939*. London: Macmillan & Co., 1962.

An Honoured Guest: New Essays on W. B. Yeats. Edited by Denis Donoghue and J. R. Mulryne. London: Edward Arnold, 1965.

In Excited Reverie: A Centenary Tribute to William Butler Yeats. Edited by A. Norman Jeffares and K. G. W. Cross. New York: St. Martin's Press, 1965.

Jeffares, A. N. "'Gyres' in the Poetry of W. B. Yeats." *English Studies* 27 (1946): 65–74.

———. *W. B. Yeats*. Profiles in Literature Series, edited by B. C. Southam. London: Routledge & Kegan Paul, 1971.

Korkowski, Eugene. "Yeats' *Vision* as Philosophic Satura." *Éire/Ireland* 12 (Fall 1977): 62–70.

Lynen, John F. *The Pastoral Art of Robert Frost*. New Haven: Yale University Press, 1960.

MacLiammóir, Micheál and Eavan Boland. *W. B. Yeats and His World*. London: Thames & Hudson, 1971.

MacNeice, Louis. *The Poetry of W. B. Yeats*. London: Oxford University Press, 1941.

Malins, Edward. *A Preface to Yeats*. Preface Books Series, edited by Maurice Hussey. London: Longmans, 1974.

Melchiori, Giorgio. *The Whole Mystery of Art: Pattern into Poetry in the Work of W. B. Yeats*. London: Routledge & Kegan Paul, 1960.

Moore, John Rees. *Masks of Love and Death: Yeats as Dramatist*. Ithaca: Cornell University Press, 1971.

Moore, Virginia. *The Unicorn: William Butler Yeats' Search for Reality*. New York: Macmillan Co., 1954.

Neumann, Erich. *Art and the Creative Unconscious: Four Essays*. Translated by Ralph Manheim. Bollingen Series 61. Princeton: Princeton University Press, 1969.

———. *Depth Psychology and a New Ethic*. Translated by Eugene Rolfe. New York: G. P. Putnam's Sons, 1969.

O'Driscoll, Robert. *Symbolism and Some Implications of the Symbolic Approach: W. B. Yeats during the Eighteen-Nineties*. New Yeats Papers, vol. 9, edited by Liam Miller. Dublin: Dolmen Press, 1975.

———. "*The Tables of the Law*: A Critical Text." *Yeats Studies: An International Journal*, no. 1 (1971): 87–118.

Olney, James. *The Rhizome and the Flower: The Perennial Philosophy—Yeats and Jung*. Berkeley and Los Angeles: University of California Press, 1980.

———. "Sex and the Dead: *Daimones* of Yeats and Jung." *Studies in the Literary Imagination* 14 (Spring 1981): 43–60.

The Permanence of Yeats: Selected Criticism. Edited by James Hall and Martin Steinmann. New York: Macmillan Co., 1950.

Raine, Kathleen. *From Blake to "A Vision."* New Yeats Papers, vol. 17; edited by Liam Miller. Dublin: Dolmen Press, 1979.

———. *Yeats, the Tarot and the Golden Dawn*. New Yeats Papers, vol. 2, edited by Liam Miller. Dublin: Dolmen Press, 1972.

Rajan, Balachandra. *W. B. Yeats: A Critical Introduction*. London: Hutchinson University Library, 1965.

———. "Yeats and the Absurd." *Tri-Quarterly*, no. 4 (Winter 1965–66): 130–37.

———. "Yeats, Synge and the Tragic Understanding." *Yeats Studies: An International Journal*, no. 2 (1972): 66–79.

Seiden, Morton Irving. *William Butler Yeats: The Poet as a Mythmaker, 1865–1939*. Michigan State University Press, 1962.

Stock, A. G. *W. B. Yeats: His Poetry and Thought*. Cambridge: Cambridge University Press, 1961.

Unterecker, John. *A Reader's Guide to William Butler Yeats*. New York: Noonday Press, 1965.

Ure, Peter. *Yeats the Playwright: A Commentary on Character and Design in the Major Plays*. London: Routledge & Kegan Paul, 1963.

Valéry, Paul. "On Poe's *Eureka*." In *The Collected Works of Paul Valéry*, translated by Malcolm Cowley and James R. Lawler. Bollingen Series 45, vol. 8. Princeton: Princeton University Press, 1972.

Vendler, Helen Hennessy. *Yeats's "Vision" and the Later Plays*. Cambridge: Harvard University Press, 1963.

Villiers de L'Isle-Adam, Philippe Auguste Mathias de. *Axel*. Translated by H. P. R. Finberg. Preface by W. B. Yeats. London: Jarrolds, 1925.

Whitaker, Thomas R. *Swan and Shadow: Yeats's Dialogue with History*. Chapel Hill: University of North Carolina Press, 1964.

William Butler Yeats: Essays in Tribute. Edited by Stephen Gwynn. Port Washington, N. Y.: Kennikat Press, 1965.

Wilson, Edmund. *Axel's Castle: A Study in the Imaginative Literature of 1870–1930*. New York: Charles Scribner's Sons, 1959.

Wilson, F. A. C. *W. B. Yeats and Tradition*. London: Victor Gollancz, 1958.

———. *Yeats's Iconography*. London: Victor Gollancz, 1960.

The World of W. B. Yeats. Edited by Robin Skelton and Ann Saddlemyer. Rev. ed. Seattle: University of Washington Press, 1967.

Yeats Centenary Papers. Edited by Liam Miller. Dublin: Dolmen Press, 1968.

Yeats: A Collection of Critical Essays. Edited by John Unterecker. Twentieth Century

Views Series, edited by Maynard Mack. Englewood Cliffs, N. J.: Prentice-Hall, 1963.

Yeats and the Occult. Edited by George Mills Harper. Yeats Studies Series, edited by Robert O'Driscoll and Lorna Reynolds. Toronto: Maclean-Hunter Press, 1975.

Yeats and the Theatre. Edited by Robert O'Driscoll and Lorna Reynolds. Yeats Studies Series. Toronto: Maclean-Hunter Press, 1975.

Zwerdling, Alex. *Yeats and the Heroic Ideal*. New York: New York University Press, 1965.

Index of Book Titles and Section Headings in *A Vision*

Only the prose expository portions of *A Vision* are listed here. Titles of fiction and verse portions are listed in the General Index.

"Blake and the Great Wheel," 67
"Blake's Use of the Gyres," 67

"Complementary Dreams," 67
"Completed Symbol, The," 66, 72
"Cones of Sexual Love, The," 66
"Cones of the Lunar and Solar Year, The," 69
"Consciousness," 66

"Daimon, the Sexes, Unity of Being, Natural and Supernatural Unity, The," 61
Dedication "To Vestigia," 117
"Dove or Swan," 15, 16, 26, 65, 71, 72, 76, 78, 116, 118, 140, 142–44, 162
"Drama of the Faculties and of the Tinctures, etc.," 60, 65

"End of the Cycle, The," 72, 158–59, 160
"Enforced and Free Faculties," 66

"Four Faculties, The," 58
"Four Principles, The," 69
"Funeral Images, Works of Art, and the Dead," 86

"Gates of Pluto, The," 15, 62, 67, 70, 71, 73, 78, 80, 156
"Great Wheel, The," 16, 57
"Great Year in Classical Antiquity, The," 66, 72, 73
"Great Year of the Ancients, The," 16, 66, 71–72, 73, 75, 88, 162, 169

"Life After Death," 67

"Mythology," 74, 91

"Objectives," 66

Packet for Ezra Pound, A, 67, 136, 145, 153, 159, 161, 165, 169, 170
"Place of the Four Faculties on the Wheel, The," 59

"Rapallo," 162
"Record and the Memory, The," 90
"Relations," 66

"Soul in Judgment, The," 54, 55, 67, 71–72, 78, 86, 88, 90, 162, 169
"Spirits at Fifteen and at One, The," 86

"Table of the Four Faculties," 61
"Three Fountains and the Cycles of Embodiment, The," 66
"To Ezra Pound," 18
"Two Conditions, The," 66
"Two Directions, The," 66

"What the Caliph Partly Learned," 15, 16, 57, 78, 111
"What the Caliph Refused to Learn," 15, 66, 78, 111

General Index

Abstraction, 149, 161, 167–69; in Blake, 45; Yeats's battle against, 23, 130, 139–40
Absurdism, 146–53, 156; in *The Herne's Egg*, 151; in *Stories of Michael Robartes and His Friends*, 152–53
Adams, Hazard, 19–21, 42, 94, 123, 183 n.111
Adams, Henry, 73, 77
Adepts, 52, 97, 99–100
A. E. *See* Russell, George W.
Africanus, Leo, 99
Aherne, John, 108–9, 140, 178 n.53; letter of, 93, 102, 112–13, 115, 135, 145, 162
Aherne, Owen, 22, 34, 38, 78, 87, 93–94, 97–98, 118, 129, 134, 152, 156; and Automatic Faculty, 89; and Christianity, 84, 102, 106–7, 114–15, 119; contrasted to Robartes, 117; development of, 101–7; role in *Vision* cover story, 112–16; as writer, 108–9, 111
Albright, Daniel, 168
Allegory, 139, 140, 146
Anatomy of Criticism (Frye), 170
Anima Hominis, 50, 68–69; and Record, 90
Anima Mundi, 50–51, 53–55, 68, 130–31, 156, 161; and Record, 90
Antinomies, 90–91, 159, 168; as derived from Cicero, 75
Antithetical era, 29, 76, 104, 117, 119, 149; and Aherne, 106; annunciation of, 122; Duddon as, 121; and energy, 144; nature of, 77
Antithetical gyre, 34–35
Antithetical influx. *See* Antithetical era
Antithetical inspiration, 89
Antithetical man, 51, 58, 62, 112, 114, 116
Antithetical phases, 22
Antithetical Tincture, 60–61, 77; and Arcon, 86–87; in fictional character types, 95, 106–7; and Huddon, Duddon and Daniel O'Leary, 134; as Platonic, 74; and Robartes, 107; and sexual relationships, 82–83
Apes of God, The (Lewis), 114
Arcon, 78, 97; and art, 88; defined, 86–87
Art, 24–25, 78, 85, 88, 105, 126, 143, 145, 156, 170; and antithetical era, 119; and contact with nature, 122–23; and Mask, 51, 97; source in the superhuman, 89–90, 105
Art and the Creative Unconscious (Neumann), 31
Artist, 52, 104, 111, 124, 130, 143, 146, 147, 168
Auden, W. H., 166
Autobiography, 128, 160, 168; as fiction technique, 143–44; in "Stories of Michael Robartes and His Friends," 127, 161
Automatic Faculty, 88–89
Automatic personality, 89
Automatic writing, 16–18, 85, 88, 94, 112, 154, 159–60, 162, 166, 173 n.6; and Automatic Faculty, 88–89; as invention of George Yeats, 163–64
Axel (Villiers), 105–6, 117, 120–21

Bachchan, Harbans Rai, 35, 158
Beatitude, 55, 79–80, 83–84, 91
Beauty: as Destiny, 69
Bell, Mary, 117, 119, 122–27, 142, 169
Bell, Mr., 118, 123–27, 153, 155
Berkeley, George, 33, 43, 64, 71, 159; prose style of, 161–62
Bird: as symbol, 123–24, 126, 130
Blake, William, 17, 19, 26–27, 30, 32, 64, 91, 123, 157, 164; influence on Yeats, 42–48, 67; and "The Mental Traveller," 48; and morality, 52; *Works of William Blake* (ed. Yeats), 40–42, 68, 159
Blavatsky, Mme. Helena Petrovna, 35, 43, 54, 101, 104, 139
Blood: as symbol, 127, 149–51
Bloom, Harold, 24, 26, 28–30, 62–63, 94, 158
Boccaccio, Giovanni, 154
Body of Fate, 36, 58–62, 65, 69, 119–20
Boehme, Jacob, 48, 164
Bond, John, 117, 123–27, 142, 169
Brancuşi, Constantin, 18, 127, 144
Buber, Martin, 27
Byzantium, 84, 154

Cabala, 28, 43, 48, 52, 55, 162, 164
Caesar, Julius, 75–76, 88, 162, 169

190

General Index

Caliph of Bagdad, 58, 66, 74
Callan, Edward, 128–31
Camus, Albert, 30, 151
Celestial Body, 69–70; and Beatitude, 83–84; and Purification, 85; and time, 71; and Waking State, 80–81
Celtic Fairy Tales (ed. Jacobs), 128, 131
Censor, 85
Cervantes, Miguel de, 154
Charmed Life, The (Jack Yeats), 140–41
Christ, 18, 42, 51–52, 67, 75–76, 87–88, 107, 150, 162–63, 169; annunciation of birth of, 122; resurrection of, 75
Christian era, 122, 126
Christianity, 28, 52, 114, 117, 140; and history, 28; and literary tradition, 20; in "The Tables of the Law," 104–5; and Yeats's system, 29–30
Chymical Marriage of Christian Rosencreutz, 138–39
Cicero, 73, 75
Cimetière Marin (Valéry), 88
Coleridge, Samuel Taylor, 17
Comedy, 147
Commedia dell' Arte, 60, 65
Communicators, 85, 165. *See also* Instructors
Complementary Dream, 84–85
Condition of air, 55
Condition of fire, 26, 55
Cone. *See* Gyre
Congal, 30, 151–52
Contrasts. *See* Oppositions
Coole Park, 123–25
Correspondence: doctrine of, 50, 53–54, 104, 139
Coven, 89, 117–18, 122, 134, 155, 165
Cracow, 110, 113, 179 n.64
Crazy Jane: poems about, 135, 143, 147
Creative Mind, 36, 58–62, 65, 69
Creativity, 22, 31
Cuala Press, 109, 136, 168
Cuchulain, 147–48, 152–53, 156, 168
Cypher MSS, 104, 110

Daimon, 20, 27, 42, 48, 62, 82, 86, 89, 121, 131, 163–65; and the artist, 55–56; and covens, 165–66; early concept of, 51; and Ghostly Self, 90–91; history of, 166; and love, 83; and Mask, 52; and Purification, 85; and psychology, 61–63; and Victimage, 87
Dance, 83, 111, 113
Dante Alighieri, 19–20, 25, 32, 42, 51, 55, 73, 87
Dead: communion with the living, 33, 86, 88, 166; as source of knowledge, 54, 130–31
Death: as price of spiritual wisdom, 133–34; 181 n.123
Dee, Dr. John, 109–10
Degrees: continuous, 40; discrete, 40–41
Deirdre, 87
de L'Isle Adam, Denise, 38, 117, 142, 155, 169; discussed, 120–21; as Love, 119, 137
"Demon est Deus Inversus," 62, 138
Depth Psychology and a New Ethic (Neumann), 29
Destiny, 69
Determinism, 29–30, 118, 127, 153, 160
Dialectical rhythm, 34, 37–38
Discord, 60–61, 75
Discoveries of Michael Robartes, The, 108
Dreaming Back, 79–81; and Foreknowledge, 85
Duddon, John, 112, 117–21, 124–27, 137, 142, 169
Dulac, Edmund, 16, 149, 150

Egg: of Leda, 102, 119, 122; as symbol, 39, 101, 126–27, 130
Eliot, T. S., 34, 37, 142, 169
Ellis, Edwin J., 41–43
Ellmann, Richard, 23, 30, 128, 139, 149, 156, 158–60, 163
Emerald Tablet, 110. *See also* Smaragdine (Emerald) Tablet
Empedocles, 64, 73, 75, 164, 166
Energy, 144, 161, 171; and farce, 146–47; in Jack Yeats's work, 142; as Will, 69
Esslin, Martin, 151
Evil, 24, 28–29, 62–63; in antithetical era, 117; expiation of, 82–83; slighted in 1937 *Vision*, 78
Expiation, 86–89; and Arcons, 87

Faculties, 36, 57–61, 64–67, 69–70, 80, 84; and antithetical era, 76; and Beatitude, 83–84; early concept of, 51; and Principles, 70; shared equally by men and women, 83; and solar darkness, 175 n.80; and Spirit, 89; wheel of, 71–72, 80, 86, 150
Fairy world, 80, 96, 131–32, 180 n.116
Fall, 60, 69; Christian, 43, 82
Farce, 144, 146–47
Farr, Florence, 51
Fate, 69, 87
Felkin, Dr. Robert W., 99
Ferguson, Samuel, 151
Fifteenth cycle, 84
Finneran, Richard J., 135, 183 n.112
Flannery, Mary Catherine, 42–43
Flaubert, Gustave, 64
Folklore, 80, 128, 135, 146; Irish, 33, 50, 80, 139–40
Foreknowledge, 79, 81, 85

Four ages of civilization, 150
Four cardinal signs, 60
Four Faculties. *See* Faculties
Four Principles. *See* Principles
Four Qualities, 65
Four Royal Persons, 112
Fourteenth cycle, 84
Freedom, 38–39, 55, 156, 159–60; from cycle of life and death, 82; and Robartes's pupils, 117
Free will, 27–29; in "Stories of Michael Robartes and His Friends," 118–19, 152–53
Freud, Sigmund, 63; Freudianism, 26, 29–30
Frobenius, 73, 77
Frustrators, 70, 78, 85, 162–63
Frye, Northrop, 19–22, 24, 27–28, 34, 37, 45, 117, 146, 157, 166, 170

Ghostly Self, 87; and Beatitude, 84; and Daimon, 90–91
Giraldus, 17, 111–13, 119; book of, 93–94, 104, 107, 113, 171; portrait of, 16, 110–11
Glanvil, Joseph, 48
God, 68, 106, 109, 114, 159–60
Going Forth, 78–79, 84
Golden Dawn, 17, 99, 100–101, 104, 138, 165
Goldman, Arnold, 49
Gonne, Iseult, 120
Gonne, Maud, 16, 95, 124, 143, 163, 180 n.104; and Denise de L'Isle Adam, 120–22, 179 n.77
Gould, Warwick, 140
Great Memory, 43, 53, 128–29, 137, 156–57
Great Mind, 53, 128–29, 137, 156
Great Wheel, 35, 45, 57–58, 69
Great Year, 66, 74–77, 162
Gregory, Lady Augusta, 51, 121, 133, 142, 146–47, 168; and Mary Bell, 122–27
Gregory, Robert, 100
Gregory, Sir William, 124–25
Gyres, 24, 60, 64–70, 77, 116, 155; in Blake, 43–45, 48; and bonds, 87; as line and plane, 43, 64; origin in Empedocles, 64; problem of visualizing, 64–65; as stationary, 80

Hanrahan, Red, 96, 100, 129
Harper, George Mills, 17–18, 48–50, 94–95, 98, 109
Harun Al-Raschid, 111–13, 124
Head, 60, 69
Heard, Gerald, 73
Hearne, John, 96
Hearne, Michael, 95–96, 98, 105, 106
Heart, 60, 69
"Henry IV," 142
Heracles, 160

Heraclitus, 64, 73, 166
Hermes, 73, 104
Heron: as symbol, 106
Hesiod, 166
Hipparchus, 73, 76
History, 67, 71, 117, 126, 148, 157, 166–67; and Christian perspective, 27–28; and mythology, 32–33; as symbolized by egg, 126–27
Holy Ghost, 87, 123; Holy Spirit of Joachim of Flora, 104–5
Homell, Dr. Fritz, 73
Horton, William Thomas, 17–18
Hood, Walter Kelly, 16–18, 109, 116
Howard, Rev. William, 94–95
Huddon, Peter, 117, 127, 137, 155, 168; discussed, 119–21
Humor: in *The Speckled Bird*, 98; in *A Vision*, 169–71, 183 n.111
Husk, 69–71, 80, 83–84; and Foreknowledge, 85; and Record, 90

Image, 39, 59, 61
Imagination, 86, 129–30, 132, 144, 154, 156, 157; and logic, 167; as means of knowing, 50; as means of unifying art, 145–46; and vehicle, 54; Yeats's, 150, 168–69, 171
Instinct, 28, 32, 116, 126–30
Instructors, 17, 20, 39–40, 70, 76–77, 85, 94, 109, 161–64, 166–67; command writing of first edition, 57; as coven, 166; invited by Yeats, 52; and terminology, 90
Interchange of the tinctures, 24, 77, 81, 119
Ireland, 110, 114, 121, 124, 129; Church of, 169; and Congal, 151; four sacred objects of, 100
Isis Unveiled (Blavatsky), 104

Jacobs, Joseph, 128–29, 131
Jeffares, A. Norman, 150
Joachim of Flora: book of, 84, 104–6
Johnson, Lionel, 87, 105, 121, 178 n.40
Joyce, James, 73, 95, 143–44, 146; and Jack Yeats, 142–43; and "The Tables of the Law," 105
Judwali, 93, 111–13, 116

Kant, Immanuel, 64
Keats, John, 51
Kelly, John S., 48–50
Knots, 81, 83
Kusta ben Luka, 17, 78, 111–13, 119, 124

"La Spirale," 67
Lawrence, D. H., 63
Leda, 117, 119
Lévi, Eliphas, 100

General Index

Lewis, Wyndham, 18, 144, 146
Locke, John, 129–30
Logic, 28, 130, 167
Loins, 60, 69
Love, 75, 117, 119
Lucifer (magazine), 138
Lynen, John F., 33
Lyttelton, Lady Edith, 17–18

Maclagan, 95–99, 107
MacLiammóir, Micheál, 138, 142
MacNeice, Louis, 37
Magi. *See* Adepts
Magic: in *The Speckled Bird*, 95, 97–98
Magician: four sacred weapons of, 100
Mandookya Upanishad, The, 91
Mangan, Clarence, 99
Mannin, Ethel, 155, 166
Marriage. *See* Beatitude
Marriage of Heaven and Hell, The (Blake), 26–27
Marx, Karl, 73, 77
Mask, 30, 36–38, 42, 56, 58–61, 65, 69–70; art as, 51; and Daimon, 62; and morality, 52; and myth, 142, 153–54; and Passionate Body, 80; in "Rosa Alchemica," 97
Mathers, Mrs. MacGregor (Moina), 31, 99, 111–12; as Vestigia, 117
Mathers, S. L. MacGregor, 43, 48, 53, 89, 98–99, 107, 110–11, 138; as Maclagan, 95–97; as Third Order Adept, 99–100
Meditation, 54–55, 79
"Mental Traveller, The" (Blake), 45, 48
"Michael Robartes Foretells," 116
Millevoye, Lucien, 120
Milton, John, 19, 21, 25, 73, 91
Mind, 69
Mirebeau: oleograph of the Sacred Heart in, 49–50
Moods, 54, 61, 68, 111, 126, 140, 159
Moore, Virginia, 42, 99, 128, 138, 163
Morality: and mask, 52; in *A Vision*, 43
More, Henry, 126, 130
Murray's dictionary (*O.E.D.*), 58, 64
Mythology, 25–26, 30, 74, 129, 138, 142–43, 158; and farce, 146; as Mask, 153–54; restoring, 91–92; as supported by historical figures, 32–33; *A Vision* as, 126, 130; Yeats's need for, 23, 32; Yeats's vs. Blake's, 157

Nest: Mary Bell's building of, 123, 145; and instinct, 125–26, 129–30; *A Vision* as, 124, 126
Neumann, Erich, 29, 31–32
Nietzsche, Friedrich, 148, 182 n.51
Noh, 33

Occultism: and classification, 138; as dangerous, 102–4; difficulty in expressing, 40–41, 48, 49–50; as source of poetry, 19, 43; as source of prose style, 140; Yeats's attempts to find proof for, 49–50
O'Donnell, William H., 43, 52, 95
O'Driscoll, Robert, 158, 175 n.80
Oedipus, 18, 165
O'Leary, Daniel, 101, 117, 124, 142; discussed, 118–19
Olney, James, 166, 183 n.99
"On Poe's *Eureka*" (Valéry), 170
Oppositions, 60
"Ordeal by Gold and Love" (Villiers), 120
Order of the Alchemical Rose, 102, 103, 115
O'Sullivan, Owen Roe, 96
Otherworld, 132–33

Passion, 80
Passionate Body, 69, 70, 71, 80, 83, 91; and Foreknowledge, 85; and Sleeping State, 81
Personality: antithetical, 37; in art, 170; as artistic stance, 37–39, 50, 53, 56, 60, 143; as Will and Mask, 60; in Yeats's work, 168
Phantasmagoria, 79
Phases: Phase One, 24, 34–35, 37, 59, 167; Phase Eight, 35, 59, 167; Phase Fifteen, 24, 34–35, 37, 59, 63, 86, 88, 167; Phase Seventeen, 59, 76; Phase Twenty-two, 35, 59, 167; Phase Twenty-three, 30, 142; Phase Twenty-eight, 59
Phases of the moon, 18, 35–36, 57, 167
Philosophical Essay upon Human Understanding, A (Locke), 130
Physical primary, 90, 117, 121, 142
Pirandello, Luigi, 142, 144
Plato, 39, 73, 74, 75, 76
Plotinus, 28, 43, 73, 75
Pound, Ezra, 140, 143, 155, 160, 162, 169, 179 n.65; cantos of, 145; influence on Yeats's style, 142–43, 168; style of, 161
Primary man, 51, 58; as fictional character, 95, 112, 114, 116
Primary tincture, 60–61, 77; and Aherne, 106, 107; and Arcon, 86–87; gyre of, 34–35; and Huddon, Duddon and Daniel O'Leary, 134; phases of, 22, 145; as Platonic, 74; and sexual relationships, 82–83
Principles, 58, 66, 67, 69–70, 80; and solar darkness, 175 n.80; wheel of, 71, 72, 80
Prometheus Unbound (Shelley), 26
Prose Fiction of W. B. Yeats: The Search for 'Those Simple Forms,' The (Finneran), 135
Psychoanalysis, 26, 63
Psychoanalysis and the Unconscious (Lawrence), 63
Ptolemy, 76
Purification, 79, 84–85

Radcliffe, Elizabeth, 49
Raine, Kathleen, 42, 53, 100, 138, 166
Rajan, Balachandra, 147–48, 152, 168
Rapallo, 169
Record, 68, 88, 157; discussed, 90–91; and Sleeping State, 80
Reincarnation, 29–30, 158
Return, 79, 80, 81, 84
"Return, The" (Pound), 18
Revelation, 25, 27, 70
Ritual, 92, 98, 111, 154; and farce, 146; in Golden Dawn, 138, 147
Robartes, Michael, 34, 38, 78, 89, 93, 94, 98, 103, 105, 110–11, 117, 127, 129, 134–36, 152–53, 156, 167, 171, 177 n.4; as author, 108–9; development of, 102, 107–8; as literary device, 67, 112–16; models for, 96–97, 99; as tarot hermit, 101; as Third Order Adept, 100, 102; and war, 119, 151
Romanticism, 27, 63, 71, 136, 160, 162, 167; Yeats's rejection of, 144–45
Rosencreutz, Christian, 138
Russell, George W. (pseud. A.E.), 110, 133, 136, 155; as model for Robartes, 98–99

Sage, 67, 80, 82
Saint, the, 51, 53, 55
Sara, 106, 117, 120
Satire: in *The Speckled Bird*, 98; in "Stories of Michael Robartes and His Friends," 94, 118; *A Vision* as, 170
Scrying, 109–10, 126
Self-dramatization: Yeats's in *A Vision*, 56, 60, 92, 155–57, 158–59, 160–61, 167, 171
Seiden, Morton Irving, 74
Separation of the Four Principles, 79
Shakespear, Olivia, 95, 108, 121–22, 150, 154; and Mary Bell, 124–25
Shelley, Percy Bysshe: works of, 21, 26–27, 100
Shemesh, Ara ben, 99
Sherman, John, 94–95
Shiftings, 79, 80, 82–83; and Beatitude, 83; Spirits in, 85
Sidnell, Michael J., 111, 179 n.68, 179 n.71, 179 n.76
Smaragdine (Emerald) Tablet, 104
Society for Psychical Research, 17, 48, 50, 177 n.10
Socrates, 73, 75
Song and Its Fountains (A.E.), 136
Space, 43, 67, 71, 77; difficulty in visualizing, 64–65
Speculum Angelorum et Hominum, 94, 111, 113
Spengler, Oswald, 73, 77, 129
Sphere, 64, 159, 160; egg as, 127; as ultimate reality, 90–91

Spirit, 49, 50, 57, 69–71, 77, 88, 103, 163–64, 166–67; and Automatic Faculty, 88–89; and Beatitude, 83–84; between death and birth, 86–87; and book of Joachim of Flora, 104; in Purification, 85; and Record, 90; separation from Husk and Passionate Body, 80–81; in Shiftings, 82; in Waking State, 80
Spirit of the Thirteenth Cone, 82. *See also* Teaching Spirit
Spiritism, 53–54
Spiritual primary, 90, 142
Steiner, Dr. Rudolf, 99
Stevens, Wallace, 27, 63
Strzygowski, Josef, 73, 77, 169
"Stylistic arrangement," 22, 171
Subjectivity, 61, 64
"Supreme Choice, The," 106, 120
Swedenborg, Emanuel, 32, 42, 45, 48, 64, 67, 87, 164, 167
Symbolism, 158; Egyptian, 101, 111–12; in Jack Yeats's work, 141; as a literary movement, 33–34; in occultism, 137–39; in *A Vision*, 58, 156–57, 173 n.8; Yeats's early, 146
Synge, John, 51, 146–47, 170

Tarot, 100
Teaching, the, 79, 80
Teaching Spirits, 79, 81
Terminology, 20, 21, 68, 69; difficulties with, 90–91; dropped from 1937 edition, 78; in Meditation, 79
Theatre of the Absurd, The (Esslin), 151
Third Order, 99–100
Thirteenth Cycle (Cone), 30, 37, 38–40, 54, 77–78, 90–91, 126, 157, 159–60; and Holy Ghost, 84; and Purification, 85
Thoor Ballylee, 114, 115, 125
Time: as basis for gyre, 43, 64, 67, 77; in organization of *A Vision*, 71
Time and Western Man (Lewis), 144–45
Tinctures, 32, 58; opening and closing of, 60, 65. *See also* Interchange of the tinctures
Tragic joy, 148
Tragedy, 147
Tree of Life, 53, 100
Truth: as Fate, 69
Twenty-eight incarnations (embodiments), 65, 71, 76, 107, 162; relationship to Yeats's work, 81
Twenty-seven heavens: Blake's chart of, 43–45

Ulysses (Joyce), 142, 145
Unconscious, 63, 146; and Anima Mundi, 130; and Automatic Faculty, 88; and Daimon, 89, 165; and instructors, 85, 163; in Jung, 62, 166; and Record, 80, 90; as

source of beauty, 61–62; as source of *A Vision*, 164; and Teaching Spirits, 81, 87
Unity of Being, 26, 42, 62–63, 65; and evil, 82
Unterecker, John, 37, 38
Upanishads, 42, 73
Ure, Peter, 149
Ussher, Arland, 100

Valéry, Paul, 88, 169, 170–71
Vehicle: of soul, 54, 55, 89, 130
Vendler, Helen, 21–24, 135, 163, 170; and mysticism in *A Vision*, 164; and *A Vision* fiction, 94
Vico, Giambattista, 73, 77, 149
Victim, 67, 80, 82
Victimage, 86–88; for the Dead, 87; for the Ghostly Self, 82, 87; for a Spirit of the Thirteenth Cone, 87
Villiers de L'Isle-Adam, Philippe Auguste Mathias de, 105, 120
Virgil, 73
Vision, 19, 38, 39–40, 65, 157; evoked by symbols, 137; as means of perceiving truth, 42; moment of, 72; nature of, 130; as path to the spiritual, 53
Vision of the Blood Kindred, 79, 80, 85
Vision of the Clarified Body, 84
Vision of the Friends, 78–79, 85

Wade, Allan, 108, 109
Waking and Sleeping States, 79, 80–81, 88–89
War, 117, 119, 126
"Waste Land, The" (Eliot), 142
Water: as symbol, 133, 150
"Way of the Soul between the Sun and the Moon, The," 113
W. B. Yeats: A Critical Introduction (Rajan), 147
W. B. Yeats and Occultism (Bachchan), 35
Will, 36, 58–62, 65, 69, 76
William Butler Yeats: The Poet as a Mythmaker, 1865–1939 (Seiden), 74
Wilson, Edmund, 39, 79
Woodford, Rev. A. F. A., 104

Yeats, Jack, 118; paintings of, 143; prose style of, 140–42, 161
Yeats, John Butler, 95
Yeats, Michael, 163
Yeats, Mrs. W. B. (George), 16, 17, 23, 94, 99, 100, 109, 121–22, 127, 155; and authorship of *A Vision*, 93–94; and birds, 125; and Mary Bell, 124–25, 179–80 n.85; as source of *A Vision*, 163–64
Yeats, William Butler. Works
—"Adoration of the Magi, The," 102–4, 115, 122
—"All Souls' Night," 15, 138, 156
—"Among School Children," 111
—*Autobiographies*, 96, 128–29, 136, 161
—"Beautiful Lofty Things," 143
—"Byzantium," 111
—*Calvary*, 67, 150
—*Cat and the Moon, The*, 139, 149
—*Celtic Twilight, The*, 90, 126, 131–33, 137
—*Collected Poems*, 108
—"Complementary Dreams," 67
—*Countess Cathleen*, 140
—"Dance of the Four Royal Persons, The," 15, 58, 81, 111
—*Death of Cuchulain, The*, 148, 151
—"Desert Geometry or The Gift of Harun Al-Raschid," 15, 16, 67, 111, 112, 163
—"Donald and His Neighbours," 128, 132–33, 146
—*Dreaming of the Bones, The*, 151
—"Earth, Fire and Water," 126
—*Fairy and Folk Tales of the Irish Peasantry*, 128, 132–33
—"Fool by the Roadside, The," 15, 67
—*Four Plays for Dancers*, 123
—*Full Moon in March, A*, 24, 149, 151
—"General Introduction for My Work, A," 42
—*Green Helmet, The*, 151
—*Herne's Egg, The*, 30, 135, 147–48, 151, 152
—Huddon, Duddon and Daniel O'Leary (untitled poem), 15, 128–34
—*Ideas of Good and Evil*, 15
—"Introduction to 'The Resurrection,'" 104
—"Introduction to 'The Words upon the Window-pane,'" 128
—"Irish Fairies, Ghosts, Witches, Etc.," 137
—"Is the Order of R. R. & A. C. to Remain a Magical Order?", 165
—*John Sherman*, 94–96
—"Lapis Lazuli," 139, 148
—"Leda," 15
—"Louis Lambert," 108
—"Magic," 22, 48–49, 50, 53, 128, 137
—*Michael Robartes and the Dancer*, 93, 108, 110
—"No Second Troy," 143
—"Old Men of the Twilight, The," 106, 126
—*On the Boiler*, 116, 119, 122, 137, 141
—"People's Theatre, A," 93, 108
—*Per Amica Silentia Lunae*, 15, 17, 40, 42, 48, 49, 50–56, 163
—"Phases of the Moon, The," 15, 36, 37, 38, 58, 81, 102, 108, 109, 112–15
—"Poetry of Sir Samuel Ferguson, I, The," 151
—"Prayer for My Daughter, A," 121, 139
—"Preliminary Examination of the Script of E[lizabeth] R[adcliffe]," 48, 50
—*Resurrection, The*, 67, 150–51

—"Rosa Alchemica," 61, 88, 96–97, 102–4, 107, 108, 111, 115, 136–37, 160, 178 n.36
—"Second Coming, The," 39
—*Secret Rose, The*, 106
—*Speckled Bird, The*, 22, 95–101, 111–12, 117, 118
—"Stories of Michael Robartes and His Friends," 93, 94, 118, 125, 128, 129, 135, 138, 139, 140, 142, 143, 146, 147, 152–53, 167, 168, 170
—"Stories of Red Hanrahan," 100
—"Swedenborg, Mediums, and the Desolate Places," 49, 50, 54, 89
—"Symbolism of Poetry, The," 54, 61, 88, 126, 137, 139
—"Tables of the Law, The," 84, 87, 102–4, 107, 109, 114, 115, 117
—"Three Bushes, The," 120
—"Three O'Byrnes and the Evil Faeries, The," 131–32
—"Towards Break of Day," 164
—*Tower, The*, 31, 168
—"Under Ben Bulben," 79
—"Wanderings of Oisin, The," 148
—"Wild Swans at Coole, The," 108, 109
—*Winding Stair, The*, 31, 168
—*Words upon the Window-pane*, 98
—*Works of William Blake*, 40–47, 143, 170
Yeats and Magic: The Earlier Works (Flannery), 42–43
"Yeats and the Absurd" (Rajan), 147
Yeats and the Occult (ed. Harper), 43, 49, 116
Yeats's Golden Dawn (Harper), 95
"Yeats, Synge and the Tragic Understanding" (Rajan), 148
Yeats: The Man and the Masks (Ellmann), 23

Zodiac, 43–45, 57–58, 72, 76